D0412006

CRAIG BROWN

Craig Brown

The Autobiography

*Craig Brown and
Bernard Bale*

Virgin

First published in Great Britain in 1998 by
Virgin Books
an imprint of Virgin Publishing Ltd
332 Ladbroke Grove
London W10 5AH

Copyright © Craig Brown and Bernard Bale 1998

The right of Craig Brown and Bernard Bale to be identified as the authors of this work has been asserted by them in accordance with the Copyright, Designs and Patents Act 1988.

This book is sold subject to the condition that it shall not, by way of trade or otherwise, be lent, resold, hired out or otherwise circulated without the publisher's prior written consent in any form of binding or cover other than that in which it is published and without a similar condition being imposed upon the subsequent purchaser.

A catalogue record for this book is available from the British Library

ISBN 1 85227 756 4

Typeset by TW Typesetting, Plymouth, Devon

Printed in Great Britain by
Mackays of Chatham PLC, Chatham, Kent

Contents

CRAIG BROWN

1 Why Me?

One hot night in Rome I faced the crushing responsibility of life as manager of Scotland and I began to wonder, Why me? What on earth was I doing there at all? I was not the only one asking that question. The regulars in the press box had already posed the same query.

Nevertheless, there I was, head in hands as Italy threatened to take apart the Scotland team that I was leading – a Scotland team that was playing for pride. Much has happened since that warm night in Rome in October 1993 – but much had happened before it too.

I was born just as the Second World War was getting into its stride. At the time, my father was in the RAF and I saw very little of him. My earliest recollection of the place I called home was of a tenement in Corkerhill, Glasgow – a railway village where nearly all the men, my mother's father included, worked in the manufacture and maintenance of railway locomotives and rolling stock. My grandfather was an engine-driver – a job which, to me, was something very special indeed. He was one of my very first heroes, and I could think of nothing finer than becoming an engine-driver myself. Yes, I was one of those typical wee boys whose dreams never went far beyond becoming a train-driver – or perhaps a footballer!

My grandfather's home was supplied by the railway and it was small, but cosy. A staircase ran up the outside of the building and provided us children with a play area – which frequently caused my mother's heart to leap into her mouth. Corkerhill, in those days, was a happy village full of hard-working men. Full employment, of course, meant that nobody starved – but while there were no paupers, there were no stray princes either. There was an air of equality and a common cause.

As I said my father, Hugh, was in the RAF, having volunteered to engage the Luftwaffe in battle. However, just before the war, he had bought a house in Larbert, where Stenhousemuir play. My parents had lived there for a time before he went off to war. My formative years, however, were spent in Corkerhill, and I have vivid memories of the air-raids. As a railway repair area, we were among the Luftwaffe's prime targets. Hitler thought that it would be a good idea to paralyse the transport system of Great Britain, and his idea caused me to have many a sleepless night. I remember well the wailing siren which demanded an instant response to its warning of an impending raid. Nobody ever hesitated for a moment – adults running everywhere, it seemed, and children being hoisted up with their legs dangling and hurriedly carried to a safer place.

I, of course, was one of those children – usually carried along by my mother, Margaret. My grandmother had died before the war and I had an Aunt Jess – my mother's elder sister – who seemed to fulfil the role of the family's female guide. My mother was one of eight children and, with my father away, my grandfather had been left with quite a large brood to care for. My Aunt Jess became his chief assistant.

As the raids got under way, we would be transported to the air-raid shelter – a damp, dingy place, brightened only by the flickering candles we took along and a singsong. I'm told that, as a two-year-old, I could sing 'Onward Christian Soldiers' perfectly because I had heard the adults singing it so often in the air-raid shelter. Our faith in God was naturally encouraged, and I believe that it has stayed with me to this day. I'm not, perhaps, as devout as I should be, but I was certainly brought up with a strong Christian belief, and it should come as no surprise to know that I have a brother in the ministry.

On some occasions there just wasn't enough time to get to the shelter and, when that happened, my mother used to push me under the living-room table and then lie on top of me until the sound of the bombers had gone away and the 'all-clear' sounded. We would listen to the thuds and explosions as the German bombs rained down. When I think about it, my mother must have been very frightened, and yet she always seemed to remain so calm and therefore always gave me a great feeling of confidence.

Another feature of life in Corkerhill was the baths. No, I'm not talking about swimming baths, but a series of large individual baths. I was often taken across to the baths by my mother – to where the hot water gushed and bubbled from a pipe and all the people had the chance to clean off the grime from much of their bodies. The private bits were taken care of at home – in a tin bath on the living-room floor! Going to the baths in Corkerhill became quite an outing for me.

You can imagine from what I've said that life in Corkerhill was not exactly living in the lap of luxury – and yet this is not any sort of hard-luck story. There were many in those days who were a lot worse off than we were. We had a roof over our heads and shoes on our feet – there were many, many more people in Britain who were not so well taken care of. I must say that I do like to remember how things were then, because it means that I never lose my appreciation for what has been achieved over the last fifty years and, more to the point, how things are for me today.

We were a very close family in those days, as I believe most families were at that time. All the privations brought on by the war drew people so much closer together. Family life in Scotland has always been an important thing – it is still important today, but in those turbulent years of the war it seemed to be even more so.

Whenever my father came home on leave during the 1940s, I was always overjoyed to see him – even though there were always those awkward moments when he had to take in how much I was growing and I had to learn just a little more about him. Prior to going into the RAF, he had played football professionally for King's Park – now known as Stirling Albion. He was a hard, tough-tackling midfielder – or full-back – who never shirked it when the going got rough and would fight to get a result for the full ninety minutes. He also played for Hamilton Academicals and even guested for Wolves when he was stationed nearby during the war. He became very friendly with that famous Wolverhampton Wanderers manager, Ted Vizard, and I well remember Ted visiting our home in later years when he came to Scotland in search of players. He stayed at our home and it was a great honour for us to have the manager of the great Wolves team of the 1950s under our roof.

Needless to say, my first encounter with the game of football was through my father. He always spared a few treasured minutes of his precious time during his visits home to introduce me to this wonderful game that was to play such a major role in my life. Almost as soon as I could stand, my father had introduced a ball to my feet.

Another aspect of tenement life of the 1940s was getting dressed up every Sunday to go to church. The service was always held in the local village hall. I used to stand on a chair and could just about see what was going on over the heads and between the shoulders of the rest of the congregation. I can remember just how hot it used to get with my woolly hat and gloves on. There was no air-conditioning in our village hall in those days – unless someone broke a window, that is!

So, my abiding memories of Corkerhill are of cleanliness, togetherness, family, and air-raids – plus, of course, those very special times when my father came home on leave and we were all united for a short while.

My father did quite well in the RAF. Having started as a PE teacher, he eventually reached the status of squadron leader and was in charge of the RAF School of Physical Education at Cosford near Wolverhampton, where he specialised in parachuting skills. I think his wartime job certainly helped his postwar career, as his CV from the RAF was very impressive.

Meanwhile, my mother had four brothers taking part in the war. The eldest was in the Education Corps in the army, another was an RAF mechanic, and the third volunteered for the RAF whilst still at school and trained as a pilot. During his war years he was awarded the DFM, AM and DSO. The youngest, who after the war took me to watch Queen's Park, trained as an air gunner and was kitted out for Japan when the war finally finished. So there was much anxiety in my family during those turbulent war years.

When the war ended my father became head of physical education at Marr College in Troon. There was a tied house that went with the job, and so we all moved there and lived on that beautiful part of the Ayrshire coast. The house in Larbert was sold, meaning that we were not too badly off. Before my father taught at Marr College it was a rugby-playing school – but it wasn't too long before the goalposts came out and the school found itself specialising in football and golf.

After moving to Troon, I started at the local primary school. I had two brothers by this time – Bob, who was born in Glasgow when I was about two, and then Jock, who arrived in Kilmarnock about three years after Bob. When I started going to school I was the big lad of the family and began to feel quite grown up – not that I was in any hurry to do that. Going out early every day and leaving my little brothers to enjoy their time with my mother was not my idea of a good deal, but I got used to it in time.

My father's big interests outside his PE teaching were football and golf. My brothers and I were encouraged to take part in both sports as early as possible. The back gate of our house opened on to the school playing field, a vast area which was just like an enormous back garden to us.

I liked Troon and I still do, but we were not there for very long because my father was offered an even better job as Physical Education Adviser for the whole of Lanarkshire. It was quite a job because the county was the biggest in Scotland and therefore had a vast number of schools and colleges.

For his new appointment, my father had to be based in Glasgow, and so we were soon all on the move to take up residence in Rutherglen. I moved to another primary school and began to play competitive football in Stonelaw Park. I had got used to kicking a ball about on the lush grass of the college playing field, so it came as quite a culture shock when I discovered that my new 'home ground' was an ash pitch!

I had been accustomed to playing with the older boys at school, who didn't seem to mind me taking part in their games, so it was natural that I should join them in their games in the park. The only problem was that to get to the park you had to cross a very busy cobbled road which had trams running back and forth every few minutes. You had to take your life in your hands every time you crossed the road, and I knew that there was a danger that I would be banned from going altogether unless my mother was able to see me safely across.

With all due respect, and with all the love in the world for my mother, no lad wants to be seen turning up for a game of soccer with the bigger lads having been escorted by the hand across the road by his mother. It can make your aggressive tackles seem just a little less formidable. I hate to admit it, but I resorted to sneaking off and, if I was asked where I was going, I would say that I was going to play football with the other lads but didn't know exactly where. Luckily, it seemed to work.

A neighbour of ours in Troon was one of the most famous – if not *the* most famous – referees in Scottish football, Jack Mowat. He used to stop at the gate, or sometimes come in for a coffee, and he and my father would talk about football for hours. He was another man of powerful character, whose love of the game served to fuel further my burgeoning enthusiasm for all things to do with football.

My father always wanted the best for his three sons and he decided that we would get a better education if we lived in Hamilton, where he thought the standard might be higher. He was opposed to private education and, despite him having such a good job, I doubt if he could have afforded the fees for all of us – anyway, he decided that Hamilton schooling would be better for all three of us. Coincidentally, the Lanarkshire office in which he was based also decided to move to Hamilton, so it all worked out rather well in the end.

I was still at primary stage when we moved, being aged about ten, and so I went to the St John's primary school. Fortunately, the people of Hamilton were very keen on football and so there was no shortage of the game that I had come to love. My father bought a house that was only three minutes' walk away from the famous Hamilton Academy. Right next to our house was an area of waste ground, covered in a base of red ash, which proved to be such a good training ground that I often wondered whether my father had bought the house because he liked it – or because he could see the potential of that area of waste ground at the side.

That ground was in the shape of a triangle – which meant that you could only put a goal at one end. However, you could get crosses in and there was the added advantage of the wall of our house which ran alongside our improvised pitch, providing a great place for target practice, wall passes, and various other soccer-skill games. I played for countless hours on that ground. As long as we had a ball, my pals and I never once complained about being bored, and we would play football on that red-ash pitch as often as we could. The good thing about our love of the game was that our parents always knew exactly what we were doing and where we could be found. My father made us a wooden set of goalposts – and even put a net on it.

If there was any drawback at all to our 'ground', it was the fact that the mainline railway ran alongside it. The Hamilton–Glasgow train regularly thundered past, separated from us by a tall metal fence. The trouble was that, although we were kept out by the metal fence, the ball wasn't. If we became a little careless it could become quite a costly business in stray footballs. But as it happened, we discovered a saviour.

There was a professional footballer with Hamilton who was also a train-driver – he used to take small cargo trains up and down the line on a fairly regular basis. His name was Stan Anderson, and he became quite famous with Hamilton, and later with Clyde and Rangers. Later in his career he became manager of Clyde. Every time Stan saw one of our footballs on the line he would stop his train, climb down and then kick the ball back over to us. In fact there were even times when he would abandon his train altogether, climb over the fence and give us a few tips. I often saw Stan in later life and have always remained grateful to him for the kindness and patience he showed to us as teenagers in those days. Sadly, in November 1997, after bravely enduring a long illness, Stan passed away, aged 58.

Sometimes, of course, a ball would be irretrievably lost – or else become worn out. When that happened, my father, or one of the other boys' parents, would invariably come up with a replacement. Remember, these were the heavy leather footballs of yesteryear – and the very fact that we were able to wear them out gives you some idea of how much work we gave them. The red ash, the rough-cast house wall, and the incessant booting by us boys meant that the lifespan of our footballs was well below the average.

My father was eventually promoted again, this time to become the director of the Scottish School of Physical Education establishment at Jordanhill, which trained all the PE teachers in Scotland. Naturally, he was an extremely busy man and became quite preoccupied by his work. I did occasionally go with him to see Hamilton play, but these were invariably mid-week matches because on Saturdays he was fully occupied by the Jordanhill football set-up. They ran five teams at the time and all the organisation was down to him and his superb colleague, Roy Small.

I was really interested in my father's work, and it certainly foreshadowed the job I would be doing in later life. It often amuses me to listen to people talking about my job now. Many people think that all I have to do is pick a Scotland team, spend a few days with them, play the game and then go on holiday, watching football matches in other parts of the world. Oh, how I wish! . . . Let me assure anyone who thinks that this job is a bed of roses of one thing – that even the most beautiful petals are surrounded by many painful thorns!

Because my father's work kept him so busy, I was dependent on my Uncle Jim Caldow – my mother's youngest brother – to take me to senior games at weekends. His was a famous footballing name because of Eric Caldow, Rangers captain and Scotland international. He was a Queen's Park fan and so we used to travel to Hampden to see them. They had a good team at the time. I seem to remember that their regular side was Weir, Harnett, Hastie, Cromar, Valentine, Robb, Reid, McCann, Church, Dalziel and Omand. I learned a great deal from those trips to Hampden to see Queen's Park with my uncle.

During holiday times my father was able to take me to see Hamilton Accies. The manager, Jackie Cox, was a good pal of my father and was an extremely well-known character in Scottish football. He had played at a good level himself and was a cousin of Sammy Cox – a very popular Scottish international who played for Rangers.

Jackie had some wonderful phrases which I can still recall clearly – even though I was just a lad on the fringes of the conversations at the time I first heard them. His team talks were littered with the most amazing expressions and were audible to anyone within a hundred yards. Just to give a couple of examples of his verbal skills, he once told his men, 'I could frichten 'im just by clearin' mah throat!' That was in reference to a winger whom Jackie thought to be cowardly. He used to totally destroy the opposition verbally. I heard it all because I was just down the passage giving all the boots a good clean – it's amazing what you'll do just to be involved!

One day, when Jackie Cox was playing for Hamilton against Rangers, he caused some consternation. Now Jackie used to love to mix it a bit and take the big scalps and, on this particular day, he had given most of the Rangers side a hard time. Then there came a very strong tackle on the talented inside forward Jimmy Caskie, which resulted in Caskie being stretchered off. As he was leaving the pitch, Jackie ran over to him and said: 'Jimmy, while you were in the jeelie-pieces, I was on the porridge and the breast of the pheasant!'

Hamilton's big rivals were Motherwell, who were just the other side of the bridge over the Clyde – and they had a fine team managed by Bobby Ancell. Guys like Willie Hunter, Ian St John and Pat Quinn were playing for them in the 1950s, so we sometimes used to sneak over and take a look at them.

My boyhood hero was playing for Hearts so, whenever the opportunity showed itself, I never missed the chance to go and see him in action. He was the one and only Dave Mackay and, whenever he was playing in the Glasgow or Motherwell area, I would plead with my Uncle Jim, my father, or just about anyone else who might be persuaded, to take me to see the game. I idolised him, and if any one player could be said to have made a huge impression on me in the formative years of my life, it was Dave Mackay of Heart of Midlothian. Every time I saw him I knew that I wanted to be just like him. The course of my future career was clear to me, and I was beginning to burn with ambition. Would I be good enough?

It was a question that would have to remain unanswered for some time. My exploits on the pitch were, at that stage, limited to the kind of games I've already mentioned, and so there could be no knowing whether or not my brothers and I were destined for careers in the game. Nowadays, of course, it is all very different, with lads as young as eight being marked by clubs and then wooed for years until they are ready to become full-blown trainees.

My father took a strict view of the exposure of youngsters to too much sporting activity too early in their lives, and this applied as much to golf as it did to football. He was a very keen player, but even so he would not let me actually play until I was eleven years of age. I used to caddy for him, which meant that I did learn about the game and its etiquette – but not until I was eleven could I actually take part. I could hardly wait and often used to trudge around the Hamilton golf course yearning for the day when I would be allowed to tee off.

I was learning the game of football in a similar passive way from my trips to watch Hamilton, Motherwell, Queen's Park and Dave Mackay. I remember great games and great players at Hamilton, but I also remember a great groundsman, Bobby Shearer, father of another Bobby Shearer who played for Rangers. Shearer senior was known as 'Bush', but I never found out why, although I suspect his hair had something to do with it. I do know that he kept the Accies ground – Douglas Park – in absolutely immaculate condition. He took great pride in giving the players the best possible playing conditions, and he certainly succeeded.

The Hamilton side of those early 1950s contained a number of names probably well remembered by some of you – Jimmy Cron, Bobby Cunning (an outside left who went to Rangers), Jim McLean (who later became well known as manager and chairman of Dundee United), Andy Paton, the centre-half, Pat Holton (who was later to join Chelsea) and Sam Hastings. They were all players whom I remember watching, enjoying their skill and determination.

That, then, was my football upbringing. I was a Hamilton supporter and a Queen's Park supporter with a long road ahead of me.

My childhood memories are of bombs, baths, boot rooms, a friendly train-driver, a close family, moving house, having two younger brothers, and watching Dave Mackay. I also remember the luxury of the occasional daydream that perhaps, one day, it would be possible that I could become a professional footballer myself. Being a train-driver could have been fine, and even joining the forces or following my father into physical education might have been acceptable – but the power and the sheer magic contained in the game of football had already begun to work its charm on me.

2 A Star in the Making

My father had this strict policy that we should always support our local club. That was no problem to me because I never needed any encouragement at all to be an Accies supporter – I really liked the club and its ground. Of course, if everyone's father had taken the same view as mine, then clubs like Manchester United, Liverpool, Celtic and Rangers would never have had the widespread following that they all enjoy today. However, it was my father's policy and both my brothers and I stuck to it.

Throughout my life I had supposed that it was quite a well-known fact that we were Hamilton supporters and so, years later, it came as quite a surprise to receive a sharp letter as a result of a favourable comment I made in support of another club. It came in 1994, when Clyde moved to their new ground in Cumbernauld. I had previously been manager of Clyde for over nine years – although my good friend Alex Smith was currently in charge at this momentous time in the club's history. I was interviewed about the exciting new era in the story of Clyde and was asked what I thought would be the outcome of their first game in their new stadium. I replied that I hoped there would be a good crowd for such a gala occasion and that Clyde would win their match.

The chairman of Hamilton at that time was George Fulston – now the chairman of Falkirk. Apparently his wife had heard, or was told about, the radio interview, and she wrote to me – and I do believe that it was without George's knowledge. She stated that, in her opinion, what I had said was deplorable, and how could I expect the support of the Scottish people for the national team if I was showing favouritism to one team or another.

Needless to say, I quickly wrote back to Mrs Fulston – who, incidentally, is a very charming lady – and explained to her that I had been a Hamilton supporter for a long time and had remained so. Having worked at Clyde for so long, as both manager and a director, and with the club moving to a lovely new ground, it should be perfectly understandable to anyone that I would want them to win their opening match. I do hope that she thought my letter was a pleasant one – it was meant to be!

That incident demonstrated to me just how important it is to be careful about your comments to the press – especially when you are in charge of something as important as a national team. I always try to make my comments constructive, unbiased and objective – but there is rarely any response when people are in agreement with you. It is only when you say something that strays beyond your own confines that people seem to take umbrage if your comments don't support their own particular viewpoint.

I must point out that I have remained on good terms with both Mr and Mrs Fulston – and I certainly have nothing but respect and admiration for George Fulston's tireless efforts for Hamilton and Falkirk.

I see that I have digressed yet again, but it seems that the present is always tied up with attitudes and events from the past.

As my years advanced into double figures, the two big loves of my life, namely football and golf, had grown even closer to my heart. When I was eleven years of age I was finally unleashed into the world of golf – and I really took to the game. I played at Hamilton Golf Club and steadily improved until I had a handicap of four – while I was still at school. I was runner-up in the Lanarkshire Boys' Championship and reached the last eight in the Scottish Boys' Championship, as well as playing for the West of Scotland boys' team.

There never seemed to be any question but that I would pursue a career in golf, but I have to say that even though I was very enthusiastic, I was not quite good enough. However, my love of golf continued to develop and has endured to this day. In fact, it proved to be a very useful tool to me on a number of occasions during my playing days.

At around the same time, I played my earliest competitive games with St John's primary school, where one of my teachers was Curly Thompson. Naturally enough, he was called 'Curly' because he was completely bald. Another of my teachers was Bob Roan, who was in charge of the football team at St John's.

It was Bob Roan who also had the unenviable job of taking us for swimming. He had developed his own technique for teaching youngsters how to swim. Once you had learned how to 'sprachle' – a Scottish term for getting about in the water at the shallow end without drowning yourself or anyone near you – Bob would take you to the deep end and order you in, sometimes with the assistance of a discreet push. Naturally you didn't argue, and the primitive urge to live took over. Your innate sense of survival helped you to sprachle your way from one side to the other – or even back to the shallow end. Either way, when you finally clung breathlessly to the side of the pool – after what seemed like a battle across the Bay of Biscay – Bob would be there, smiling down at you. 'There you are, son, I told you that you could swim!' He was absolutely right, of course – you were still alive to prove his point! To be fair, I never heard of any fatalities as a result of his 'scientific' approach to the art of swimming, and we were all able to swim shortly after becoming his pupils.

Swimming was very popular in Hamilton because we had such good facilities. The town was also very proud of Eleanor Gordon, who had won countless national and international breaststroke championships. She was a very famous swimmer, and her exploits inspired many youngsters throughout Scotland, especially in her home town of Hamilton, where the baths were one of the most popular venues for young and old alike.

So you see I enjoyed my golf and I enjoyed my swimming, but it was football that was the most important to me. If ever I had to choose between the sports, football would always be the winner.

As I grew up, I played in all the Hamilton Academy school football teams. We had a variety of coaches, who were also teachers. I recall Cliff Bruce, science teacher; Alf McCracken, our

English teacher; Eddie Young, also an English teacher who was keener on rugby but was, nevertheless, a good football coach; and the principal teacher of PE, Willie Liddell. Mr Liddell encouraged all sports at the school and, certainly, football was no exception.

I played constantly throughout my school years and took part in trials for the Scottish Under-15 team, which was a great experience even though it was unsuccessful. Joe Baker was also around at the time and was centre-forward in the Under-15 team. It would have been great for me if I could have joined him, but it was not to be. I was disappointed, but I have always considered that disappointments only put you down for as long as you let them. If you use them as a springboard to better times ahead, then they become much more bearable.

A couple of years later I was offered a trial for the Scotland Schools Under-18 team. There were some excellent players in the squad. The goalkeeper was Fred Renucci, who went to Partick Thistle. We had Phil Lynch, who went to Celtic, and Davie Hilley, who went to Third Lanark and then on to Newcastle. He still writes a column for the *Sunday Post*. We also had Sandy Turpie, who played for Queen's Park, Brian McIlroy, who went to Rangers and then Kilmarnock, and Hugh Brown, who also went to Kilmarnock. But probably the most famous of that particular squad was Billy McNeill, who went on to become the first British captain to hold aloft the European Cup when he led Celtic to their historic triumph in 1967.

To my immense delight I found myself selected to be among these guys, and I played for my country at the age of seventeen. We scored a memorable 3–0 victory over England at Celtic Park. It was a tremendous experience for me – quite awesome to be walking out at Celtic Park, and very emotional too to be wearing the shirt of my country. I think I must have had a reasonable game because I kept my place in the squad. As you might imagine, my family were nearly as thrilled as I was about the whole thing.

While I was at school I was also playing for one of the very best amateur teams in the country. Willie Waddell, the former Rangers player, was manager of Kilmarnock at the time, and he had a firm belief in youth development for football clubs. To this end Kilmarnock Amateurs were formed, and this was the team that I played for – one of the strongest sides in Scotland at that time. There was probably only one team to rival us at the time – and that was Drumchapel Amateurs. There were certainly some epic matches between us.

I used to go down to Kilmarnock for training. It was about an hour's journey from Hamilton and, of course, it was an invaluable experience to be training there. I was also invited to train at Celtic Park, and I went along with Billy McNeill. The coach of the Celtic youth players at that time was the late, great, legendary Jock Stein – who was then in the early stages of his management and coaching career. He was something of a father-figure even then, as he took a personal interest in each one of his charges and coached them as individuals. Jock also had an amazing memory and, from our very first meeting, he remembered everything about me. Even when I hadn't seen him for ages he still remembered that our first encounter had been when I was a young hopeful visiting Celtic Park for the first time.

The manager at Celtic Park in those days was Jimmy McGrory, but he didn't offer terms to either Billy or me – which turned out to be quite ironic, really, when you consider how great a name Billy was to become at Celtic. As it happened, they later had a change of heart and did offer to sign him. As for me – well, I was pretty confident in my ability and I lived in the expectation of some club offering me a career in the game. I was hopeful, and I was informed repeatedly that this or that club had phoned my father to establish my availability. However, my father liked to keep my feet on the ground and didn't tell me of the enquiries.

Not long after running into the Celtic cul-de-sac I was back in the Scotland Schools Under-18 side. One of my teammates was to go on and make himself very famous indeed. He was Alex Ferguson, who was then playing for Govan High School and was an extremely good attacking player. We were to play against England again, this time at Dulwich Hamlet, the home of one of England's most famous amateur clubs. Jim Cruikshank was our goalkeeper and he went on to play for Hearts and Scotland as a senior. We lost the game 4–3 as it happened, but it could have gone either way, and there was the special memory for me of scoring from the penalty spot.

To be really honest I was playing far too much football, what with school matches, Kilmarnock Amateurs, training with the big clubs and the internationals too. It was a lesson to me that you can have too much of a good thing. I don't think it was good for me to have so many physical demands placed on my body. I believe that the same thing applies today. A boy who is still developing physically should not have his body overtaxed by the rigours of too much competitive football. No, I'm not one of those people who say that the competition should be taken out of youth football – I think that competition is very necessary – but you should keep a balance. Sadly, I feel that little has changed over the years, and that many of today's youngsters are often overworked with competitive games.

I eventually joined Rangers at the age of seventeen. The newspaper headline at the time read 'Rangers sign the boy they all wanted'. It was a fact that there were quite a few clubs in the frame for me.

Rangers did not have a youth team as such, but would farm out youngsters to clubs in the Scottish junior leagues where they could gain some experience against semi-professionals. I was sent to Coltness United and was at the same level as Billy McNeill, who was playing for Blantyre Victoria. Our careers seemed to be moving in parallel – if anything I had the edge because I was also later picked for the Scottish Junior squad.

At this time, in 1958, I was concentrating on playing football and golf, and I didn't really know much about what else was going on. My father did all my talking for me, and he often neglected to tell me everything because he didn't want me distracted from developing my game. Had I known that there were clubs on both sides of the border chasing after me, it could well have gone to my head.

In the *Daily Mirror* of 15 July 1958, Jimmy Stevenson wrote: 'The future of a teenage Scot who has been the rage of soccer scouts for a year was settled yesterday. Craig Brown signed for Rangers.' He also quoted Bob Jackson, a top scout and former Portsmouth manager, as saying: 'Whoever gets the lad gets the best proposition I've seen in years.'

My father was well respected in the sports world because of his rise through the academic world and because he talked a lot of sense. He had helped and guided me since childhood, and I had no reason to think that he would not be the best person to act as my personal guide through the rest of my career. I listened to what everyone had to say, but it was my father's words that really counted. As he told the *Evening Citizen* a month after I had joined Rangers, 'Craig has been brought up in an atmosphere of football. He has played in the garden with a ball at his feet since he could toddle.'

I continued to play in the garden with a ball at my feet – and on my head as well. I knew that there was always room for improvement and, even though I was training and playing matches all the time, I still wanted to put in extra work at home. One of my exercises was to take the dining-room chairs out into the garden and line them up as obstacles, then I would slalom my way through them with the ball at my feet and repeat the exercise whilst heading the ball.

I continued my studies at Hamilton Academy and quite fancied my chances of gaining a BSc degree in engineering when I left school. At 5 feet 7½ inches and 10 stone 2 pounds, I also wanted to build myself up a bit, and so I began to do some labouring work at a steelworks. I was probably burning the candle at both ends, but not in the same way that many youngsters do today. All my activities were to do with my career. My efforts finally gained me a ticking-off! The Rangers manager, Scot Symon, called me to one side and cautioned me against doing too much. I was playing three times a week and training at least once every day.

'You need to take it a little easier. There's such a thing as overdoing it – even in football,' said Mr Symon. He did have a twinkle in his eye as he said it and so I knew that I wasn't really being told off but was being offered some genuine advice. It was a valuable lesson – and it is one that I pass on to youngsters today if I feel that it is appropriate. When the newspapers heard of my 'ticking-off' they immediately began drawing parallels with Pelé, who had been told exactly the same thing by his national coach. Pelé was big news at the time because of the 1958 World Cup, and I was honoured to be considered worthy of being mentioned in the same breath. I didn't take the comparison too seriously, though – I was already learning that you should have a pinch of salt with your newspaper, even without the fish and chips inside!

As things progressed I was selected for the Scottish Junior squad to play against the Irish Junior side – which was quite an achievement for a youngster of my age. One of my proudest possessions is the cap I earned for that match. I keep it at my house and always get a thrill when I look at it.

When I went to Ibrox I found myself amongst players I had only ever heard of. They were big stars and I was quite overawed to be mixing with them – players like Eric Caldow, Alex Scott, Bobby Shearer, Ralph Brand, Jimmy Millar, Billy Stevenson, and the other heroes of Glasgow Rangers. These men were like gods to the fans, and to me. They were people whom I had read about and talked about – but never, ever contemplated as becoming my teammates.

After a year with Coltness I was called up to Ibrox as a full-timer. My studies for my BSc were shelved and I was ready to see what the journey on the magic carpet of football was going to be like. I was put into the reserves squad – and even there I was playing alongside great players like Sammy Baird, Johnny Hubbard, Ian McColl, Billy Ritchie and others. Most were in the twilight of their careers, but they were still great players and big stars nevertheless. The reserves had their own manager, Bob McPhail, who was legendary throughout Scotland as a pre-war international. An amazing man – at the time of writing this he is still attending matches at Ibrox, even though he is well into his nineties. Assisting Bob was Joe Craven and, between them, they kept a happy and successful squad going strong. It was a very happy time for me because I was wearing the shirt of one of the greatest clubs in the history of the game and learning something from my coaches every day. With all those great players around me I felt that everything was going brilliantly for me. I was playing football all the time and I couldn't have wished for life to be any better.

At a reserve game between Rangers and Celtic in 1997 there was a crowd of 33,000. In the back end of the 1950s we could expect crowds of 20,000-plus for reserves Old Firm clashes, and almost the same for all the other fixtures. As a result, there was never any disgrace in being listed among the reserves every week.

I was quick to learn that star footballers are only human after all. Sometimes the stars of stage, screen and sport can seem to be a race apart and nothing like the rest of us. However, as I became friendly with the internationals at Ibrox, I found them all easy to get on with. We talked about all the normal things of life – what sort of pet dog this one had, which horse to back at Newmarket, and so on. I was included in all these conversations about everyday matters and soon settled in.

There were, of course, little cliques at Ibrox – as there have always been at every club. Because I lived in Hamilton I fell into the clique of players who lived near me, among them Eric Caldow, Willie Telfer, Doug Baillie, Stan Anderson and Bobby Shearer, the captain. We also used to pick up Davy Wilson on the way in – he stayed in Cambuslang. We all travelled in from Hamilton to train at Ibrox, which brought us together in all sorts of ways.

These were happy days for me at Ibrox with the company I was keeping, my playing progress and my golf. I was also making progress on another front. I've already mentioned giving up on my engineering course, but I did switch to taking a PE course at Jordanhill, because it was more in keeping with my footballing career.

There was an odd atmosphere at Jordanhill in those days. There were strict doctrines like never showing that you were injured, never allowing an opponent to know that you were hurt. Trainers were never allowed on to the football pitch to attend the injured. There were no substitutes so you were expected to play on regardless. I'm sure that only broken legs, broken necks or death were regarded as acceptable reasons for not completing the full 90 minutes. That wasn't the end of the discipline – everything from your boots to the rest of your kit had to be kept scrupulously clean, and it was your responsibility. Everything took place with military precision.

Quite a few professional players were taking courses at Jordanhill at that time. Graham Leggat was one, and he was a fair influence on me. He played for Aberdeen and then Fulham. When I was in my final year at the Hamilton Academy he had arrived there as a student and, of all people, he influenced me the most and made me take a serious look at the possibilities of a PE teaching course. I suppose it was because he was such a wonderful sportsman, a great all-rounder and an excellent gymnast. He excelled at every sport he took part in. He was also in the spotlight because of playing for Aberdeen and Scotland at the time.

There were other professional players at Jordanhill, too. Bobby Clark, a top goalkeeper with Aberdeen and Scotland, Ian Riddell of St Mirren, Roger Hynd, a nephew of the Shanklys who played for Rangers, Doug Houston, who played for Dundee, Dave Hilley of Third Lanark, Frank Coulston and Dick Staite of Partick Thistle, Joe Gilroy of Dundee, Derek Whiteford of Airdrie, and many others, who I hope will forgive me for failing in my struggle to bring their names to mind.

We often had games between the professionals and the top amateur players and these were usually held on a Wednesday on one of those red-ash pitches that were prevalent in Scotland at the time. They were tough matches, and very often my direct opponent was a young man by the name of Archie MacPherson, who later became a top commentator with the BBC. I found him a difficult opponent. He was a very fast winger who was very clever with the ball and, quite unashamedly, I used to have a kick at him to try to slow him down a bit. I saved some of my hardest tackles for Archie.

My PE course was to last three years. It was very thorough and rigorous. For instance, three times a week we went to Cranstonhill baths and started our day with swimming instruction in cold water – and I do mean *cold* water! We went up and down that pool until we were too exhausted to notice just how cold it was. In those days my Ibrox training happened during the evenings and, even though I was working so hard at my PE course, I was still able to drag one leg after the other. When I think back, I must have been pretty fit in those days! The Ibrox training was hard enough in itself. Our fitness trainer was Davie Kinnear, a military-type gentleman who was very strict and had us running round the track wearing spikes to maximise our ability. He was quite a taskmaster but he did have a sense of humour. I remember once when Johnny Hubbard broke away and ran up into the terraces. 'What are you doing up there?' asked Davie Kinnear.

'I've come to collect some of Sammy Baird's long passes,' replied Johnny.

We all held our breath, waiting for the explosion we were sure would follow. It didn't come. The trainer just burst into laughter. So, we had some fun as well as our hard work. Ibrox was a really happy environment – and I'm glad to say that it still is.

Johnny Hubbard, or 'Hubby' as he was predictably called, still does a wonderful job coaching youngsters in Prestwick and Ayr and his acute sense of humour prevails. I recall when, yet again, he was accusing his inside forward, Sammy Baird, of being a selfish player. After a match against Aberdeen he said to Sammy in his distinctive South African accent: 'Sam, there were 58,742 spectators out there today!' Sammy replied: 'How the hell do you know that, wee man?'

'Because I was counting them when you were on the ball, you greedy b . . .!'

However, I did have one problem at Ibrox. My best position was that of left half – or left midfield as it is now called. It was a position in which there were some very good players, and I always make a joke and say that I was third choice. The first choice was an amputee and the second one was a Catholic!

On that subject I have to say that I always found the religious differences that surrounded Rangers and Celtic to be despicable. It isn't so bad these days with both clubs playing down that factor in their Glasgow coexistence. In the past it was a different story, with the religious divide being quite a serious problem. Yet it never seemed to be a problem in the dressing room. The players of both clubs have always mixed well socially and, when called up for their country, the subject never seemed to be on the agenda. It appears to be something that has been carried through the generations by the supporters. I never heard anything about religious differences in the Rangers dressing room, and I'm sure it was the same in the Celtic camp.

The Old Firm games were a cauldron of hate – much more than I realised in the innocence of my teenage years. I used to have an umbrella that could have been mistaken for a white-and-blue design – although it wasn't. In fact it was a Bank of Scotland umbrella. I was a young player at Ibrox at the time and was using the umbrella in the rain when I was accosted by a couple of Celtic fans who told me what to do with my umbrella . . . 'or else!' It came as quite a shock to me. I had always looked at the rivalry as a natural condition between two clubs in the same city. I had never realised that there were greater undercurrents than just seeing who was top dog in Glasgow football. I soon learned that it was better not to identify yourself with one club or the other when you were out and about in Glasgow – it was safer that way. As I've said, there was no such animosity between players and my friendship with Billy McNeill continued even though we were in opposing clubs. Our friendship prevailed and still does to this day.

In my present job I am sometimes accused of favouritism towards one or other of the two Glasgow giants. It is a ridiculous charge, of course. In the summer of 1997, my brother Jock became general manager of Celtic, and that caused more than a little consternation because it was suggested that he was a Rangers fan. He has never been a Rangers fan. I can assure you that he, and the rest of the family, have always been Hamilton fans. There is hardly a day that goes by without some rumour or other getting started in the football world. Most of them are very wide of the mark.

Both my brothers are smashing guys, really decent chaps, and although both are well qualified academically this is never apparent in their attitude or speech in their dealings with other people.

My middle brother, Bob, is a Church of Scotland minister in Queen's Cross Church in Aberdeen. He has an MA degree from St Andrews University which involved four years of study, a Bachelor of Divinity from Glasgow University which required three years of study, and a Master of Theology degree from Duke University in North Carolina. Bob was in fact a student for eight years, during which time he took various jobs to supplement his income. He was always committed to joining the ministry.

People who know that my brother is a minister often say to me that I must be a devout person also. However, if my brother was in Barlinnie Prison, that wouldn't make me a criminal. That is probably a very flippant remark because, while I don't consider myself to be a devout person in the extreme sense, I like to think that I have a degree of faith, although I can never aspire to the tremendously strong Christian beliefs that my brother Bob has.

My other brother, Jock, also has great academic qualifications, and he must be a really clever guy because I never ever saw him study. He left school in Hamilton and went straight to Cambridge University where he gained his MA degree in law. That, of course, was English law and, when he returned to Scotland, he had to sit the Law Society of Scotland exams to be qualified to practise law in Scotland. After gaining dual qualification he went on to embark on a very successful legal career. While at Cambridge he captained the university soccer team and, unlike me, he has played at Wembley three times in the annual varsity fixture against Oxford. He acquitted himself very well as a rugged, dirty centre-half playing in a high standard of game for Cambridge.

Now that he is general manager of Celtic, I hardly ever see or hear from him. He spent much of his first period there travelling abroad to see players and set up transfer arrangements recommended by the Celtic coach, Wim Jansen. So, although Jock and I get on very well, our contact has been greatly reduced.

When the job was first mooted he asked for my opinion. I, rather selfishly, said: 'I don't think you should take that job because I get enough abuse when I go to Rangers as it is, and if my brother is at Celtic it is only going to get worse. No doubt the abuse I get at Celtic will increase as well if the team is not doing too well. Please stay out of it. Stick with your legal world and your role as BBC football commentator.' He was the top man for BBC Scotland, after all.

The next day I phoned him again and changed my tune.

'I've phoned because my reply to you yesterday was very selfish. I was thinking of how it would affect me, but I never gave a thought to how you felt about it. I should be strong enough to take whatever comes and I'm sure I can handle any comments that come my way. So, if the job appeals to you go for it, don't worry about me.'

Jock admitted that I had put him off but then told me that he felt that at this stage in his career a new challenge would be rejuvenating for him. Not long after our phone conversation he contacted Celtic and accepted their offer.

I think the press and the public have grown to realise that there is no reciprocal influence whatsoever, any more than there was when he had to interview me for the BBC once in his capacity as a football commentator.

Those are my brothers and, of course, I'm very proud of both of them.

All this was still a long way off for a young Rangers player and third choice for the left half position at Ibrox. Billy Stevenson was first choice for my position and Stan Anderson, my old friend, was second. Then, after I had been at Ibrox for about eighteen months, Rangers signed another player with whom I had to compete for the No. 6 shirt. He was to become the most famous of them all, but he certainly didn't look like the part when he and I first shook hands. Anyone who remembers his first day at Ibrox will tell you that he was a very nervous young man. When he and I said hello, little did I know that I was meeting a legend in the making – the one and only Jim Baxter.

3 Hello, Jim! . . . Goodbye, Rangers!

Jim Baxter became one of Scotland's biggest-ever stars, and by coincidence I was the first player he met when he arrived at Ibrox. I was getting treatment for the first of many knee injuries and that is why I was there when Jim arrived. It was during the summer of 1960, and I met him for the first time when the manager, Scot Symon, was showing him around the Glasgow Rangers stadium.

Jim was noticeably nervous, and when Scot left him with me in the treatment room we had quite a long chat. He had just joined Rangers from Raith Rovers for £17,500, which was quite a lot of money in those days, especially for a club like Raith. They had paid £200 when he had first joined them a few years earlier, and he had certainly become something of a sensation. His displays included a great game against Rangers in 1958 which had resulted in a shock 3–1 win for Raith. Rangers began tracking him after that and eventually they got their man.

On the pitch, Jim Baxter was supremely confident, but that first day at Ibrox showed me another side of his character, a side that very few people know. I remember him saying to someone else a bit later on that he had felt like a country yokel at the time of his arrival. He later offered this explanation:

'I know that I've been called arrogant and I can't help what people say. I know that's probably how I have looked. But when I was eighteen I was called up to play for the Scotland Under-23 side against Wales at Tynecastle. I was with Raith then and it was a big day for me. I travelled to Edinburgh to meet up with everyone else. I was feeling quite pleased with myself until I saw the other lads. They all looked really something, very sharp and exactly as professional footballers should look. I felt out of place . . . a nobody.

A couple of kids asked me for my autograph and then I saw them looking at their books to see who I was. That was the day when I decided that everyone would know who I was. I knew I could play, but I had to make sure that everyone else knew too. But I never tried anything that I didn't know I could achieve.'

The legend of Jim Baxter has been told many times. He was undoubtedly a brilliant player, and one of the greatest to wear the Rangers and Scotland shirts. When we reported for pre-season training it seemed natural that his peg should be next to mine – partly because the pegs were arranged in alphabetical order, but also because we already knew each other. As the season wore on, players changed their pegs to be near their best pals, but Baxter and Brown always remained together. We became good friends. I discovered that inside that flamboyant and brash exterior was a very warm human being.

Whenever we chance to meet, I always get the best of greetings and hospitality from Jim Baxter, and I always try to reciprocate. I had the marvellous privilege of watching him play for Rangers and to see at close-hand the magnificent talent that he had. He made an instant impact in the first team. The Scottish League Championship was won for the 32nd time, the League Cup was also won, and the FA Cup was only just lost, thanks to a battling Motherwell side. Rangers also took part in the inaugural European Cup Winners' Cup competition, and reached the final in which they faced a cynical Fiorentina side. As it happened, Fiorentina did win by the odd goal, a wonder strike by Kurt Hamrin, a Swedish international. You can see from all this that Jim Baxter's first season at Ibrox was exciting to say the least.

While all this was going on I was becoming even more anonymous. My knee injury, which at first appeared to be just an annoyance, was beginning to look a little more serious. I kept on getting fluid on the joint. I was ordered to keep on working at strengthening the quadriceps, which I did, but I still continued to get the fluid problem. When I trained with Rangers it appeared, and when I was working on my PE course it appeared – and it was beginning to become a bit of a worry.

I was not a very important player at the time and so I did not receive the urgency of treatment that might have helped me to recover a lot more quickly – and possibly permanently. It is simply the way of things in football, not just then but now as well. If I had been a first-team player, I would have received the care and attention that was due to my status, but I was not and I understood my situation perfectly. Many a player has been told, 'Go on, lad, get yourself sorted!'

David Kinnear was an excellent remedial gymnast, but he was not a qualified physiotherapist and so it was not his fault. My knee problem refused to respond, and so my chances of first-team football became limited.

It didn't stop me playing, but I did have to live with this knee problem, which kept niggling at me incessantly. I was quickly beginning to realise that, unless something very dramatic happened, my career was going in one direction only – and it wasn't up. Everyone tried to be encouraging, but I had this awful feeling that my dreams of winning the championship and playing in Europe as a regular first team-player at Rangers were destined to end in tatters.

Before I signed for Rangers, one of the other teams that tried to take me on board was Third Lanark – now defunct, but regarded then with great affection by everyone interested in Scottish football. Their manager at that time was Bob Shankly, brother of the great Bill Shankly. He was a fine man but, at the time, I was dazzled by the Ibrox marble staircase and the smooth, gentlemanly encouragement of Scot Symon – not to mention being well aware of the fact that wearing a Rangers shirt could earn me more status and a little more money.

However, Bob Shankly did not forget me and, when he left Third Lanark, he became manager of Dundee. He and his brother Bill were not only great managers but also took a very personal interest in just about everyone who was playing the game, no matter who they were playing for. It had not escaped Bob Shankly's notice that I was not getting first-team football for Rangers, and so he asked them if they would transfer me to Dundee.

I was extremely surprised when Bob Shankly was turned down by Rangers. My surprise was all the greater because Rangers at that time were certainly not short of players and I was not among the top ones. I felt that I did not figure very highly on their list of priorities, and so I fully expected them to be only too glad to unload me. I don't know who was the more surprised, Bob Shankly or myself, when they said they were going to keep me.

After his initial surprise, Bob asked if it would be possible for me to join his club on loan. This time Rangers were in agreement, and I didn't mind at all. I didn't really want to leave the Rangers set-up for one minute – but I was also eager to stop my career falling into stagnation. Since it was for a loan spell only, there was no danger that I couldn't return to Ibrox, and so, in October 1960, I became a temporary Dundee player.

I hadn't been at Dundee for very long – in fact I'd played just a few reserve games – when my knee began to be troublesome again. Lawrie Smith was the physiotherapist at Dundee, and he took a good, long look at the problem. He was a great guy and an outstanding physio as well, and after studying my knee for some time he told me quite simply that there was only one way it was going to get any better – and that was through surgery.

I was sent to see a world-renowned knee specialist, Mr Smillie, who had written a number of books on the subject. After examination, he confirmed what Lawrie Smith had said, adding that surgery was not simply an option – it was essential. I was packed off to a local nursing home for the first of what turned out to be five operations on my left knee.

Nowadays, I know, there are wonderful ways of performing operations with the minimum of fuss and disruption to everyday life. Keyhole surgery has taken away those big incisions and the necessity to be confined to bed, sometimes for weeks. It was not the same when I had my operations – it was necessary then to have several weeks of recuperation before there was any possibility of getting back to any serious work, and in my case that meant getting back to being considered for first-team football.

Dundee were very good to me and extremely patient. Rangers also kept a sharp eye on my progress and were very encouraging. Fortunately, I did recover before the end of the season and I played in the reserves at Dens Park to prove my match fitness. Whether or not I had done enough to secure a place in first-team football with Dundee remained to be seen.

Even though I was a Rangers player and knew that I would be returning to Ibrox once the loan period was over, I felt really at home at Dens Park. I was still finding it quite difficult to understand why the Ibrox club were so unwilling to sell me, and even began to think that it was possibly because I was so useful in the Rangers golf team. We had been very successful in various competitions. In fact, in the month before I joined Dundee on loan, Harold Davis, Bobby Shearer and I had won the *Daily Record* Footballers Golf Team Trophy for Rangers with an eight-stroke win over second-placed Hibernian. Just for the record, Dundee had finished third in the competition.

I had never had any trouble in being accepted at Rangers – and I am sure that my golfing ability went a long way towards that acceptance. A lot of Rangers players were keen on the game. When the team went out on golf outings, I usually managed to finish in the top four – which was pretty good really because a lot of the team were class players, and the manager, Scot Symon, was very good indeed, besides being very enthusiastic. Bobby Shearer had a very low handicap, as did Harold Davis. Max Murray was a scratch player and there were several others who were a force to be reckoned with on the golf course. I always seemed to do well and, even if my soccer skills didn't earn many plaudits, my golf had certainly raised my esteem among my Rangers colleagues.

We had a few interesting golf outings while I was at Ibrox, many of which I can recall. I shall never forget one in particular. Let's be absolutely frank – the etiquette of golf had been quite lost on many of the players, who would do things that would have golf officials holding their heads in despair and disbelief. Players would share clubs and a caddy car, some wouldn't have golf shoes and would wear trainers with tracksuit bottoms tucked into their socks. Normally you wouldn't get on too many courses dressed like that – maybe it was because it was Rangers that many a blind eye would be turned?

On this particular occasion we were playing at Erskine Golf Club and the lads had been out on the course. The last four to go out were Ralph Brand and Jimmy Miller against Willie Henderson and Davie Provan. They were sharing one set of clubs and you could hear them shouting during the round – which means that they were shouting pretty loudly. So they were coming up the fairway to the last hole, long after everyone else. Their earlier shouting had mostly been about the score.

'Is that eleven?'

'No, it's twelve!'

'It never is.'

'Aye, it is!'

So it went on. I think it was Ralph who was pulling the caddy car and, as they went up to the last green, he was giving out the clubs. He took the caddy car right on to the green and up to the flag. It was a wet day and the scars from the wheels of the caddy car could clearly be seen on the green. Apparently they had been doing this all over the course but, since they were the last to go, nobody had noticed. When Scot Symon found out he was none too pleased – in fact he was furious. The club officials shared his views and, needless to say, we were not invited back to that particular golf club.

In the dressing room of a football club there is invariably plenty of what we call 'patter'. Ibrox was no exception. Friday morning was always full of anticipation because, in blue typewritten letters, the team names were pinned to the noticeboard.

On this particular Friday, the newspaper heading on the back page was 'Henderson To Get Contact Lenses'. It was well known that the outside left, deputising for the injured Davy Wilson, was Bobby Hume – one of the first professional players to use contact lenses. Our groundsman, Davie McLeod, on studying the Scot Symon selection and bearing in mind his reading of the *Daily Record*, was loud in his condemnation. He read the forward line and made his customary remark: 'I see it and I don't believe it.

Henderson, McMillan, Millar, Brand and Hume. Two blind wingers! I don't know whether to line the park tomorrow or just put kerbstones along the sides!'

Anyway, back at Dundee, I was determined to make the best of my loan spell and, when I was back in full action in the reserve team, I set out to prove myself. I felt that by doing so I would be able to reciprocate for the interest that they had shown in me. I did not really expect to be given a first-team chance at this stage, although of course there was always the hope that in the latter games of the season there would be an opportunity.

The first team had not experienced the best of seasons. Their Scottish League Cup hopes had been dashed before I had arrived at the club. Rangers had been the team to put paid to their hopes over two legs of the quarterfinals in September 1960. In fairness, Dundee had succeeded in giving Rangers quite a scare. The first leg, played at Ibrox, had ended 1–0, but the return at Dens Park finished in a 3–3 draw as Dundee refused to capitulate. Rangers had learned a valuable lesson from that experience, however, and when the two teams met again at Dens Park – in the Scottish FA Cup second round – the Ibrox men were easy 5–1 winners. The League campaign was also a disappointing one for Dundee, even though they had put in some very good performances. Despite this, they still only managed to finish in the middle of the table, in tenth place out of eighteen clubs. Rangers had won the championship but perhaps the worst blow of all as far as Dundee was concerned was that our great rivals, Dundee United, finished one place above us – in ninth position with just one point more!

Despite my injuries I was continuing with my course at Jordanhill and I certainly enjoyed a wide range of sports there. The course meant that you had to be fairly proficient in just about every sport that it is possible for a human to play. I played football and golf, of course, but I also found myself taking part in swimming, rugby, rowing, cricket, hockey, basketball, skiing and mountaineering. I once had to set off after a Dundee evening match to go to Aviemore as part of my skiing and mountaineering education. You can just imagine how amusing many of my soccer colleagues found it. I came in for huge amounts of stick from these so-called pals, who even suggested that I might be a better footballer if I wore my ski boots on the pitch instead of the regulation ones!

I did enjoy keeping fit and having a go at all these different sports. My father had instilled in all of us the benefits of regular exercise and a healthy diet. It was rare for me to eat anything but fruit at lunch-time. I'm sure that it helped me, and I would recommend it to anyone who wants to give his body a fighting chance of enduring the rigours of life.

Another big interest of mine, of which not too many people were aware, was country dancing – in fact, I became quite good at it. I even reached the stage of being a member of a 'jig-time' dance team which appeared regularly on Scottish television. I still do like country dancing, but these days it is mostly for the music, as I don't have the knees for 'pas de bas'. When I'm at a wedding, or some similar social event, I'll still have a go, however – after all, those are the times when it's almost obligatory for you to make a fool of yourself, aren't they?

Anyway, we finally came to the end of the season, and I had really enjoyed my time at Dundee. I was impressed with the management style of Bob Shankly, who was quite different from Scot Symon. I would hate to have to say which of the two men was the better manager because, after all, they both had so many fine attributes. Suffice it to say that they were both good at their jobs. I prepared myself for a return to Ibrox and was determined that I would have another go at proving that I was worth a try in the first team.

As it turned out, I never did get to say goodbye to all my new friends at Dundee. Just before I was due to return to Ibrox, Bob Shankly made a final attempt to sign me on a regular basis – and this time Rangers agreed.

We called Bob Shankly 'The Wily Old Fox' – and with considerable justification. He used all his astute managerial skills to get me to Dundee for as small a fee as possible. Early on during my loan spell I had played well in a reserve game against Willie Henderson but, when Rangers were due to play us again in a second-eleven match at Dens Park towards the end of the season, our boss came to me and said, with a knowing look, 'Henderson can have a better game tonight, son!'

I had started that season as a reserve with the club that had finished as champions of Scotland, and now I had become a reserve with the club that had finished below the halfway line in the table. Certainly on paper it did not look to be the best thing that could have happened to me, but nevertheless I could not help feeling that there were going to be better days ahead. Bob Shankly really knew his business, and he was more than enthusiastic. It seemed to me that Dundee were experiencing the dawning of a very exciting time in the club's history.

My family were all very encouraging, as they always were, but ultimately the decision was mine. I was not being forced to join Dundee and I didn't have to go there if I didn't really want to, but at the time it seemed to be the right move to make and so I signed the necessary forms. In the end I was right to make the move when I did, but I have to admit that, when I said goodbye to Glasgow Rangers, I was not really all smiles.

4 Champions!

I felt that there was a much better opportunity for me at Dundee to play a part in a team that I considered to be destined for much greater things. I was delighted to sign for Dundee because I felt that here was a club that was going places. There was such a strong squad at Ibrox that I felt sure my chances would have become more and more limited as time went on. I had been very impressed with the drive and ambition of Bob Shankly, and I knew that he was not the man to settle for second best in anything. I wanted to be there when he guided the Dark Blues to success.

The excitement began almost as soon as we reported for pre-season training. A tour had been arranged for us in Iceland – a country that I had only read about and been fascinated by, never considering that I would actually be seeing it for real one day.

On the tour we played against the Reykjavik side and also against the Iceland national team, and I felt that I was settling in quite well. There had been a few changes to the playing staff as Adamson, Horsburgh, Jardine and May were released, but the biggest surprise for the Dundee fans was when Doug Cowie was placed on the transfer list. Doug, then 34, had been at Dundee for sixteen years and had become one of the club's all-time greats, having been capped for Scotland twenty times. He had rarely turned in a bad performance, either for club or country. I think he was very disappointed at being placed on the transfer list, because he felt that he still had a lot to offer Dundee. As it happened, he was not idle for long because Morton quickly signed him as player-coach.

Coming into the club was another veteran player – and I hope he doesn't mind me calling him that – Gordon Smith. Twice before, Dundee had tried to sign him and now it was a case of third time lucky. There was no doubting his talent. He had played eighteen times for Scotland and had won the Scottish Championship with both Hearts and Hibs. Some of the Dundee fans were surprised at the signing, however, because Gordon was 37 – and therefore older than Doug Cowie, who was being transferred. They need not have worried, as it happened. There was never any need to doubt a Shankly signing, whether it was Bill or Bob that was involved.

I wanted to be considered as a first-team choice but Dundee had a pretty settled side, despite all the comings and goings. The team sheet was almost always the same during the opening games of the season, and I remember it well – Liney, Hamilton, Cox, Seith, Ure, Wishart, Smith, Penman, Cousin, Gilzean and Robertson. No doubt you will remember some of those famous names. I wasn't at all sure how I was going to get my big chance, but I still felt a lot closer to it than I had at Rangers, so I was not worrying unduly.

There was a mixed start to the season because Dundee fell early in the Scottish League Cup competition, but put together a few good opening League results – including a 4–1 win at home to our local rivals, Dundee United. Kilmarnock and Rangers led the table after a couple of games but we were soon up with them. Alan Gilzean had been the club's top scorer the previous season with 32 League and Cup goals, and he just continued where he had left off. In the centre of our defence was the mighty Ian Ure – so there were giants of the game in both of the most important positions in the team.

I was continuing to play in the reserves but I was already in the reckoning for the first team. It was an amazing season, really, because in addition to those eleven players I have already mentioned, the club used only four others. If that was the first eleven, then I was hanging in at No. 12.

We were scoring plenty of goals – five against Kilmarnock, four against Motherwell – and Bob Shankly was enjoying himself. He was a very similar character to his brother Bill and rarely missed an opportunity to tell the world how wonderful his players were. It was all going very well for the club, but not quite so well for me because I had yet to play for the first team in a competitive game. Had substitutes been allowed in those days I reckon I would have created a record for the greatest number of appearances as a sub, because I was always with the squad both home and away.

At long last I got my chance when our skipper, Bobby Cox, was injured. I was not at all happy about his injury because I was a club man and wanted us to be at our strongest at all times, but I can't deny that I was excited when I was told that I would be playing. My only problem was that I would be out of position at left back. It was something that I was asked to do a number of times and it did prove to be a successful switch for me, even though I was more at home in the left half position.

The newspapers were very kind to me. I played in the return away game at Kilmarnock where we drew 1–1. One writer, Jimmy Stevenson, introduced his match report with the headline 'Stand-in Sets An Example'. Another writer said of Dundee: 'They got a point because of the rugged defence of Ian Ure and the speed and tackling of young Craig Brown, a big hit in his first top team game.'

I was thrilled to read such things about myself and, if I look at those press cuttings now, I still get pleasure when I read about 'young' Craig Brown. There were other descriptions of me as 'the crew-cut Craig Brown'. Yes, I had a crew cut in those days, and I was young and, yes, we are talking about the same Craig Brown. It's not the years – it's the mileage!

Those were thrilling days at Dens Park. A 5–1 win over Rangers had demonstrated to everyone that Dundee meant business and, as the season wore on, it became more evident that our position at the top of the table was no mere flash in the pan. Even when we lost Alan Gilzean with a broken jaw, the goals continued to flow.

Alan was a big element of that early success. He was a tremendous goalscorer, a typical bustling centre-forward who was excellent with his head as well as his feet. He had all the courage that you expect from a top goalscorer whom every defender in the country was determined to stop. Even when he broke his jaw, he was not out for long.

Things were a little different in those days. Games were played in conditions that would have meant very definite postponements today. If there was snow on the ground, as long as the lines were visible and the snow didn't come up over your ankles, the game would still be on. I remember 'Gillie' once wearing sandshoes on a frozen pitch and scoring two goals while everyone else struggled to keep on their feet.

I don't really think that I was to blame – I hope not, anyway – but after I came into the side we seemed to go through a bit of a slump. We were beaten 3–0 at Partick and then had a stern test away to Celtic. We lost that one as well, 2–1, but I was pleased with my own performance, and one of the journalists at the game wrote: 'I was particularly impressed by young Craig Brown. The former Ranger showed something of the play which, as a youth internationalist, hinted at taking him right to the top.' Another newspaper made me Dundee's top player for that game and I, of course, took great encouragement from such things. It didn't go to my head, but it didn't do my confidence any harm either.

I might have guessed that it was all going too well for me by now. There had to be another blow just around the corner and, sure enough, it was waiting for me when we played away to Raith Rovers. My left knee let me down again and I had to go off. Another trip to hospital beckoned and, as you may imagine, I was pretty distraught. I desperately wanted to continue in the side as we entered the run-in to the season. It had developed into a two-horse race between ourselves and Rangers, and I wanted to do my bit to bring home the championship to Dens Park for the first time in the club's history.

There was nothing that I could do except enter Fernbrae Nursing Home and keep reading the newspapers, listening to the radio, and watching television. I was forced to sit in that Dundee nursing home, hungry for any news of what was happening to my team. Our rivals, Dundee United, actually did us a very big favour. Rangers seemed to have taken the initiative in the title chase even though we were still picking up points. Our standard of play seemed to have slipped a little, while theirs was gaining in momentum. Despite all that, Ibrox was stunned when Rangers came up against our rivals Dundee United and slipped up. On the day that we scraped a 1–0 win over Hibs, mighty Rangers went down 0–1 against United. I was overjoyed at the news but more than a little sad that I had not been able to play. It is very frustrating to be in a hospital bed while your teammates are playing their hearts out.

Dundee United might well have done us a favour with that spectacular victory away to Rangers, but they were no less determined to beat us in the return local derby game in April. A 20,000 all-ticket crowd witnessed a great game which Dundee won 2–1, with Alan Gilzean driving a sensational shot past Rolando Ugolini to get the winner with just four minutes left. With two games remaining, Rangers had to go to Aberdeen and Dundee were at St Mirren. When the news came through that Rangers were trailing 1–0 there was a buzz of excitement around the ground which reached the ears of the players. Pat Liney, in goal, must have been inspired by it because he saved a penalty with a spectacular leap which stopped St Mirren skipper Jim Clunie's shot going right into the top right-hand corner of the net. It was 1–0 at the time and touch and go. The relief of that penalty save encouraged Andy Penman to score our second goal, bringing the championship even closer to reality.

The last game of the season was absolute agony for me as so much was at stake. Everything hinged on getting at least a point from a visit to St Johnstone – who also needed points to save them from relegation. It is amazing how often history repeats itself. Just thirteen years earlier, Dundee had been in a similar position, needing to take points from the last game of the season or risk Rangers stealing the championship at the last gasp. On that day everything went wrong and a 4–1 defeat saw Dundee having to make do with the runners-up spot.

I have never been one to bite my nails but, if I had, I would have been down to my elbows before the final scores came through. Rangers had been held to a 1–1 draw by Kilmarnock, while Dundee had gone through a battle royal with St Johnstone, who included in their line-up the very same Alex Ferguson who has demonstrated so often since how much he hates the taste of defeat. St Johnstone gave Dundee a number of scares early in the game as the tension seemed to get to everybody but, in the 24th minute, there was a flood of relief when Alan Gilzean headed home. 'Gillie' scored again in the second half and then Andy Penman drove home via the crossbar to make it 3–0 and signal the start of the party.

The whole of Dundee celebrated that piece of football history while I was still in my hospital bed. It would have been very easy for everyone at the club to have forgotten all about me during those ecstatic celebrations, but the manager made sure that I was not neglected. We were all paid in cash in those days and on the first pay-day after that championship-winning game he came to see me personally with my brown envelope.

'I've brought you this, son,' he said as he put the envelope on my bed. I stared at it – it looked very much bigger than usual. I thought for a moment that he had brought me a letter telling me that my services would no longer be required by the club. Tentatively I opened the envelope while he watched me with a smile on his face. Inside was a big bundle of cash.

'That's your bonus for winning the championship, son!' said Bob Shankly. 'You played your part just the same as the others.'

I was amazed. It wasn't the money – it was the fact that I was being treated no differently to the other members of the side who had played in many more games. They were the big shots as I saw it, and yet here was the club treating me in just the same manner. I was one of the exclusive band of only fifteen players who were involved in Dundee's first-ever Scottish championship. I received the same bonus as everyone else and – more importantly – I also received my championship medal, something which I cherish to this day.

I also cherish the experience of having worked for such a great manager as Bob Shankly. He always expected the best from his players, but he invariably gave them the best too and I learned an enormous amount from him. He also got me into a habit that I have maintained to this day.

After winning the title, Dundee went on a summer tour to New York. The manager took the trouble to send me a postcard because I was still undergoing treatment for my knee injury. He wrote: 'Sorry you couldn't make this trip but I hope all goes well and that you are trouble-free for pre-season training.'

That card meant a lot to me. Bob Shankly was a busy man and I really appreciated the fact that he had taken time out to get in touch with me. It was also a thrill to get a card from someone whom I had grown to respect and admire so much.

Yes, but you were talking about a habit! . . . I can almost hear you say it. Well, receiving that card meant so much to me that it taught me a lesson. It taught me that there are those left at home when you are away on your travels and they could well do with a card from you – even with the smallest of notes. I picked up the habit of sending cards to friends all over the world whenever I was on my travels. I have become quite famous for it among my circle of friends – and it all started with that postcard I received from Bob Shankly, one of the finest managers and men it has ever been my privilege to know.

I don't just stop at sending cards to friends either, because I also learned then what a morale-booster such a message can be. To give you an insight into how I run the Scotland team – if I have to leave a player out of my plans because he is injured, or just not suitable for a particular game, I always try to make sure that he does not feel rejected. I arrange for him to be sent postcards, faxes and anything else that will help to make him feel that he is with us in spirit at least. I learned that from Bob Shankly, and I am sure that it has gone a long way to helping with the great team spirit we have in the Scotland camp.

I must tell you a little more about life at Dundee when I wasn't injured, because it was a great set-up. I had been among friends at Rangers, and that certainly didn't change when I joined Dundee. I stayed in digs run by a lady called Mrs Garvie, who had four other Dens Park players staying at her place. We quickly became known as the 'Garvie Five', and consisted of Ian Ure, George Ryden, Tommy Mackle, Hugh Robertson and myself.

We were notorious for being late for training because we all used to travel in the one wee car – which had a habit of refusing to start. We had all sorts of fun together while we were at Mrs Garvie's. My next digs were at Mrs Duncan's in Sagar Street, and then later Doug Houston and I moved to Mrs Clark's digs in

Americanmuir Road in Downfield, Dundee. So you see, during my time with Dundee I was in three different lots of digs, but, I hasten to point out, I was never evicted from any of them!

Another thing that happened while I was at Dundee was that I completed my PE course at Jordanhill and also another one-year course which I looked upon as a kind of insurance. The latter course qualified me to teach subjects at primary level in schools, and I considered that it would be useful to have that as well as my PE qualification. I did actually start to teach while I was at Dundee because we used to train only in the mornings for four days a week, which left me with the afternoons and the whole of Monday free. I was what was known as a peripatetic, or itinerant, PE teacher, because I went round various schools in the Dundee area. I thoroughly enjoyed myself in the teaching profession, even though I was still classed as a full-time professional footballer. It was not uncommon in those days, but today, with so many more fixtures and other commitments, players would find it virtually impossible to have such a part-time career – even if they wanted, or even needed, it.

While all this was happening I was still very much a part of the Dundee first-team squad, which was not only trying to defend the championship in the new season, but was also making its debut in the European Cup. This meant that there were quite a few problems with my teaching work as I often had to change my appointments, and that, in turn, would throw out some of the timetables at the schools where I was working. The other problem was that the PE work also caused my knee to swell up once more. I discussed the problem with the education authority, and they suggested that it would probably be better, and more convenient all round, if I concentrated on my primary teaching instead of my PE teaching. I took their advice, and that really is how I got started in primary teaching.

Meanwhile, there was plenty happening on the football pitch. The New York visit that I mentioned earlier was planned to enable us to take part in a soccer tournament involving teams like Reutlingen of West Germany, Hadjduk Split of Yugoslavia, Guadalajara of Mexico, Palermo of Italy and America of Brazil. It provided some valuable experience in playing against foreign sides. Doug Houston, whom I mentioned earlier, had joined Dundee from Queen's Park, and the well-known goalkeeper Bert Slater had also signed for us. Three players had left us and there was a cloud hanging over the club because six of the top Dundee players had not signed new contracts. The club had offered £25 a week but Hamilton, Penman, Robertson, Seith, Ure and Gilzean were not yet committed, and there was the obvious worry that they might go elsewhere. That £25-a-week offer was not bad in those days. The two Glasgow giants, Rangers and Celtic, would possibly have paid more, but nobody else in Scotland would have done at that time. As it happened it was all a storm in a teacup anyway, because all six of them eventually signed on the dotted line, meaning the team was intact when we opened our campaign against our arch-rivals Dundee United at Tannadice.

It was a League Cup game, and I'm pleased to say that I had recovered sufficiently from my knee problems to be picked for the team. Unfortunately we lost 3–2, which was a blow – but we made up for it a few days later with a 1–0 win over Celtic.

I have to admit that we struggled during our remaining League Cup games, and not even a civic reception at Dundee's Chamber of Commerce, in honour of our championship's success of the previous season, could rekindle the flame that had burned so brightly. A lot of our confidence did return, however, when we beat Dundee United 2–1 in the return League Cup game, and it was probably that victory that set us up for our very first European Cup game. We had been drawn against Cologne – one of the most daunting challenges any side could be asked to face on their European Cup debut. The manager decided that the best policy would be to go for experience rather than for enthusiasm, and therefore four other younger players and I found ourselves left out to make way for those with possibly cooler heads.

On the face of it we were in for a hiding by the Germans. There is no shame in the fact that we were pretty well written off, with questions being asked about how many Cologne would score rather than if they would score. Scottish football has always been a game full of surprises – not all of them pleasant ones. In recent times, Scottish clubs have struggled in European competitions. We cannot use the English excuse of being banned for so many years because we have never had a break in continuity but, somehow, these days it does not seem to pay off for us.

I thought that Celtic played very well before going out to Liverpool in the 1997/98 UEFA Cup, but I could not honestly say that about others – Rangers included. They should have done much better. The clubs' management and coaches, along with their players, also seem to find it a mystery that no serious progress has been made in any of the European competitions for so long. We can only put it down to not being 'all right on the night', and hope that, soon, a psychological barrier can be broken down and that Scottish clubs will set the matter right by once again making their mark on the European football stage.

We have had our European triumphs, of course, and I'm sure that we will again – but we are certainly starved at the moment. Anyway, let us turn the clock back and follow the fortunes of Dundee in the 1962/63 European Cup competition, to a time when the first hurdle was looking more like one of those nightmare fences in the Grand National.

What was about to happen in that tie against Cologne nobody really knew – how could they? As I said, we had already been written off by many people. However, since the event, it has become one of the most talked-about clashes in European football history.

5 Marching on Europe

Nobody could possibly have written the script for Dundee's first European encounter. There had been a buzz of real excitement when we heard that we had been drawn out of the hat with FC Cologne. They were a well-known side and the tie was eagerly awaited. You can imagine that as the time approached for the first leg – which was at Dens Park in September 1962 – the newspapers were carrying daily bulletins on the build-up to the big day. They were given some real gems by a gentleman called Karl Frohlich, who was the advance guard for Cologne and had been sent ahead to take a look at the hotel and training facilities. During an interview he said one or two things that could hardly be thought of as flattering towards Dundee. The newspapers loved it and their banner headlines whipped up even more frenzy for the approaching clash.

Not only did Dundee fans feel insulted by Herr Frohlich's remarks – which he later denied making, by the way – but they also lulled Cologne into an air of complacency. He had insinuated that they only had to turn up to get through to the next round of the European Cup.

I was not playing in that game but I was in my customary place with the squad – not on the bench, of course, because substitutes were not allowed then. I did not make the eleven on the team sheet but I was involved in all the preparations as usual – just in case. The match began at a frenzied pace. Dundee, roared on by the fans, were determined to go for the jugular from the very start. The Germans were startled, so much so that after ten minutes their experienced defender, Matt Hammersbach, put the ball into his own net while under pressure.

About a minute later we scored again with one of the most incredible goals that I have ever seen. Bobby Wishart found himself in a position to have a go. He let fly but completely miskicked the ball, his foot ploughing into the turf. Instead of rocketing towards the goal, the ball merely trickled along – but Fritz Ewart, the German goalkeeper, dived in the opposite direction. Bobby had sent a large divot into the air and the goalkeeper had mistaken it for the ball. He flew in one direction and caught the turf as the ball gently rolled in at the other post. Long-term Dundee fans will remember that goal for as long as they live – as will I.

It didn't end there either, because Hugh Robertson took advantage of the Germans' dismay to put us 3–0 ahead with only thirteen minutes gone. Alan Gilzean and Gordon Smith both scored too, putting us 5–0 ahead when we went in for half time. That scoreline must have sent shock waves all around Europe. Emotions were running very high indeed during the interval, and not just because of the goals. Alan Cousin and the German goalkeeper had both gone for a high ball and the Cologne man had ended up on the ground, rolling about as though he had been pole-axed. In fairness, he did go to the local hospital later for treatment to a head injury, but Alan denied that he had made any deliberate contact with Ewart. The German newspapers had other ideas, though, and a photo of Alan Cousin punching their goalie hero was splashed all over the media. It was not a fake photo but it was a misleading one. Photos taken from a different angle showed that there was no question of a punch being landed.

At the end of that first leg we had conceded a deflected goal but Andy Penman had got one for us and a brace from Alan Gilzean completed his European hat-trick. I think that we all had to rub our eyes to make sure that we hadn't been dreaming; the final score was Dundee 8, FC Cologne 1. The Germans returned home seething. Their supporters did not not blame them – they put it all on Dundee. Even one of their officials stated that if the goalkeeper happened to be injured early on in the second leg, a complete reversal might be on the cards. We shrugged that off, even though the newspapers made something of it. On reflection, I think that we were a little naive. Prior to that second meeting, we took it that the problems over our accommodation and training facilities were simply down to language differences and our own inexperience. We never even considered that there might be something more cynical behind it.

On the night of the match things had reached boiling point in Cologne. The Dundee directors and officials were virtually ignored by their German counterparts, even down to having to find their own seats as their hosts refused to have anything to do with them. At the very least it was extremely ill mannered but, once the game was underway, we quickly learned that there was a lot more to it than that. Once again I was not in the team, but even from the side of the pitch you could see that some of the German antics were far from gentlemanly. There was kicking, punching, spitting and even scratching going on – all with the total support of about 40,000 home fans.

Cologne took the lead after Ian Ure mistimed a tackle and had a penalty awarded against him. Habig scored from the spot. A few minutes later we were two goals down when Mueller scored what was, to be fair, an excellent goal. Then, with the game 27 minutes old, our goalkeeper, Bert Slater, dived to save a low ball and Mueller came in feet first with no hope of getting the ball. Sammy Kean, our trainer, rushed on to see blood running down Bert's face and he knew that it was serious. Andy Penman took over in goal as Bert was stretchered off, but then the real drama began as the German ambulance drivers attempted to get Bert into the ambulance – which had been parked behind the goal – and off to hospital. Bert jumped off the stretcher and went with Sammy Kean to the dressing room amid a lot of shouting and arm-waving. I like to think that this was all a coincidence, but many remembered what had been said after the first leg about the possibility of our goalkeeper being injured.

Andy Penman did his best in goal but by half-time the Cologne side were three goals ahead on the night and the overall scoreline was now 8–4. The Dundee players trooped off the pitch blazing with anger at the German team's conduct, and it was left to Bob

Shankly – even though he was obviously angry himself – to calm the situation down. Meanwhile, Lawrie Smith had managed to patch up Bert Slater and had wrapped so much bandage around his head that he looked as if he were wearing a turban.

'I look like Lana Turner,' joked Bert, and that managed to take some of the heat out of the mood in the dressing room. The very fact that he was returning to action also gave everyone a lift. He played on the wing for a while, just to make sure that all was well, and then went back in goal – much to the relief of Andy Penman. Later, Bert claimed that he had been a better winger than Gordon Smith – another example of the famous Slater wit!

The second half was played in much the same style as the first, but the Dundee side had grown up a lot during the interval and refused to give in to the provocation. We mounted much more pressure on the Cologne goal and came close to scoring several times. Ian Ure unfortunately scored an own goal, but that was the end of the scoring and at the end we had won the tie 8–5. It was not the end of the drama, however! As the final minutes ticked away there was a vast gathering of German fans around the touchlines. Taking throw-ins was difficult to say the least, and yet the German officials assured everyone from Dundee that this was quite normal in Germany. We weren't convinced, and our worst fears were realised when the final whistle went and the pitch was invaded. The Dundee players were marooned together in the middle of the pitch as the home fans began to swamp them. Fists began to fly and it began to look very nasty indeed until the next part of the drama unfolded – as our skipper Bobby Cox explained: 'Above all the noise I suddenly heard a voice say: "Don't worry about this lot – the Jocks are here!" It was like the relief of Mafeking. It seemed that every British soldier stationed within a radius of a couple of hundred miles had come to the game and, at the end, they swept on to defend us. They were all in civvies but there was no mistaking them. They fearlessly wrapped themselves around us and practically carried us off the pitch to safety.'

It was quite a scene, I can assure you, and one never to be forgotten – although it was later forgiven. Immediately after the game there should have been a banquet, but the Dundee party boycotted it. Years later the two sides met again in the UEFA Cup, and this time there was a much greater feeling of *entente cordiale* – and Dundee won again, 5–4 on aggregate.

Much of the ill feeling in that tie had been caused by the German press, and that was another lesson I learned. I try to be very careful in what I say and to whom I say it. One false move and you can have all sorts of problems on your hands. That doesn't mean to say that I blame the media for all the troubles of the world, but it does mean that certain members of the journalism profession could act a little more responsibly.

I suffered an example of this early in my career as Scotland manager when I left Davie McPherson out of the squad and called in Colin Hendry. When asked for the reason for Colin's selection, I included in a list of his attributes that he was slightly younger than Davie. Imagine my consternation the next day when, beside a large photograph of Davie McPherson, was the heading – 'Too Old At 29!'

So, Dundee survived their first sortie into Europe with honours, and we were all looking forward to the next round. The League season wasn't going too badly – we had a good run which kept us within four points of the leaders, Hearts. It was a fairly confident Dundee side that went to Portugal to face Sporting Club of Lisbon in the next round of the European Cup. It was an exciting game, and we had gone into it to defend, which I felt we had done quite well. Two minutes from time, Sporting scored with a controversial goal. Everyone was sure that Bert Slater had punched the ball on to the crossbar and away, but the referee decided that it had crossed the line and he awarded the goal. We didn't protest too much because in reality the Portuguese side deserved their victory, even if it was only 1–0. We felt that the possibility of turning the game around in the second leg was well within our capabilities. As it turned out we were right. About 32,000 turned up to see the side beat Sporting 4–1, with Alan Gilzean scoring another hat-trick and Alan Cousin getting the other. The 4–2 aggregate scoreline meant that Dundee were in the quarterfinals, and suddenly everyone began to sit up and take notice.

On the League front our form had slipped a little – although a

10–2 win over Queen of the South in December helped a bit. Alan Gilzean's seven goals in that match equalled a club record. Unfortunately, the gap between the leaders and ourselves was beginning to widen.

Anderlecht were to be our next European Cup opponents. They had beaten Real Madrid in the previous round, so the Belgians had built quite a reputation – especially with nine internationals in their side, including Paul Van Himst. The first leg was at the Heysel Stadium in front of about 60,000. They were all set to cheer their team nearer to the European Cup final, but there was a stunned silence when Alan Gilzean met a Gordon Smith cross and put us ahead after only 60 seconds. Anderlecht were rocked for a moment but soon got their act together and played some great football. However, Alan Gilzean fired in another goal on twenty minutes and, even though Anderlecht pulled one back from the penalty spot before half-time, the dressing room was buzzing during the interval. Alan Cousin added to the Belgians' woes just after the interval but, to their credit, Anderlecht kept cool and continued to play some attractive football. The Dundee defenders held firm, with both Ian Ure and Bobby Cox clearing off the line on the rare occasions when Bert Slater was beaten. When Gordon Smith scored our fourth goal with only nineteen minutes left, the game was all but over. It is to the credit of the Belgian fans that when the final whistle went to end the game they gave the Dundee side a standing ovation.

The return match at Dens Park a fortnight later was also a classic, with almost 40,000 people packed into the ground. Anderlecht put on another great display of football and took the lead in the first half. However, after the break, it was the home side who dominated, and the pressure eventually told when Alan Cousin equalised with twelve minutes left. A few minutes later Gordon Smith hit the winner and the final scoreline was 6–2. Part of the reason why Anderlecht had conceded goals at Dens Park was because they had been following the wrong man. They knew that Alan Gilzean would be the danger and they put two men on him – which gave freedom to our other forwards. What the Belgians didn't know was that 'Gillie' had gashed his foot in the first leg and had only had the six stitches removed a few hours before the return game. He had been used as a decoy and it had worked handsomely.

At the start of the season, the thought that Dundee would make it to the semifinals of the European Cup would have produced smiles from even the staunchest of supporters – and yet here we were in the last four. I was in and out of the side for League matches and I was present as one of the fourteen-man squad at every European game, home and away. Never getting on the pitch for any of those special games is something that I really regret. I do take some consolation, though, from being a part of the squad, and therefore in the dressing room and alongside the pitch at every game. It is frustrating when you are not actually playing, but it would have been much worse to have been left behind in Scotland while the side was engaged in battle in Germany, Portugal and Belgium.

Our semifinal opponents were to be AC Milan, expected to be the toughest yet of our European opposition. The first leg was away, and 78,000 fans were there in the famous San Siro Stadium. Bobby Cox was injured, and it would have been the natural choice for me to stand in for him but, unfortunately, I was injured as well, and so it was decided not to take the risk.

Dundee were a goal down after three minutes of the game starting – but they kept their heads and Alan Cousin finished some great work by Andy Penman and grabbed us an equaliser. Spirits were high in the dressing room at half-time because we felt we could contain the Italians and set up a great second leg back at Dens Park. AC Milan had other ideas, however, and soon scored two hotly disputed goals to go into a comfortable 3–1 lead. I say that the goals were controversial because there were suggestions that the ball was out of play before being crossed to Bariston who made it 2–1. As for the third goal, there was a Milan player standing in an off-side position on our goal line. The referee had given off-side but then changed his mind and awarded the goal. Milan scored again later in the game and we were disappointed to leave the pitch at the end of a 4–1 defeat.

It always sounds like sour grapes and so I try to make a point of not criticising officials or even crying over spilt milk. What's done is done! Others, though, complained bitterly about the

Spanish referee, and it does have to be said that the slightest hint of a tackle from a Dundee player did seem to bring forth an immediate whistle! Later, it was discovered that he had accepted gifts from AC Milan before the game, and he was eventually banned after some other charges of bribery, which were nothing to do with our game, had been revealed. At the end of that first leg, the Dundee players were dismayed and could not really understand how they had come to lose 4–1 to a team they considered to be inferior to the other three teams they had already encountered and beaten.

Milan were programmed to defend their lead when they came to Dens Park for the second leg, and they did it almost perfectly, although their tactics were rugged, to say the least. It was impossible to get any rhythm into the game because the Italian players continually broke it up with fouls and niggling incidents. As it was, Alan Gilzean scored just before half-time to reduce the aggregate deficit but, after having a later goal disallowed, a blatant penalty denied and a frustrated player sent off, we were forced to concede. It had been a great experience in the European Cup, and I think that Dundee had done Scotland – and indeed Britain – more than proud. I would not have missed it for the world.

Our League form suffered as a result of the pressure of the European games and in the end we finished at ninth place in the table, despite finishing quite strongly. Sadly, there would be no European football for us the following season.

Dundee Football Club was very good for me. I have already mentioned how much I admired our manager Bob Shankly, and that I learned so much from him. He was a very honest, straight Ayrshire man who had played for the famous Glenbuck Cherrypickers in the mining village of Glenbuck, where he and his brother Bill grew up with the rest of their football-mad family. Bob was also a close friend of Jock Stein, and they were all of the same mould. Bob Shankly was never one for giving out a lot of praise. He would sometimes put a hand on my shoulder before a game and say: 'Nothing clever from you today, son!' It might sound like a very negative way of motivating someone when all the psychologists say that positive affirmation is what is required, but we all knew what he meant and became accustomed to his special phrases. As an example, if someone said: 'I think I'll pass the ball inside the full-back for our winger to run on to', Bob would say: 'Christ, there's nae need to get complicated!'

The lads always joked because he never ever called me Craig. He always exalted me to a deity and called me 'Christ Craig'! Even on the rare occasions when I had a good game he would come to me after the match and say: 'Christ Craig, that wasnae bad today, son.' Also, if a player was being a bit bombastic in the bath, boasting about his prowess, Bob would come in and cut him dead by saying something like: 'Will you shut up, we've all seen you playing!' He had a perfect way of putting you down if you were getting too big for your boots, but he always had kind words when they were needed.

Another of Bob Shankly's favourite sayings would be heard when a pressman asked him the team selection for the next game. Bob's wife was named Greta, and he always gave the pressman the same answer – 'Oor Greta hasnae picked it yet!' It was just an amusing way of saying that he was keeping his cards close to his chest and would not reveal anything until the last possible moment before the game.

Sammy Kean was his right-hand man, coach and trainer. He was a former Hibs player and he knew his stuff all right. Between them they gave us training sessions that were long on hard work but probably a little short on imagination. There was little or no time spent on tactics. The players themselves worked those out, and some of us used to stay behind after official training to plan a few things. The senior players, particularly our right half, Bobby Seith, who had won the English League championship with Burnley, would evolve the set pieces from throw-ins and free kicks and we would practise these without supervision when the regular training had been completed. I would suggest that this was pretty unusual – not only then, but also now.

Of course, there were many light-hearted events too. One of the many other lessons I learned was never to take on a supporter in the crowd. I made that mistake playing against Celtic once. It was at Celtic Park, probably around January 1962, a cold, wet afternoon, but with the usual huge crowd. I was given the job of marking a young Celtic lad making his debut for the club. Bobby Lennox was his name, and he later went on to become one of the famous Lisbon Lions.

I was given the job of keeping him out of the game. Bob Shankly knew all about him and realised that he would be a threat. He had a saying which sounds quite chilling – 'One from eleven is ten'. As there were no substitutes in those days, if a player was ineffective you were stuck with it for the whole game. At least, that's what I like to think he meant! Being absolutely blunt, I had been given the job of kicking Bobby Lennox every time there was an opportunity – and to make sure that he made no real contribution to the game.

You can just imagine how the Celtic supporters responded to that. I came in for a lot of stick from the home fans – and that is when I made my mistake. One fan in particular took tremendous exception to the way I was doing my job. He questioned my parentage and hurled all kinds of other abuse at me. I was aware of what he was saying about me, and so was the Dundee full-back, Alex Hamilton. He was quite a character, as well as being a great Scotland international. He came over to me and said: 'You see that guy in the crowd? If he shouts at you again, and you get a wee chance, tell him that he's a mug because he's paid to get in.' It would have been a stinging retort because Celtic were struggling against us at the time.

Sure enough, the moment came when the ball went out of play and landed in a big puddle in front of where this guy was. The ball-boy was a bit slow getting to the ball because it was in the puddle, so I just went in and retrieved it. As I did this the guy started up again, telling me what a terrible player I was, the worst he had ever seen, and this game was the worst he had ever seen. I took Alex's tip.

'Well, pal,' I said, 'you're the mug because you paid to get in!'

Quick as a flash, he replied: 'Aye! But you'll be paying next season!'

It was a great answer and I felt very small indeed because I had absolutely no reply. It taught me never to try to mix verbals with the crowd, and the Dundee lads kept telling me that the guy was likely to be a prophet! It also taught me never to listen to Alex Hamilton again!

Talking about Alex Hamilton, he was the player who originated the back-handed insult that players today are often heard to repeat in jest. For instance, he called Ian Ure over once and said: 'Well, Ian, you and I have got thirty-three Scotland caps between us – and I've got thirty-two of them!' It is a much-used leg-pull between players, but it was Alex who started it. He was always joking, and not just with his teammates either. He used to love winding up the opposition, and especially enjoyed tormenting the stars of Rangers and Celtic whenever he got the chance. One of his jokes was to take a complimentary ticket and put it in his shorts. He pulled this stunt on both John Hughes, the Celtic winger, and Davy Wilson, the Rangers outside left. He waited until there was a lull in the game and would then go up to his victim with the ticket in his hand, saying: 'Here, John, here's a ticket for you to get into the game.' He also used to joke with them that they ought to have paid to get in for the privilege of being a spectator watching him play!

There was quite a bit of humour at Dundee, with everyone getting his chance as well as being on the receiving end. During that 1962/63 season I was given my nickname of 'Bleep' or 'Bleeper'. It originated during a game against Partick Thistle. The Jags goalkeeper, John Freebairn, sent a long, long clearance way down the pitch over all our heads and I chased after it. Because I had my back to the rest of the pitch, I decided to try a fancy overhead scissor kick as I had seen the continentals do. I completely mistimed it and, instead of the ball going back up the field, it just went straight up into the air like a rocket. It seemed to hang way up there for some time over our penalty spot, almost as if it had gone beyond our sphere of gravity. While we were all waiting for it to come down it reminded Alex Hamilton of the Russian Sputnik that was in the news at the time, and he began shouting: 'Bleep bleep! Bleep bleep!' That's how I came to be given such a unique nickname.

We had another interesting excursion that season when we played against Arsenal in a testimonial match for Jack Kelsey. We played two games against them, both home and away, and I was involved in both matches. The Arsenal side had some very famous names – Geoff Strong, George Armstrong, Alan Skirton, George Eastham, John Barnwell and Eddie Clamp among them. We had two very good games, and it was a delight to play at a wonderful ground like Highbury. We drew there 2–2, with Alan Gilzean scoring both Dundee's goals which, I think, led to his eventual transfer to Tottenham where he – quite rightly – became a hero.

On the eve of the Highbury game we all went to Chelsea to see them play Blackpool. Tommy Docherty was manager of Chelsea at the time, and I remember the game well. We stayed at the Mount Royal Hotel, which was in a noisy part of town but very pleasant nonetheless. It was an especially enjoyable trip because we were not there for a cut-throat competition and were therefore able to relax and enjoy the visit to London and two of the most famous grounds in the game.

It was a great honour for us to be invited to play in such a high-profile testimonial, and it shows the esteem in which Dundee was held after their European Cup and Scottish championship exploits. In 1997, Nigel Winterburn's testimonial at Highbury produced a big crowd for the visit of Glasgow Rangers. It was a parallel with our 1962 visit. As many a Dundee fan has said in recent times: 'Those were the days!'

6 The End of the Beginning

fter our visit to Highbury there was newspaper talk of me signing for Arsenal. Ian Ure and myself were both in the frame, it seemed. I felt that I had performed well against the Gunners, but I could not imagine that they were seriously interested in me, although I could clearly see why they would be keen on big Ian. As it happened, I was officially told that there had been some interest in me, but as I had no wish to leave Dundee and the club were not particularly keen to unload me, I stayed where I was.

Dundee, like most clubs at that time, were in good financial shape. Players were earning nothing like the astronomical figures of today, and I believe it was to use up some surplus cash before the end of the financial year that the club would take us away for training. We were told that we would be staying at a pleasant hotel in Crieff or Pitlochry, and we would look forward to going because we would train in the mornings and then have the afternoons free for golf or some fishing. It was no more exciting than that because we were never taken to places famed for their nightlife.

On those trips, therefore, we had to amuse ourselves. Some players liked to play cards – but not as many as you might think, or even as many as nowadays. So we used to have a bit of a singsong in the evenings, and the old folk who would be staying in the same hotel as ourselves loved it. We would get round the piano and sing all their favourite songs. One or two of the guys were quite musical. Alex Hamilton played the piano, Hugh

Robertson played the guitar, and a couple of the others could sing very well, and so we would stage an impromptu concert around that old piano, doing all the old-time songs as well as a few Beatles favourites.

As I said, the other people at the hotel would enjoy this immensely – and so did we. It was good fun and gave a great boost to our camaraderie and team spirit. I would like to think that it went a long way to helping Dundee to be successful on the pitch. After all, team harmony has often been the secret of many a club's successes. It is something that I have always tried to foster in my various roles as coach, club manager and national team manager. It has always been my objective to make sure that there is a good relationship amongst my players.

So, there we were singing our heads off each evening, until gradually it developed into six of us becoming a singing group. A local musician, a guy called Johnny Battersby – who had a sixteen-piece orchestra in the JM Ballroom in Dundee – asked us if we would go into the ballroom and sing as a special attraction. We thought it might be a bit of fun, and someone wrote a couple of songs for us. It was hardly the start of any threat to Frank Sinatra, but it was certainly the start of an interesting diversion.

Murdoch Wallace Junior was the local businessman who ran the JM Ballroom, and he was in the process of forming his very own recording company. The pop business was really booming at the time and Murdoch was keen to have his share. We were becoming quite well known for our singing group, led by Alex Hamilton, but, really, we only thought of it as another way of amusing ourselves. We had started by singing in the bath, then progressed to the hotel lounge, and now the JM Ballroom. We had no plans for going any further than that – but Murdoch Wallace had other ideas.

Alex involved Kenny Cameron, Alex Stuart, Andy Penman, Hugh Robertson and me. For engagements we wore the club blazer and a bow tie, but it was a bit of a mouthful to try to introduce us all individually and so we became known as Hammy and his Hamsters. The gigs came flooding in and we could probably have taken up many more offers but, after all, we were essentially professional footballers just out for a lark!

All this was developing in the 1963/64 season. By now we had lost Ian Ure, who had fallen out with the club. He had refused another contract and attempted to go on the dole, before being given a sales job by John Bloom, the famous washing-machine tycoon – who was a keen Arsenal fan – and eventually signing for the Gunners just after the start of the season for what was then a record Scottish fee of £62,500. We missed Ian on the pitch and also away from it because he was always a good leg-pull. In digs, we tormented him constantly.

He was a very clever guy with an excellent education record at Ayr Academy. He had a wealth of general knowledge and liked to tax his mind with crossword puzzles. Each night in digs we had a crossword competition. We would each get a copy of the Dundee *Evening Telegraph* and, starting the puzzle together before our evening meal, we would see who could complete it first – or who had filled in the most before our landlady called us down for the meal. Doug Houston, Tommy Mackle, George Ryden and I were the others involved, and of course Ian was always the best at it, so we hit on a scheme to wind him up a little bit. The four of us took to buying the early edition of the paper and getting the crossword mastered among ourselves – then we would go through the motions in the evening, taking it in turns to be the winner for the night. The big man, Ure, used to rage because we would keep an eye on him and, just as he was about to fill in the last answer, our 'winner' would say, 'Aye, that's me finished.'

Ian would jump up and shout, 'Och, ye so-and-so!' He got really mad about it. It was a long time before he realised the secret of our 'success'.

Another of our little games with Ian Ure was to tear a piece out of the sports pages of a newspaper that he didn't have and, when he asked us what it was, we would casually say, 'Oh, it was just a piece about you going to AC Milan or somewhere. We tore it out to give you in case the paper was lost.' We would then discuss among ourselves what had been done with the cutting, each one saying that the other had put it for safe-keeping somewhere. Eventually one of us would go off to pretend to look for it, only to return with a shrug of the shoulders, apparently unable to find it. By this time the big man would be beside himself and would jump into his car and go off and tour the newsagents until he found a copy – only to discover that he had been conned again. He fell for that one only once. It is no reflection on his mentality that he did so – he was just far too trusting. We even used to get people to put on foreign accents and phone him, pretending to be from top foreign clubs like Juventus or Barcelona, and ask him if he would be interested in joining them. Yes, we certainly missed Ian Ure, who was a great guy and a wonderful defender for his clubs and his country.

Despite the loss of Ure and one or two other comings and goings, our season was going well. We recorded some very big scorelines and kept pace with the leaders, Kilmarnock and Rangers. Alan Gilzean was still finding the net regularly and, by the end of the season, he had broken Alan Stott's record League goals tally in a season, which had been standing for nearly twenty years. Gillie scored 52 in the League that season and we had some great results, including a 9–2 home win over St Mirren and a 6–1 victory over St Johnstone. We scored a total of 92 goals in 36 league matches and, had our defensive record been a little better, we would surely have finished higher than the sixth place we finally occupied at the end of the season.

The biggest excitement was probably in our Scottish Cup campaign. We began by knocking Forres Mechanics, a very good non-League side, out of the competition with a 6–3 away win. Next we were drawn to play Brechin City away and we beat them 9–2. Our third-round tie was against Falkirk, at home for once. We defeated them 6–1 and were thus in the quarterfinals, having scored 21 goals in three games. Motherwell were our opponents for the next round and they provided quite a test, holding us to a 1–1 draw at home. Four days later we played them again in the return match and beat them 4–1 at Fir Park.

The four semifinalists were Rangers, Kilmarnock (then managed by Willie Waddell), Dunfermline (who had Jock Stein in charge in those days) and us. Dundee were to play Kilmarnock on the neutral ground of Ibrox. A look at the scoreline now will tell you that Dundee won 4–0 – but that was not a true reflection of the game. The two sides were even in the first half and it was really only in the last quarter of the game that supremacy was gained by the Dark Blues.

April 25th was the Hampden date for Dundee to play Rangers in the final of the Scottish FA Cup, and the whole of Dundee was excited because it was the first final appearance for the club since 1952.

It was an exciting time for Hammy and his Hamsters too! Yes, while all that had been going on we were still making a name for ourselves. It was decided that we would record 'My Dream Came True' on the new JM Records label. The song was a romantic number and we were backed by the Johnny Battersby Showband, who provided a tasteful melody line. On the 'flip' side – you see I was even into the pop jargon – was a much more up-tempo number with a great beat. It was entitled 'She Was Mine'.

The recording session was held in a studio in Edinburgh and it took a lot of rehearsals and takes before we finally got it 'in the can'. Murdoch Wallace knew his way around the publicity machine and the record was given a lot of exposure – especially since it was released just four days before the Scottish Cup Final. Although we were called Hammy and his Hamsters, everyone knew that we were Dundee players so, in a way, it was probably the start of the tradition of footballers recording songs before major events like cup finals, World Cups and so on.

It was a very busy time for us because there were the record promotional events as well as preparations for the Cup Final. Even on the day after the Cup Final – Sunday, 26 April – we were due to appear in a special show at Dundee's Green's Playhouse. Others in that show included Harry Douglas and the Deep River Boys, Stratford Johns, the actor, Eileen Keegan, compere Charlie Sim and the Johnny Battersby Showband. It was a great show and we enjoyed it – although we were not in the best mood for fun as Rangers had won the Scottish Cup by beating us 3–1. It was heartbreaking to see our opponents score twice in the last 90 seconds when it had looked as though a replay might be on the cards. The rain-soaked crowd of some 120,000 had enjoyed a thoroughly entertaining afternoon, and I don't think our side let their fans down in any way. A lapse of concentration at the very end proved to be fatal.

Some consolation was provided by the fact that our record sold well and, even though we were losers on the pitch and Rangers had completed a clean sweep of the championship and both major cups, we were not down-hearted, because Dundee was still there among the top clubs in the country. Besides, if all else failed, we knew we could earn a living busking on street corners!

Dundee was at that time a fine example of how a football club should be. I believe that it was the best footballing side I've ever known, and the harmony among the players was exactly how I like my teams to be. There were stars, but not one of them ever elevated himself above anyone else. Even those, like myself, almost permanently on the edge of the first-choice eleven were considered to be a part of the team. You expect that these days with substitutes and a squad mentality – but in those days it was much more rare, and a credit to the manager and his coaching team.

It would be remiss of me if I did not give a further mention to Gordon Smith, who was a hero of that side and a famous outside right who, as I said earlier, had already won the championship with both Hibs and Hearts before doing the same with Dundee. He was a terrific example of fitness, and of courtesy. Bearing in mind that he was the wrong side of his mid-thirties when he was performing for Dundee, he was truly outstanding in every respect.

Gordon was also very encouraging to the younger, less experienced players like me. When we were on that trip to Iceland he gave me a lot of tips to improve my game, but he also weighed in with one or two other items of advice. He once asked me what kind of shaver I used.

'I've got the very best kind of electric shaver,' he told me – and, indeed, he had a top-of-the-range Ronson which, I have to confess, I admired.

'Some day, when you've had a really good game, I'll buy you a Ronson like this,' he told me. I must admit that I didn't take him too seriously and soon forgot all about it. Some time later, we were playing alongside each other against Kilmarnock. He had the No. 7 shirt and I had the No. 6 – which meant that we were next to each other in the dressing room. It was quite a good game and I managed to give a reasonable account of myself. A few days later we were at home to Rangers. I arrived at the ground and went to my place in the changing room. There at my seat was a box – and in it was a brand-new Ronson electric razor, together with a note that read simply, 'I thought you had an outstanding game last week.'

Gordon had not forgotten what he had promised, even though I had, and it was a magnificent gesture which was so typical of the man.

These were the halcyon years of Dundee and, in my present job, the experience that I gained with that club at the time has proved to be invaluable. The European experience and the coaching, preparation and methods were an education to me that money would have been unable to buy. Yes, of course, I would have liked to have been one of the regular eleven who were constantly at the forefront of the manager's plans, but I was, after all, in the top fourteen, and therefore always involved in some way with everything – and I'm extremely grateful for that.

I was still teaching through those heady days as a Dundee 'star' and a 'pop icon', but I continued to have trouble with my knee. I decided, after I had been at the club for about six years, that I would pluck up the courage to ask the manager if I could go part-time officially. I explained that, with my knee still giving me problems, I was not expecting to have a very long playing span, and I wanted the insurance of my teaching career. He agreed with me and I was allowed to do my training with Hamilton Academicals. I continued to play for Dundee, but mostly as a reserve player with just the occasional first-team excursion. Meanwhile, I was gaining experience in my teaching work.

It was around 1965 when Falkirk, at the bottom of the First Division, made an approach for me. I talked to Bob Shankly, who was still Dundee manager, and asked for his advice, because I was due a benefit payment from the club. He looked me straight in the eye and said, 'Son, I'm getting the hell out of here – and I would advise you to do the same!'

I think he had fallen out with the chairman by this time, but I took his advice and agreed to join Falkirk. I had been the first signing that Bob Shankly had made when he joined Dundee, and I was his last transfer away from the club before he left. It was the end of a great time for the club and for me personally.

The deal went through and I did get my benefit payment, plus a little bit, which enabled me to buy a new car and still have some left over. I was also pleased to hear that Doug Baillie, with whom I had been at Rangers, was also joining Falkirk from Third Lanark the same week.

As I said, Falkirk were bottom of the table when we joined, but we managed to get some good results in the last weeks of the season and successfully steered the club to the safety zone away from the threat of relegation. I had been nursing my knee and disguising the fact that I was really only performing on one leg. I had been playing as sweeper, and I enjoyed myself because I found it a simple position in which to play.

Our last home game of the season was particularly memorable because we were visited by Celtic, and we delighted the Brockville Park crowd by beating them 6–2. It was an important end to the season for us because the club wanted to show its supporters how much it appreciated their loyalty when relegation was looking to be a certainty. There is no better way to send a crowd home happy than to give one of the biggest clubs in the game a real thumping.

I had three managers while I was at Falkirk. The man who signed me was Alec McCrae, and then he was sacked and replaced by Sammy Kean. That was bad news for me because Sammy had been the trainer at Dundee and, while there was no problem between us on a personal basis, he knew all about my injury problems. I remember that when we turned up for pre-season training, our coach – the excellent Willie Ormond – brought him into the dressing room to introduce us. We were all sitting around in our brand-new tracksuits and I was the first person that he clapped his eyes on.

With no hesitation, Sammy borrowed Bob Shankly's name for me and said, 'Christ Craig, you're not a full-timer, are you?'

I replied: 'No, boss, I'm only here during my school holidays.'

He said: 'Thank Christ for that!'

The players all laughed, and they knew that I wasn't going to figure too prominently in the forthcoming team selections. To be fair, Sammy was not an unreasonable man and I did get into the side. Unfortunately, he was later sacked and replaced by a well-known manager called John Prentice – one-time Scotland manager.

John Prentice had been an impressive manager in his day and was actually in the Falkirk side that won the Scottish FA Cup in 1957, so you can imagine that he was a very popular manager for the club. He had a tremendous knowledge of the game and the respect of everyone. By the time he arrived I was really struggling and spending nearly all my time with the second team. In fact, in the programme notes for first-team games, references to me usually said something like: 'Craig Brown, the "Auld Heid", is doing a great job in the reserves.'

I was still only in my mid-twenties but I was already classed as an 'Auld Heid'! I was captain of the reserves but I was still struggling, and it was quite good news for me that substitutes were to be allowed for the first time. I was now able to start a game and then, when I could not go on any longer, I would put up my hand and my replacement would be prepared to take over. Before the advent of substitutes I would either have not been able to play or been something of a lame duck during the latter part of the game. If substitutes had been allowed some years earlier, my playing career might have lasted much longer.

I had another knee operation when I was at Falkirk which slowed me down again – and then came the moment that every player dreads. I was told that I was being freed by the club. I was very disappointed that the news was given to me by Gibby Ormond, the reserves' coach and brother of Willie. He handed me an envelope. Inside was a letter that said that my services were no longer required.

It hurt that the manager had not told me face to face, and I learned another lesson. Having suffered the ignominy of being given a free transfer, I would never do the same to someone else without talking to him in a direct fashion, face to face, man to man! The letter I received was just a brief note thanking me for my services, which were no longer required. It went on to tell me to make sure that I only took one pair of boots with me! The letter came after a reserve game against Rangers at Ibrox, and I did feel that I had been treated rather badly. It wasn't the matter of being freed, but the manner in which it was done. I have never knowingly treated any player in my charge in such a fashion, and I never will.

So, Falkirk didn't want me any more. I thought long and hard about my situation and decided that my playing career was over. The knee was still playing me up and I felt that I was enjoying my teaching career enough to be able to turn my back on the game as a professional footballer. While at school I was coaching youngsters and so I was still involved in a very pleasant aspect of the game – giving tips to boys who might well turn out to be the stars of tomorrow.

It turned out that my playing days were not entirely over, however, when I had a surprise approach from Stranraer Football Club. They asked if I would be interested in trying to resurrect my career. I thought about it again and decided to have a go. I received a small signing fee and turned up for work. I started to train at Shawfield Stadium, the home of Clyde, where the physiotherapist was Lawrie Smith, who had been the first person to identify my knee problem when I was at Dundee. Lawrie was now at Clyde where the manager was Davie White, who later went on to manage Rangers.

So I trained at Clyde and began my Stranraer career with a friendly match against Larne, the Irish team. I was delighted, because I found that football at that level was very comfortable and I had high hopes of a good season with Stranraer. I should have known that it was all too good to be true. During training I received yet another knee injury, and I went to the Law Hospital in Carluke where I saw the surgeon, Mr Garden. He was a top man who knew his job, and he gave my knee a thorough examination, inside and out. Finally he came and talked to me with a very serious expression on his face. I could feel the tension rising within me as I waited to hear the result of the exploratory operation.

'I'm sorry, Craig, but your knee is a mess. It will not withstand any more wear and tear – and it is arthritic. I have cleaned it up the best I can but you have a condition known as exostosis, a bone problem. The truth is, you will have to give up playing.'

I swallowed hard. I had been expecting something like this but it was still painful to hear. Was that it? Never again to be able to kick a ball in anger? It was a bitter blow, but I knew that there was no point in arguing. The medical facts were evidence enough that my playing career was over – this time for good. I did not dwell on feeling sorry for myself. I felt bad for Stranraer. It was now August 1967 and the season was underway. They had paid me a signing-on fee and had started to pay wages. I felt that I had given nothing in return, and I well knew that for clubs like Stranraer there was a constant financial struggle. They had been good enough to offer me the chance of getting my career back together and it had not worked out. I knew they needed every bit of cash they could muster, and that was why I spontaneously paid back all they had given me. I felt that it was wrong for them to be out of pocket for something that was not their fault. For me, it was bad enough being told that I would never play again, but I would have found it very difficult to live with myself if I had gone out of football with the feeling that I had taken money under false pretences from such a friendly club as Stranraer.

Unlike many players, I had no need to worry about where the next penny was coming from or, indeed, what to do with my time. I would now have more time to devote to the teaching profession. While undergoing various courses during my Dundee days, I also attained my Scottish FA coaching certificates, my preliminary badge and my 'A' licence badge at Inverclyde, Largs, so I was already qualified enough for professional coaching had I chosen to pursue this option. If I might just give a bit of advice to today's players, it is a good idea to take your coaching certificates while you are still playing, because you have both the time and the money to invest in your future. In Scotland, the Professional Footballers' Association, whose dedicated secretary is Tony Higgins, is a big help, because it contributes two-thirds of the cost, which I believe is a very generous way of giving players extra options when they find it is time to be hanging up their boots.

I could name many among today's top football management and coaching staff who took the trouble to take their coaching courses quite early on in their playing careers. Men like Alex Ferguson, Walter Smith, Archie Knox, Jim McLean, Alex Smith, Jimmy Bone, Tommy McLean, Murdo MacLeod, Tommy Burns,

Paul Sturrock, John Blackley, Terry Christie, Jim Leishman, Bobby Williamson, Billy Stark, Wilson Humphries and John Haggart. Some of today's younger managers have followed the same pattern, planning well ahead for a continuation of their football careers. We are very proud in Scotland that virtually all the managers in senior football have taken their coaching courses at Largs and hold the 'A' or 'B' badges of the SFA. We encourage that, and we are also moving on to the higher course for a European pro licence which is co-ordinated by UEFA. It is a very good course at Largs, and we continue to promote it, both for the good of Scottish football and for the good of those players and others who want to coach at the highest possible standard.

For me, the summer of 1967 proved to be the twilight of my playing career. I had my championship medal, my youth and school caps, and many adventures and experiences to treasure. Now, it seemed, I was destined to be a schoolteacher who used to play football.

7 What the Doctor Ordered

There is no prescription for football. It was 1969, my professional interest in football was over and I was happily continuing my role as primary and PE teacher when I was invited to join the coaching team at Largs by Roy Small, who was running the courses there. I was asked along with my present colleague, Frank Coulston, who was – and still is – an excellent coach. The staff at Largs included Eddie Turnbull, Aberdeen manager, Jimmy Bonthrone, who was then at East Fife, Wilson Humphries, then at St Mirren, Archie Robertson, the manager of Clyde, Willie Ormond, then in charge at St Johnstone, and Peter Rice, who was a former player with Hibs and became a lecturer at St Andrews College.

All those men I have just mentioned have been fine coaches in their own right. Everyone has different ideas – which is why I maintain that there is no prescription for football. It is something that I have kept in mind since then. I have had it as a belief throughout my coaching career. You have a philosophy of football that suits you and you stick to it. It is totally wrong to criticise someone else's beliefs because what might work for one coach may not work for another – and vice versa! Flexibility has to be a highly important factor – you cannot be hide-bound to one system, one set of rules for set pieces in attack or defence.

All this was brought home to me once when I had a minor disagreement with the late Peter Rice, who was in charge of the course at this particular time. Peter had been No. 2 to Roy Small and, as Roy was away at this time, Peter was in charge. I was watching one of my coaches taking an excellent session. He was Eddie Thomson who later became coach of Australia after he had finished for Hearts and Aberdeen. Eddie was very successful with Australia and gave them a much higher profile on the international scene than they had previously had. When he left the job he became a coach in the J League of Japan. I have often wanted to be a fly on the wall at one of his sessions, just to see how the Japanese and other nationalities coped with his team talks. The last time I saw him they were still being delivered in one of the most pronounced Edinburgh accents you could ever wish to hear – I sometimes had difficulty in understanding him myself!

Eddie was coaching the use of a sweeper behind a back four. Peter came along and said: 'What's he doing, Craig?'

'Well, you can see what he's doing, Peter,' I replied.

'Surely he's not using a sweeper behind the back four?'

'He certainly is,' I responded.

'Well, you never do that!' Peter said.

I rose to defend Eddie's right to try his own methods. 'I think that's a bit of a sweeping statement, Peter.' One thing led to another and Peter and I disagreed over it. Eddie's idea was unusual but it was working for him – and it has since worked for Willie McLean and me when I was assistant manager at Motherwell. If we had a tricky away match we would use Eddie's system to good effect. Peter felt that Eddie should fail his exam because it was an unrealistic system – but I strongly disagreed.

In the end, Eddie completed an excellent session and I passed him. Later, both Frank Coulston and I were dropped from the coaching staff at Largs. I think it was a direct result of my disagreeing with Peter, who said that he was going to use a pool of coaches instead of having the same people involved all the time. I don't think anyone has been dropped since then, so I think I am probably correct in my assertion that it was all down to my backing Eddie.

I am sure that Peter, fine coach though he was, felt that there was a prescription for football and that if you used a sweeper it had to be behind a two- or three-man defence, and adopting any other system was unthinkable. Since then I have always kept an open mind while doing my own coaching thing. I have my own thoughts and systems but I am always prepared to have any aspect of my knowledge of the game improved by sensible suggestions. There is no set formula for anything, whether you are scoring goals or stopping them, and I defy anyone to show me a long-term success story involving anybody who is not prepared to adapt, adopt and try to improve.

While I was adding to my coaching experience I was working tirelessly with school and youth teams as well. I was also working to further my teaching career. When I finished my professional playing, the Open University was starting up and so I took a degree through that medium. I had been taking course after course for some time in my thirst for knowledge and qualifications, but there always seems to be a stigma attached to the role of a PE teacher – everyone thinks that you are an ignorant acrobat! People don't seem to realise that the academic qualifications needed to get into a PE teaching course were a lot more stringent than those needed for a primary teaching course in those days. I knew from my father's experience that qualifications were of the utmost importance if you were going to have a good career in teaching and, as with everything else, I did not see the point in getting involved with anything unless it was with a full commitment.

I thought I'd better get some academic respectability, so I took a BA degree through the Open University. I also did some additional courses that were relevant to my job – courses such as the development of reading, geography, and so on. Studying was becoming something of a hobby for me. I was really enjoying it and it provided me with something totally different from my PE and football coaching – which were taking up most of my time, of course.

As a result of all this – and possibly also because there was a shortage of teachers in Lanarkshire where I was working – I became deputy head teacher in Bellshill. Things seemed to move quite quickly because not long after that I became, for a short time, head teacher in Uddingston, and then later applied for a post as lecturer at the Craigie College of Education in Ayr.

This prompted a move from my home in Hamilton where I had

lived since I was married to Johan at the age of 24. So we moved to Prestwick and started a new kind of life in Ayrshire. My relationship with football, was still continuing with me managing and coaching football teams. This early experience has proved invaluable to me in my current job as the technical director as well as the team manager for the Scottish Football Association. For example, when I was at the Macalpine School in Dundee, while I was still playing, I ran three teams, which was quite an undertaking. I did get help from some of my Dundee playing colleagues, in particular from Terry Christie, who is now manager of Stenhousemuir Football Club and also rector of Musselburgh Grammar School. Doug Houston, my room-mate in digs, Ian Ure and Tommy Mackle all helped me with the school, so I had my own coaching team even in those days. I was determined to give as many youngsters as possible a taste of the enjoyment of playing football.

I often wish that I had known and realised the value then of the seven-a-side games and mini-festivals that we now encourage youngsters to play. In those days it was all eleven-a-side games. In the playground little has changed. The youngsters still like to be identified with their favourite teams and players, just as they did when I was a schoolboy myself. Lads love to get the chance to wear their team's shirt – and that means the school shirt as well as their favourite club's.

Today, we at the Scottish Football Association want everyone to take part in small-sided football while they are still under twelve, as we feel that it is a much better introduction to the game during those developing years. We also promote mixed soccer because the game is such a good recreation for everyone. Women's football is really taking off, and we have no wish to do anything other than encourage it in Scotland. Just as in men's football, you cannot be too young to learn the basics of how to kick a ball and to get some healthy exercise from doing it at the same time.

During my teaching days in Dundee, the rivalry between the two local sides – Dundee and Dundee United – was as keen as ever and, in the classroom after a local derby, there was much banter between the supporters of the two sides. In those days

Dundee was the stronger and more successful of the two sides but, in recent years, the pendulum has swung the other way – mostly because of the great effort put in by Jim McLean, and more recently his younger brother Tommy.

I can remember walking along the corridor at the Macalpine School on one occasion. I was talking to another teacher, Bill Young, at the time, when a parent appeared at the end of the corridor. He looked at me and said: 'Are you Craig Brown?'

I thought that he was about to congratulate me on our team's performance the day before, so I smiled and said, 'Yes, that's me.' With that this huge guy hit me with a right uppercut and down I went. I was pretty fit and not short of aggression myself in those days, but he had taken me by surprise. I didn't leave it at that, though. I caught hold of him, wrestled him to the ground and started to repay the 'compliment' – which meant that quite a nasty fight ensued in the foyer of the school. By this time the head teacher had arrived on the scene along with all the cleaners and various other people.

The head teacher told the man that if he wanted to interview any of his staff he should see him first. The man told the head teacher exactly what he thought of him and then threw him along the corridor. Once again chaos broke out until we were able to restrain the man. It transpired that he was the father of a boy to whom I had administered some corporal punishment earlier in the day. I had caught the boy hitting another lad across the face with the end of a climbing rope when they were supposed to be packing away the PE equipment, so I dealt him the appropriate punishment of the time – the belt!

It was a measure of my inexperience that I had punished the boy at the end of the day. It was the first time I had administered the belt, which was an acceptable part of school life in those days. The boy went home with his hand stinging. His father had been working in the fields collecting potatoes, casual work which was common in the area at the time. The workers were paid cash in hand at the end of the day and invariably spent it much more quickly than they had earned it, with the local hostelries proving to be the ultimate winners.

By the time this guy had met his son he was already half cut and, when he heard that it was Craig Brown who had punished his lad, it was like a red rag to a bull – because this guy was a Dundee United supporter and there was no way that he was going to let a Dundee player get away with such a thing. Along he came to remonstrate with me. Eventually he managed to struggle free and started to run away, all the time pointing at me and shouting: 'I've not finished with you.'

I had to report the matter to my manager, Bob Shankly. He listened patiently while I told him the story, then he took a long, hard look at the bruise under my eye.

'Is that what he did to you, son?'

'Yes, boss, I wasn't expecting it,' I replied.

'What did you do to him? I'll tell you this – nobody messes with any of my players like that!'

His concern was not for the ignominy that might be brought upon the club by the incident but the fact that one of his players at least gave as good as he got. That was the Shankly philosophy. The whole episode was soon forgotten and I heard no more about it until months later when I went into my digs one day and one of my teammates was reading the evening newspaper. The headlines read 'Dundee Player Assaulted'. It was Ian Ure, the avid newspaper reader, who was sitting with the paper, so I asked: 'Who's that, Ian?'

He laughed and replied, 'It's you!'

The story was all about the court case that had followed the incident. Because the guy had pleaded guilty I had not been called to give evidence – in fact, I didn't even know that there was to be court action. He was fined £10 – a significant figure because it comprised £6 for hitting Mr Baxter, the head teacher, and £4 for assaulting me. It wasn't the severity of the assault which counted, it was the rank of the person who had been attacked!

The following Saturday we were playing St Mirren and I was fouled by one of their players. As I was getting up from the ground I heard a voice in the enclosure shout: 'Go on, Brown, get your strap out!' The supporters never miss a trick!

It didn't do me any harm in the educational world because, in those days, corporal punishment was the accepted thing and, although I didn't condone it, I followed instructions and, on that particular occasion – as well as on very rare others – I used it, albeit very sparingly.

My time as a teacher, and in particular at the Macalpine School, taught me a lot about the great enthusiasm in Scotland for playing games and for football. When I moved to Lanarkshire I also ran the school teams. At Blantyre I had a very good football team, and also a very fine gymnastics display team of which I was very proud. Our main rivals were envious of our facilities and the way we were turned out for all our sporting activities – a reflection on our head teacher, who was not only a great educationalist but also extremely keen on the recreational aspects of school life. His name was Mr David Crawford, a wonderful man. With him and our janitor, Mr John Baird, I had two very strong allies in providing the best for the youngsters at the school. We tried to encourage them in sport as well as in every aspect of education.

I must have had a charmed life as a teacher because when I went to Bellshill, to the Belvedere School, I had enthusiastic support from the head teacher and the rest of the staff. We excelled in football, swimming and gymnastics and had some great individuals. One of my pupils at that primary school was not only in my football team but also in the class of which I was appointed teacher. He went on to become a top player and in 1979 was named Scottish Footballer of the Year. You know him as Andy Ritchie, and his career spanned Celtic, Greenock Morton and eventually Motherwell. He was impressive even as a boy – a very big lad who was obviously destined for an exciting career in football.

Andy Ritchie was a prime example of the argument against eleven-a-side football on big pitches for young kids. All Andy had to do was to get into the opponent's half and shoot. Because of his size, and the size of the goalmouth when compared to the lack of size of the goalkeeper, he would grab a handful of goals every time he played. You could get a jumbo jet to fly under the crossbar and over the young goalkeeper's head, and Andy soon learned where to place his shot. He was a prized asset to us because he could score so easily but, because his size and ability gave him such an advantage over other boys of his own age, he effectively ruined the game each time he played. It wasn't his fault, but it did show how inappropriate it was to have eleven-a-side matches in that primary age group. I tried to even the games a little by making arbitrary rules such as that he could only score with his head one day, or from outside the area on another. It succeeded in evening up the games and hopefully furthered his football education too.

While at Blantyre, I also ran the local Hamilton district schools side along with a priest by the name of Father Glachan. Between us we had the privilege of selecting the best boys from the local schools – and it would have been totally enjoyable but for the various parents who continually tried to influence our selection. The best example of this is provided in a series of award-winning short stories written by William McIlvanney. He wrote about the single parent watching his or her son playing football. Whereas the rest of the 21 players appear merely as a blur to that parent, his son remains in sharp focus throughout.

Because I was so busy with my schools coaching, I gave up coaching seniors for a while, but I was still remembered in Dundee as being a player and a coach, and also as being semi-literate. As a result, D. C. Thomson, the well-known publishing company based in Dundee, got in touch with me with a view to my writing a column. They produced all manner of newspapers and magazines, ranging from the *Sunday Post* and other newspapers to the *Weekly News*, the *Topical Times*, the *Beano* and miscellaneous women's and children's publications and assorted journals.

I was asked if I would comment on one of the matches of the previous weekend every Monday in the *Dundee Courier*, and I was delighted to do so. Then I was asked if I would write actual match reports for the *Sunday Post*. I was no longer playing at this time, and I was thrilled to be involved in the game from a completely different angle. So, for the next eighteen months, I was a regular in the press box. It taught me a great deal. I was sometimes given one of the top games, but I was always getting First Division matches – remember that there was no Premier Division in those days.

Once again, I consider this period as part of my education. I was able to listen to the comments of the press men and join in with their discussions, which gave me a great insight into the way the press viewed things. As well as commenting on the match I used to write the introduction to the piece and learned that you have to make it brief, to the point, and interesting enough for the reader to continue through to the match report, rather than just flash-read the scorers. I quickly learned the value of those people who write the actual headlines in the newspapers.

Usually, your introduction is something that you think up during the second half of the game when you can see how the match is going. You may already have been given your introduction by goals, sendings-off or injuries. I was once at a game between Airdrie and Aberdeen and it was, arguably, the worst game of all time. It was 0–0 with a minute to go and I had been struggling to dream up my intro before finally settling on resorting to William Shakespeare and his famous work *Much Ado About Nothing*. I had branded the game a bore with nothing to say for itself.

Not long before the final whistle, Drew Jarvie scored to break the deadlock – but my intro still held because the rest of the game was totally forgettable. I just added that Jarvie of Airdrie popped up to give us the only bright spot of the whole game. It was then that I realised the importance of those headline writers because, when the report appeared in the *Sunday Post*, the heading read 'Jarvie – Merchant of Menace' – totally in keeping with my Shakespearean intro.

I have often been amused by – or admired – newspaper headlines since then, although there have been times when I have been disgusted by the inaccuracies or innuendo contained in stories that are way off mark – or headlines that are meant to sensationalise the unsensational.

Anyway, I learned the ways of the press box. I would hear John Begg, the famous freelance writer, say, 'Who scored? . . . Left leg or right leg? . . . Who passed it to him? . . . What time was that?' It wasn't that he didn't watch the game, but he would be so busy telephoning constant reports to seven or eight newspapers that he didn't have time for the details. The other reporters would shout him the answers to his questions. When a goal is scored these questions are usually flying around the press box so that everyone is in agreement – even if they all have it wrong! I found also that it was easy to influence the reports if you just made a chance remark to someone near the end of a game. As an example, I might say, 'Doug Houston is having some game for Dundee today. Some of his passes have been great.' If you say it at the right time, when the reporters are considering which players have done well, you will almost certainly read the next day that the player you were touting 'put on a great performance'.

Most managers co-operate with the press – but not all. I can remember being asked to get a statement on injuries from one manager who was fairly new to that particular job, and whose side was playing in Europe a few days later. I waited for an hour and ten minutes after the game only to be told to 'F*** off' by the manager when I asked him if he had any injury worries. He didn't know who I was, and really it would have made no difference if he had. There really is no need for anyone to be uncivil – after all, we all have a job to do. I made up my mind, then and there, that if ever I was in a similar situation I would not speak in that manner to any journalist who was just trying to do his job. As far as I am aware, I never have.

To get back to my job at the college in Ayr, part of my role in lecturing on primary education was to watch students teaching in schools. It meant that I was out quite a bit, and when you add to that all the work I was doing with football teams, it doesn't take a genius to see that I was not at home very much. We had long holidays from the college, but I spent most of those involved in football coaching at some level or another. There was a lot of hard work done, but at various times of the year I would have a month off, which gave me the freedom to still be involved in football almost as a full-time occupation.

I have always liked to be busy all the time. I can't stand having nothing to do. It was no different in my teaching days – or even in my childhood. If I wasn't actively doing something, then I had to be thinking about things. During my time at Craigie College in Ayr, I would involve myself in football and golf – as well as catching up with all the latest paperwork and guidelines involved in my teaching profession. If there was an evening when I found that I was free I would have a game of golf – or dream up some new coaching idea to try out when next I got the chance.

The doctor had ordered me to stop playing football and I had done exactly as I had been told. I did not even take part in any of the training games I organised as part of the coaching work. If I kicked a ball at all, it was to demonstrate a point or just to pass it to someone who needed it for an exercise. I kept myself fit by taking part in the training and indulging myself in a bit of golf or swimming.

For all that, I could not stop thinking about the game. I was not bitter about the way my career had ended, and I was certainly grateful for the successes I had enjoyed during my all-too-short playing years, but it was frustrating not to be involved at the highest level of the game. I felt that I'd had something to offer and had been denied the chance of finding out whether or not I was right.

I had done what the doctor ordered and that was that. But then came the day when I was asked if I would like to become part-time assistant to Willie McLean, who was then manager of Motherwell, having taken over from Ian St John.

Would I?

Now, that really was just what the doctor ordered!

8 Back in the Game

I knew Willie McLean from the days before he took over at Motherwell. He was a very successful manager at Queen of the South in Dumfries where I also turned up as education lecturer to overspill students. Willie had collected some very good players at Queen of the South, talented and tough guys who gave him a well-balanced side. As an example he had Alan Ball in goal, Billy McLaren, Ian McChesney, John Murray and Rab Thorburn – who was later to become a player and my assistant at Clyde. Willie had a flat in Dumfries and I was staying in an hotel in the town, and we used to meet up and have long chats about football. I was delighted to discover that we were on the same wavelength, and I used to enjoy taking time out to go and watch his training sessions with Queen of the South, as well as seeing mid-week matches.

When Willie invited me to become his assistant, I didn't hesitate. He knew all about my commitment to my career in education but, as it happened, I was well able to fit in all that he required of me. The advantage of those long holidays was that I had plenty of time available during the period that was the all-important pre-season training time. From December to January I also had a full month off, and then again around Easter, which was the crucial run-in time to the football season, I had another full month in which to concentrate totally on my work with Motherwell.

Suddenly I had two full-time jobs again, and I was closely involved with one of the top teams in Scotland. It did not do a lot for my home life as I was always going out early in the morning and not returning until very late. My family knew where I was, but I don't suppose that was much consolation really.

On the plus side, I was able to work closely with Willie McLean and learn a great deal from him. We would sit and discuss training schedules, tactical techniques and all kinds of aspects of running a football team. There has never been a harder-working manager than Willie McLean, and his enthusiasm and drive were certainly an inspiration to anyone who came into contact with him – myself included. When I was not available he would take care of just about everything – including the reserves, who were my concern really.

With my education work and my football work, I found myself involved in three training sessions a day, morning, afternoon and evening – which, of course, is why I spent so much time away from home. I believe that it was the making of me as a potential manager because I had to follow Willie's example – there was no other way. We inherited a big squad of players, full-timers, of whom many were never seriously going to be first team-regulars – but everyone had to be treated the same. We had to spend a great deal of time looking at training and coaching innovations to keep so many players interested and motivated all the time.

You can imagine that the bulk of my reserve squad were disgruntled guys who were full-time on full-time pay, but with the knowledge that they would be unlikely to see any first-team action. They were experienced professionals and it would have been advantageous to have sold them – but they had to be seen to be sold, and that made it all something of a vicious circle. We could not afford to use the first team as a shop window, and reserve-team football is not exactly the most flattering scenario for a player that you are hoping to sell for a decent fee.

It was certainly a trying, and yet also an enlightening and instructive, time for me at Motherwell. Willie did very well for the club. He was a master of coaching, tactical awareness and man management – although I have to say that his man management skills did not extend to the directors of the club, the carpark attendants, the ball-boys, tea ladies or any of the other backroom people. Willie's efforts were focused exclusively on his players and immediate coaching staff. The players responded by always listening and exactly following the instructions given by Willie. Nobody ever formed the opinion that they knew better than he did.

I learned more from Willie McLean than I have ever learned from any other manager, either before or since.

We had a good, hard side at Motherwell in those days. When Willie took over the team they were not in a good situation. It was the very last season of the old two-division system and, if you did not finish among the top ten of the First Division, you would not be in the new-look Premier Division, which was due to commence in August 1976. I think we were around fifteenth when the new management regime took over. The emergence of Stewart MacLaren, Gregor Stevens and Willie Pettigrew from the reserves about halfway through the season transformed the side. Pettigrew ended the season as top scorer with 20 League goals in 28 games – seven of which were as substitute. We finished in tenth place and assured ourselves of Premier League football the following season.

That inaugural season of the Premier Division was an exciting one because there was the novelty of having to pit your wits against the top clubs four times in a season instead of the customary twice. Our opening League match was against my local side, Ayr. The game ended as a cagey 1–1 draw, and that was the pattern for our first five games, each one ending in a draw. We lost our sixth game at St Johnstone 2–1, but that was probably a blessing in disguise because thereafter we won and set ourselves up for quite a decent season, finishing fourth at the end of the campaign. One of my favourite results was a 6–3 win at Dundee, although beating Dundee United three times out of four and drawing the other game against them was also a bit of fun for me.

We also reached the semifinals of the Scottish Cup after knocking out Jock Stein's Celtic, Cowdenbeath and Hibs on the way. Rangers were our opponents at the last hurdle, with the game to be played at Hampden Park. They beat us 3–2 and went on to win in the final against Hearts, but we gave a good account of ourselves. It was an Alex Miller penalty which proved to be the one goal too many for us.

That semifinal match of March 1977 still leaves a bad taste in my mouth, even after all these years. It was not just the penalty. We were two goals ahead at half-time and should have been home and dry, but the penalty decision knocked the stuffing out of us. It was what is politely called 'a harsh decision' – but there are other words to describe it. We lost another goal when Stuart Rennie, our goalkeeper, overcarried the ball and Rangers scored from the indirect free kick. In the last twenty minutes we had gone from being 2–0 ahead, and cruising to the final, to losing 3–2. We left the pitch feeling totally shellshocked. I don't think that Rangers were helped by divine intervention, but I do feel that they had more than eleven players on their side.

The following season we met Rangers in the quarterfinals of that same competition and this time they beat us 2–0 at Ibrox – although they themselves lost 1–0 in the final against Celtic. In the League, our away record let us down because we only had two wins away from home – both against Hibs. We were pretty solid at Fir Park, though, and suffered only two defeats.

Those early days at Motherwell were made all the more interesting because there was a compensation battle going on between the club and Portsmouth, who were due to pay something for the signing of Ian St John as their manager. Motherwell had not wanted to lose him and there followed a disagreement between the two clubs that dragged on for some time. The Motherwell chairman, a lawyer by the name of Ian Livingstone, a fine gentleman, kept us informed of the situation, and it finally transpired that Portsmouth could not afford to pay the compensation and, instead, offered any player on their staff in exchange for Ian St John.

The upshot was that I made several trips to Portsmouth to watch them and see if they had any player who might do a job for us. I believe that the compensation finally agreed was to the value of £30,000, although it was never confirmed. It was a fair amount of money in the mid-seventies, so I had to be sure that we were not going to be sold short.

Portsmouth had one or two decent players, but the only one

that I thought might be any use to us was Peter Marinello. Now Peter had been with Hibernian until he was sold to Arsenal for £100,000 – a goodly sum in those days. Peter had been described as the 'new George Best', but, though he certainly had both the looks and the football skills, there was no way that he – or anyone else – could have stepped into the shoes of the world-class Best. I'm sure that the pressures of trying to live up to such an image did no favours at all for Peter Marinello and contributed to his being transferred from Arsenal to Portsmouth and being now at our disposal if we wanted him.

I reported back to Willie and the decision was taken to sign him. I found him to be a very nice guy, but he had some basic faults that several coaches at his different clubs had tried to remedy without success. One was that he would not play to the full width of the pitch. He would cut in far too quickly instead of staying out on the left wing as long as possible. Both Willie McLean and I used to get on to him about it, and he told us that Don Howe, his coach at Arsenal, used to say the very same thing to him. It was not deliberate awkwardness, just a bad habit of straying into the pitch and not being available in the open spaces on the wing. We warned him that if he played inside so much he was making himself a sitting duck for opposing defenders to clatter him.

Peter Marinello's other problem was that he could not cross a ball properly. He had great pace and he could take on and beat me at will with his obvious ball skills, but his final touch was poor, and so Willie McLean devised a simple exercise to help him. We would put a cone, or marker, a little way in from the corner of the pitch and Peter would practise running towards it and then putting the ball inside it before making his cross. It changed the whole angle of his last touch and gave him a much better chance of putting in a good cross than if he was trying to put the ball over from nearer the touchline. Willie had a very perceptive eye for football, and that simple measure certainly helped Peter Marinello. Some time later, when I was at Clyde, I used the same method to help Pat Nevin, and it is a tribute to Willie McLean that it helped Pat, and other players too.

Another memory of that period was our Scottish Cup

fourth-round tie against St Mirren in February 1977. Alex Ferguson was manager of St Mirren then, and they were running away with the new First Division. For their visit to Fir Park they brought most of Paisley and, of course, Fergie was his usual self, intimidating everyone and boasting of what he was going to do. We wound up our own players into battling mood with key St Mirren players like Frank McGarvey, Tony Fitzpatrick, Billy Stark and Bobby Torrance all delegated for special attention – which, I can assure you, they got. The St Mirren players didn't relish it and we beat them 2–1 – much to the annoyance of Mr Ferguson.

It is worth pointing out that Fergie did take St Mirren to the championship of the First Division that season, and thus gained promotion to the Premiership, so no doubt his famous scowl did not stay in place for long. Certainly Alex is another of those managers for whom the word 'defeat' is only applicable to other managers and their clubs. His track record speaks for itself, and is a reflection of his rugged determination always to have things his own way.

Of course, Willie McLean was delighted with that St Mirren result, and it was interesting to see the two faces of management – Willie with a grin from ear to ear, and Fergie with his scowl. I have always learned a great deal from managers and how they handle things, whether success or failure. Bob Shankly at Dundee, for instance, was very similar to his brother Bill. He never contemplated defeat – it did not exist in his mind, let alone his vocabulary. When it happened he rarely spent much time thinking about it but much preferred to move on to the next challenge.

A tip for any of today's players who might one day want to go into coaching or management – keep watching the guys who are in charge of you now. I learned from every person who ever took me for a training session or who was my manager. I didn't agree with everything, but the more you observe, the more characteristics you pick up, then the more experience you have to draw on when it becomes your turn in the driving seat. I would never presume to know all the answers, but I have certainly benefited from making a study of all the managers I have ever had the privilege of knowing.

At Motherwell, we had a groundsman who was famous for being one of the greatest characters in the game at that time. Andy Russell was his name, and there are many stories about him – most of which are true. One of my own experiences occurred the night that Celtic came visiting towards the end of the season when they were chasing their ninth consecutive championship. I remember it very well as it was a Wednesday night, and few people doubted that Celtic would clinch the title – probably on that very evening. Motherwell, of course, had other ideas.

Jock Stein arrived with his entourage of superstar players, looking every bit the reigning kings of Scottish football. One of the first people Jock bumped into was Andy Russell, and he said to him: 'Well, Andy, and what's your park like tonight?'

Our groundsman answered in a fairly provocative manner: 'G'd enough for what's goin' on to it!' There was no way he was going to be fazed by the big boys from Glasgow.

Jock didn't really appreciate that reply but he was not going to let it spoil the party. We didn't know it at the time, but he had brought some bottles of champagne with him in readiness for the after-match celebrations. Celtic went into their dressing room and Andy Russell watched as their gear was being unloaded. It was then that he spotted the bottles of champagne and hurried down to the Motherwell dressing room where Willie was giving his pre-match talk. Willie hated being interrupted at this stage, but Andy insisted that it was urgent and so the manager broke his own rule and allowed him to deliver his message.

'Jock's got six bottles of champagne in there!' he revealed.

'Oh, he has, has he?' Willie turned to his players. 'There's no way he's drinking his champagne here at Motherwell!'

It was quite a game and we put three goals past them. Two of those goals, in fairness, were own goals by Celtic's Andy Lynch, but we still deserved the victory and, as the players trooped off down the tunnel at the end, Andy said to Jock, 'What are you going to do with your champagne now, Big Man?'

It didn't help the mood that Jock Stein was in at that moment, and he launched himself at Andy. The two of them were rolling around the floor, punching and cursing, until the referee – Ian Foote – separated them. A report went in to the Scottish Football

Association but they decided to let the matter rest – which was probably the wisest decision, as it was a one-off incident and did no real harm.

That's not the only incident I recall about Andy Russell. There was another occasion when a carpet firm sponsored a game with Rangers at Motherwell. It was thought a good idea to have a red carpet for the players to walk out on. Several days before the game this magnificent red carpet was delivered to Andy at Fir Park.

When the big day arrived it was very noticeable that the carpet was somewhat shorter than it had been on the day of its arrival. Later, we found out that some of Andy's family had suddenly found themselves the better off for new lounge carpets. Still, Andy put out the remainder for the teams to walk out on – which they did with due pomp and ceremony – then he began rolling it up.

Someone shouted: 'What're you doing, Andy? The referee's no' come out yet!'

Quick as a flash Andy shouted back: 'I'm no havin' that b . . . . . d walking on my mother-in-law's new carpet!'

There were some disillusioned full-time professionals at Mother-well who wanted first-team action all the time. I never blame a player for that. It shows that they care about their job. The problem is that you need to have depth in a squad but you cannot play everyone you have on your staff. Among the players were Lloyd, a goalkeeper from Liverpool, McClymont, Muir, McCabe, Pelosi, Leishman, Pettigrew, Stevens and MacLaren. They were all fine players – but frustrated. Some of them, like MacLaren, Stevens and Pettigrew, finally did become regulars in the first team, but others were destined for only occasional chances. I did my very best to keep them all a happy bunch because I knew what they felt like from my own experiences of being in the reserves. I believe it provided me with further education in the management of players as individuals.

We managed to keep our heads above water at Motherwell – and probably would have won a few things but for some strange results going against us by the odd goal here and there. As it was, we were 'nearly men' – a very difficult outfit to beat, but not quite good enough to actually win anything. With more capital to give us a wider selection of players I think we could have become a greater power in Scottish football. It is one of those things that have to be filed under 'we'll never know' – probably the biggest file of all time!

Football in Scotland in the mid-1970s was undergoing a transformation. There were still those who did not like the idea of the League being split into more than two divisions, each with fewer clubs, but the supporters seemed to like the idea, believing there would be more interest in the promotion and relegation battles. In general, people do not like change. My dislike, however, is of change for the sake of change. If there is a definite aim and purpose, then fine, I'll go along with it.

When Scotland set up its new League system I was not opposed to it, and I have to say that the changes that have taken place since have all been for the good of the game. In England, there were many moans and groans when the old Football League system was scrapped and the Premier League introduced, but it has proved to be a tremendous shot in the arm for the game. A huge rise in available money has meant that the facilities at grounds are so much better, world-class players are attracted, and everyone is on a better deal. The standard of football in England is much higher, and England has become a force to be reckoned with on the world stage once more. I am sure that it all has much to do with the restructuring of the League.

In Scotland, there has been talk for a number of years of further restructuring, breakaway groups and all kinds of things. I'll go along with anything that gives us better football and co-ordinated youth development, just so long as that is the prime intention – rather than just a battle for power and money. There was no power battle at Motherwell. I had the best of both worlds – football with a great manager, a fine bunch of players and other staff.

My teaching work gave me the satisfaction of doing something different from football and helping young people on the road to very different careers from those of the players I was working with at Fir Park. But my ambitions towards management had grown, and the day dawned when I was in the frame for another job in which I was to be the man in the hot seat. The club was Clyde. I had played against them a number of times and had been to their well-known Shawfield Stadium quite often. I felt a bit sorry for them because they had the reputation of being one of those clubs that seemed always to be either relegated or promoted. It had not been many seasons before that they had finished third in the First Division behind Celtic and Rangers, yet since those days in the late 1960s they had been relegated, promoted and relegated again.

Now I had the chance to follow in the footsteps of my old pals Stan Anderson and Billy McNeill and become manager of Clyde, and I really wanted to have a go. I remember saying at the time how amazed I was to see Clyde in the Second Division because, only a few seasons ago during my early days at Motherwell, we had found them one of the hardest sides to play against and we had failed to beat them. Now they had slipped down two divisions in as many seasons.

One of the things I had to be assured of was that there would be no interruption to my education work if I became manager of Clyde. I have never been under any illusions about football and how it can leave you high and dry just when you have started to trust it. I have seen and heard of many players and managers who thought they were going along quite well only to have the rug pulled from under them unexpectedly. Had there been any problem with my continuing at Craigie College, I don't think I would have accepted the job but, as it was, there was no objection and so I shook hands on the arrangement.

I had managed all kinds of schools and youth teams and had been assistant to Willie McLean – but now things were beginning to get a little more serious. Suddenly Craig Brown was being described in the newspaper as 'Manager of Clyde Football Club'. I felt that I had just set foot on the 'yellow-brick road' to fame – or failure! A whole new chapter in my life was about to begin.

9 Off to Clyde

I t was a phone call from Billy McNeill that set me on the road to becoming manager of Clyde. Billy and I are old pals, as I have already said, and he phoned me to say that he had recommended me to the chairman, Tom Clark, to succeed him, as he had decided to take the job as manager of Aberdeen Football Club.

I felt honoured that Billy had done this for me, and it confirms what most people know about football – that it is an old pals' act. Clyde were in the bottom division at the time, and when I took over in July 1977 they had just finished in what was considered to be their lowest position ever – eighth from the bottom of the Scottish League. I don't think anyone can apportion blame for that. There had been a number of years of instability for one reason or another. Billy McNeill had been in charge for the last seven or eight games of the season, and before that Stan Anderson had been the manager. During Stan's protracted illness Bobby Waddell, Mike Clinton and Peter Rice had taken temporary charge. They were all good managers and coaches, but somehow it had just not worked out at Clyde.

Billy's influence had steadied things but there was a lot of work still to do and, when I began my stint in mid-July, I had sixteen players, three backroom staff and three scouts. Billy had told me that the players were very good as individuals at that level, but that they needed organising. He felt that I would not need to make many signings – if any – to win promotion from the Second Division.

When I asked Billy about the staff his response was very interesting. He told me that our physiotherapist, John Watson, was, in his opinion, the best in the country. John was also superintendent physiotherapist at Strathclyde Hospital in Mother-well. Billy said that he would have loved to have taken him to Aberdeen with him, but John had wanted to stay where he was in full-time employment at the hospital and part-time at Clyde.

Billy also told me that Clyde had a very fine and very dedicated commercial manager called John Donnelly, and that there was a very good coaching assistant in Stewart MacMillan, who could also take charge of the team for reserve-type games. I say 'reserve-type' games because Clyde did not actually have a second string at that time, but would field some of the less regular first-team players for minor cup competitions and friendly games.

I did not know any of the three scouts who were attached to the club, so I thought I had better enlist some guys whom I did know. Quite probably, the scouts who were already at Clyde knew what they were about but, as a manager, you need to have scouts who are exactly on your wavelength and know your thoughts on players. They are, after all, your eyes and ears. So I appointed Bob Weir and the late Andy Sawyers.

Billy was very thorough in his appraisal of the situation. He even told me that the club had a very good tea lady who also did the laundry, and one or two other things about the place. Sadie Donegan certainly lived up to Billy's praise of her.

Most importantly, Billy told me that if I was offered the job I should jump at it, because the Dunn family, who ran the club, were lovely people and had both integrity and dignity. To a great degree it was owing to the Dunn family that the club was held in such high esteem throughout the country.

Not long after the chat with Billy I received another phone call asking me if I would attend an interview for the job. I travelled to Shawfield Stadium, which was also a well-known Glasgow greyhound track. It was my first-ever meeting with John McBeth, who was the Clyde secretary. He was also the son-in-law of the chairman. From our first encounter, it was obvious that John along with his wife, Frances, was an extremely dedicated Clyde supporter.

In the years that followed, I have never ceased to admire the honest work that has been put in, both during my time and since, for Clyde Football Club. Mr McBeth is on the executive committee as well as being vice-president of the Scottish Football Association, and he is an insightful and tireless worker for the good of the game.

So, John met me and I was then interviewed by the board of directors, who asked me if I would accept the post on a part-time basis. I readily agreed to this because it meant that my educational work could continue. I was asked to start immediately, and I must say that Motherwell were most understanding when I explained the situation. The then chairman Ian Livingstone, was very sincere in his good wishes.

I had been training with much larger groups of players at Motherwell and it was a delight to be working with a smaller group at Clyde. I felt that it made personal attention much easier. At Motherwell I had often been involved with three sessions a day, but here it was much more concentrated with about four good sessions a week. The Clyde players were very enthusiastic and responded well.

The directors had made it clear that there was very little money available for players, but they said that they would do their best, and I would like to put it on record that they were as supportive as possible throughout my time at the club.

As Billy McNeill had told me, they had some good players. John Arrol was the goalkeeper, with Phil Cairney as his replacement. Bobby Ferris was right back and at centre-half we had Joe Finlayson, with Jim Boyd at left back. In midfield were Brian Ahern, Bobby Harvey and Steve Archibald, as well as Gerry Marshall, Neil Hood and Joe Ward. Our front players included Sean Sweeney and Arthur Grant. Stan Rankin was my first signing, and Gordon Hamilton was our captain.

Anyone who knew anything at all about the game could see that we had quite a good squad, and it was still a bit of a mystery as to how the club had fallen into such a relatively lowly position. Unfortunately, these things do happen, and it was now my job to try to change it. I wanted to get the supporters more involved, to let them see that we meant business, so I invited them to come and watch training sessions. The response was quite good, and you could feel the spirit at the club starting to lift as the new season approached.

We had a particularly good pre-season friendly at home to Preston, which ended as a 1–1 draw. It confirmed that we needed more confidence in front of goal because we had controlled the game throughout and should have won. Friendlies are never as good as competitive matches to pinpoint your deficiencies, but when you are the new manager it gives you the chance to assess what you have – especially since most players want to make a good early impression.

The season began on 13 August 1977 with a 0–0 draw away against Albion Rovers. It was not an inspiring match but it did set the ball rolling. A week later we had our first home game, and I was delighted when we beat Stenhousemuir 3–0 in front of eight hundred supporters. From then on we seemed to gather momentum, and it was not until our seventh game on 24 September that we suffered a defeat, and even that was partly due to our defender, Eddie Anderson, scoring an own goal.

By the turn of the year we had worked our way into a good position at the top of the table with just four defeats in our first twenty games. However, every silver lining has a dark cloud, and I was asked to see the chairman around that time so that he could explain our financial situation. He told me that the club had no money and that they did not want to go into the red – then he asked if I might be able to do something about it by selling a player.

I had only three players whom I thought might be worth selling from the point of view of bringing in enough money to make it worth losing them. I told the chairman so and named them – Joe Ward, Brian Ahern and Steve Archibald. Mr Clark asked me if I could perhaps contact a few people and see if I might be able to make a sale or two.

I phoned round several of my colleagues to gauge interest in my players. I promoted Steve Archibald in particular, because he was doing very well for us, and several Premier managers and their representatives came to look at him. I was told by one of them, a very well-known and respected manager, that Archibald would never make a top player.

It was Alex Stuart, manager of Ayr, who showed some positive interest, and we arranged a fee of £15,000 plus Jim McSherry – but the deal fell through because McSherry refused to come to Shawfield, considering that our ground was not a football stadium but a dog track. I was disappointed, of course, and I phoned Billy McNeill to have a chat about Archibald. He advised me that he had used him as a sweeper and that he had been quite successful in that position. I could see the sense in that and I must now confess that the one thing I had never considered was to try him as a forward. We were well served in that position and I had therefore never needed to experiment, but he had scored goals for us from his midfield position.

After a bit of discussion with Billy, I agreed to sell him Steve Archibald for the princely sum of £20,000. I don't think Steve will mind me saying that he was to receive £3,000 as his share of the deal, which was to go through on 3 January 1978, after the New Year fixtures. The board pleaded with me not to play him in our two fixtures just before the transfer in case he should be injured and the deal collapse. However, I wanted my strongest side for the games against Albion Rovers and Queen's Park. Steve played well in both games and we took maximum points. Against Albion Rovers he even scored two of our three goals, so he had a very pleasing send-off with his old club consolidating a position at the top of Division Two.

Steve was delighted to find himself at Pittodrie, having broken through to 'big-time' football. I was very pleased for him too. To his credit, he never forgot his early days and later, when he moved to Tottenham, he sent wonderful boxes of chocolates to me at Clyde.

By accident, in a training match at Aberdeen, Steve played up front – and he was a revelation! Billy McNeill put him into the side as a striker and, of course, he took to it like that famous duck to water. Tottenham later paid more than £800,000 for him. In those days the transfer contracts were much simpler and there was no extra cash for Clyde when Aberdeen made such a profit on him. I like to think that I was quite a resourceful young manager, but I did not have enough initiative to dream up the add-on clause that has become commonplace in modern football finances. I did use it in later transfers, but not with Steve Archibald's move – so, to a certain extent, we got our fingers burned.

Having said that, the £20,000 that Clyde received was crucial, and the remaining players did not let the transfer make any difference to them. We had a very good second half of the season, including a 7–0 defeat of Meadowbank. Our home attendances gradually increased, and our best crowd of the season was our penultimate game at home to our Second Division championship rivals, Raith Rovers. Nearly two thousand supporters were in Shawfield for that game and we were very disappointed to lose 0–1 – only our second home defeat of the season, but a crucial game in which to fail.

On the last day of the season, just three days later, we were playing at home to Stranraer, and we really wanted to win this one – especially as they had beaten us at Stair Park. This time there were 1,200 supporters at Shawfield Stadium. We were a goal up through Joe Ward at half-time and then, in the second half, we took complete control and ended as 4–0 winners. Ward, John Brogan and Neil Hood each scored in the second half, and there were many celebrations at the end of the game – especially since our only rivals, Raith, had been beaten 2–0 at Dunfermline.

We were confirmed as champions, with Raith finishing on the same points as runners-up. The 21 goals scored by Neil Hood had made all the difference. The success had made a difference to our finances as well. The pools money was distributed on the basis of points gained during the season and, since we had done very well with 53 points, we had a good share. We also drew Celtic at home and away in the Dryburgh Cup and, with the money we earned from that, Clyde went from having nothing in the bank at Christmas to being in a very comfortable financial situation six months later.

Just as an aside, I was very pleased that Raith had been promoted with us because I had a great respect for their manager, Willie McLean. He had fallen out with the chairman at Motherwell but, after a short time out of work, Raith had snapped him up and he had soon knocked them into shape.

Ironically, our first League fixture of the following season was at home to Raith Rovers and we beat them 3–1. Our season began remarkably well, and by mid-September we topped the First Division table with five victories and one draw from our first six games.

Around Christmas-time we were still going well and were among the leaders, although we had dropped a few silly points. I was still learning the trade, and I did receive one short, sharp lesson in mid-September 1978. We were playing away to Dundee and Eric Schaedler, their left back, tackled our best player at that time, Joe Ward, very crudely indeed – with the result that Joe had to be carried off. He was out of the game for most of the rest of the season. The referee was George Smith from Edinburgh, a man I respected both then and now, but I did not agree with his handling of that particular situation and I told him so.

A couple of months later he was put in charge of one of our home games and he came in and said to me: 'How are things, Mr Brown?'

I replied: 'Well, not too good, actually.'

'Why? What's the matter?' he asked.

'We've not yet recovered from losing our best player because of your incompetence a couple of months ago.'

I realised that I had overstepped the mark because he just walked away from me without saying another word. During the game, which was against Raith Rovers, he allowed what I thought was a blatantly off-side goal and I wondered if I had made a big mistake in saying what I had before the game – but to have suggested that Mr Smith was reacting to my statement would, I know, have been an unfair accusation against one of the most sincere officials in the game. Ever since, I have tried not to fall into the trap of criticising referee performances – although I must admit, to my embarrassment, that I haven't quite managed to stay on the straight and narrow. I regret that falling-out with George Smith, who was an outstanding referee and is a very nice chap. Even the best of referees can make mistakes, though!

I was very upset about losing Joe Ward because he was our top player at that time, but later in the season I sold him to Aston Villa for £85,000. That, in a sense, was another mistake because I was naive enough – or perhaps cocky enough – to think that I could sell our best player and still replace him quite easily to maintain our form in the First Division. I didn't think that I needed to ask the board for any of the money we had received – I just relied on using reserve players. The consequence was that the second half of the season was very poor for us in comparison with the first half, and we picked up far fewer points. We finished in mid-table when we might have been challenging for promotion again.

It was an eventful first season in a higher division and I had continued my learning process. I was kicking myself for the fact that we could probably have done better, but the board seemed quite happy because we had increased our attendances and our transfer dealings had shown a good profit.

Around the New Year of that season, the Ayr manager, Ally MacLeod, left to become manager of Scotland. I was hotly tipped to replace him at Ayr, and I was interviewed by the chairman, Myles Callaghan, at his sumptuous home. He offered me the job on either a full- or part-time basis, and I was deeply honoured to be given the chance to be manager of my home-town club. I declined the offer, though, because I was very happy at Clyde, and felt that the club had much more potential still to be realised. I was also still lecturing at Craigie College and I thought it would be inappropriate to be lecturing and to be manager of the football team in the same town. Ayr had made me a very generous offer – certainly a great improvement on my income from Clyde – but I always feel that, in football, the satisfaction you get from working in an environment and with people you get on with is far more important than the riches of the game. Perhaps it would have worked out at Ayr, but I could not possibly have been happier than I already was at Clyde!

I had several other clubs approach me during my time with Clyde, but I am not going to name them. It would be unfair on the managers who were eventually appointed, and I have always tried to be as discreet as possible in all my dealings with clubs or people in this game. Players have talked to me about their business and personal problems over the years at both club and international level, and I have always kept their confidences.

Having said all that, there was one offer that came to me while I was at Clyde which I found to be both amazing and startling. It was an invitation from Ernie Walker, then the secretary of the Scottish Football Association, to meet him at the Haggs Castle Golf Club. When I got there, he went straight into the reason for the invitation and asked me how I would feel about becoming assistant to Jock Stein, who was by then manager of Scotland.

It was in the early 1980s, and Jock had established himself as the top man for Scotland. I was quite stunned at being asked, and felt deeply privileged even to have been considered for such an important post. However, I kept a level head and declined the offer. I did not think that I had sufficient experience at that time, and I was also concerned about job security. Scotland had gone through five managers in a decade and, if I had taken the job, it would have meant going full-time, and that would have meant the end of my academic career.

Some ten years after Jock Stein died, I was at a press meeting in Glasgow on the anniversary of his death and was asked if I had any Jock Stein stories to relate. I told them the story of Andy Russell's encounter with Jock, and also about how I had been invited to go and work with him at the SFA. The reaction from one or two of the journalists present was as surprising as it was disappointing. Their attitude seemed to be: 'Do you really expect us to believe that?' or 'Who does this guy think he is?'

There was never a problem in confirming my story because Ernie Walker was still around and would certainly have verified it, but it was the scepticism of those journalists that disappointed me. It was a clear sign of the age in which we live. It also highlighted the fact that when I was later appointed as Scotland manager, the appointment might have been made more accept-able. There are some journalists whose only quest in life is destruction and, even when you level with them, they still have to go one step beyond.

Jock Stein knew me well. In fact there was no one in football, especially Scottish football, whom Jock didn't know, but I believe that the person who had further recommended me for the job with him was a very good friend of his, Dr James Crorie. He was a very well-known legislator in Scottish football and had seen the set-up at Clyde and our methods of coaching and discipline. He was also, incidentally, an outstanding pianist. A favourite story concerning him was when one of our players, our striker Neil Hood, suffered an eye injury. John Watson, our physio, took him in, prepared the wound and shaved his eyelashes off so that the doctor could see where to apply the stitches. The doctor came in smoking a large cigar which he had to put out before he could get to work. He threw it into the pedal bin, not realising that John had been throwing swabs soaked in surgical spirits into it already. The flames shot up out of the bin and singed the hair and eyebrows of the good doctor, so that he was almost as bald as his patient when he came to put the stitches in. The boys used to joke that the stitches would be spaced about an inch apart when he'd had a few. Yet they loved and respected him – and with good reason, because he was an excellent chap and a very fine sports medico.

During my time at Clyde we had our ups and downs. I don't like to advertise the fact that we were relegated once during my spell at the club – but it is in the record books for all to see. We seemed to have a lapse of confidence, especially in goal, where I used four different goalkeepers in that 1979/80 season. I started the season with Dennis Connaghan, a really nice chap, now with Neilston Juniors, whom I had signed from Morton. Dennis had a confidence crisis and I brought in David McWilliams from Airdrie. David was a former Scotland Under-23 international but he didn't excel either. I asked Bobby Clark, the ex-Aberdeen Scotland international, to come out of retirement, and he played four games for us before deciding that he really had finished his career. Then I brought in Greg Young. Goalkeeping changes like that have an effect on the entire team, so we lost our way and fell back to the Second Division along with Arbroath. If we had turned a few more of our drawn games into victories we would probably have been safe, but the lack of confidence went from defence to attack and we scored nothing like our usual tally of goals.

There was one highlight from that season, and that was a very creditable 2–2 home draw with Rangers in the Scottish Cup third round. We had played them earlier in the season at Shawfield in the League Cup and they beat us 2–1. The Clyde players were delighted when they were given a second chance in the Cup and, but for a penalty, we would have beaten them 2–1. As it was, the players performed extremely well and deserved the home draw. The replay ended in a 2–0 win for Rangers, both goals scored in the final ten minutes, but there was no disgrace in that.

The following season we were reassembling. We had a good crop of youngsters coming through, and it was time to introduce some of them to first-team football. As a result we did not win any medals during the 1980/81 season. We had a couple of good games in which we scored six against Montrose and against East Fife, but we gained the most satisfaction from seeing the younger players beginning to blossom.

When I was first at Clyde no strip sponsorship was allowed, but after a while some experiments in junior football resulted in the green light for teams to wear sponsors' names on their shirts. Along with our commercial manager, John Donnelly, I was thinking about where we might get some suitable sponsorship when an incident occurred that triggered off an idea. It took place in Polmadie Road, where the British Oxygen Company had some works. One night, as I was travelling to training, there was an explosion there and the road was soon blocked by police cars, ambulances and fire engines. The following weekend I picked up a copy of the local newspaper and found in it an absolute condemnation of BOC, which I considered to be very unfair because the incident had been a minor one, made to look much worse by the understandable presence of so many emergency vehicles. The whole thing escalated, with petitions designed to rid the area of the works. Local councillors became involved as their support was sought, and the whole matter became a major local talking point.

I saw this as a great opportunity, and drove over to their works and asked to see the managing director. After about an hour of kicking my heels I finally saw a guy named Gordon Moultrie, who was in charge. He was extremely pleasant and listened carefully as I put it to him that his company had alienated the local community and that a way of getting back into favour might be by doing something for that community. He asked me what I had in mind.

'The local school is John Bosco and I know the headmaster,

John Mulgrew. I suggest that you give a donation to the local school, to Gorbals United Boys Club, whose president is Kenny Dalglish and whose leading light is Pat Harkins, Kenny's father-in-law – and how about sponsoring your local senior football team?'

He asked me if I had any figures in mind and I said that I had no idea what the board would accept, but I think I mentioned a figure of £10,000 for BOC to go on the team shirts. Remember, this was in 1981. He asked me to talk to the board, which I did the following night. Our elderly honorary president, Mr William P. Dunn, was there, chairing the meeting. I gave my usual report on the players and so on and then broached the subject of sponsorship.

Before I was able to get very far into my presentation, he interrupted me.

'I have to say that our jerseys have won the Scottish Cup three times. They are white and we don't want to deface them with advertising. They are sacrosanct!'

'But it's the coming thing, Mr President,' I pleaded.

He absolutely refused to discuss it, however. Also on the board was Professor Bob Jack, the professor of mercantile law at Glasgow University. He came into the conversation.

'Excuse me, manager, but you haven't mentioned money. Did you mention money to the British Oxygen Company?'

The old president-chairman had made it quite clear that there was no way he was going to agree to any sponsorship, so I replied, 'It doesn't seem now that the money is relevant – but I did mention the sum of £10,000 as being appropriate!'

The president-chairman now interrupted again and cried, 'Manager, I would put BOC on my bare torso for £10,000! Please carry on!'

So I did negotiate the deal and the upshot was that we became only the second club after Hibs, who had a deal with Mitre, the sports manufacturer, to use a sponsor's name in Scotland, with BOC brightly emblazoned in red on our shirts. That sponsorship only lasted for one year, but once again Clyde certainly benefited from moving with the times. The only reason we did not have the sponsorship renewed was simply that we were not high-profile enough. I was told that the company gained more publicity mileage from sponsoring a caber-tosser who regularly toured North America and Australasia demonstrating his skills. So the sponsorship of Clyde was not renewed by BOC, but was taken up by Solripe.

Talking of sponsorship, five or six years ago I was going to watch a game between Motherwell and Rangers. I drove into Ian Skelly's garage in Dalmarnock, from where we obtained our sponsored cars. I was talking to Stewart MacLaren, a former Motherwell player, who was now the sales manager for Ian Skelly. He asked me if I was going to the game and then told me to take a good look at the Motherwell jerseys. 'It will be the last time that you will see Ian Skelly's name on a Motherwell jersey!'

Naturally I was curious to know why, and he explained that Ian had just sold his firm and, as he no longer owned it, the sponsorship was over. Stewart told me that Ian had received quite a few millions for the business – though he could not be specific as many differing figures had been mooted. As we chatted, a tea lady was pouring us a cup of tea each and I joked about how good it was that Ian had given all his staff £5,000 each as a reward for their loyalty. I noticed that she seemed to be taking some time pouring the tea, but her expression didn't change as I repeated myself. Finally she just turned to us and said: 'I must have been off my work that day!' – a typical piece of Glasgow humour.

We were into the 1981/82 season and our young players were beginning to grow in confidence. Pat Nevin in particular was becoming a bit of a show-stealer, but the whole side was gelling together very nicely. We were undefeated in our first eleven games. Then we suffered two defeats and a draw in consecutive games, which dropped us from top to second place in the Second Division. After that there were few blips, and we regained that top spot in mid-November and stayed there for the rest of the season. We were champions once again and back in the First Division.

The following season was one of consolidation once again. I have seen many teams go charging up the League and then come charging back down again, so I have always tried to keep cool in my team-building and not inflate the balloon so fast and so far that it bursts. That was something I learned all those years ago when I was taking my various sports courses.

We had a very interesting cup tie against Motherwell in the 1982/83 season. It was in the third round of the Scottish Cup and we were at home. The result was 0–0. The replay came a few days later, and it was quite a match in which seven goals were scored – and we hit four of them. It was a blow to Motherwell, who were a Premier Division side, managed by the great Jock Wallace, but we, of course, were absolutely delighted. Our Cup designs were short-lived, however, because we faced Partick in the next round. We played well and drew 2–2 at Firhill, and the replay was equally stirring with extra time needed since there were no goals after 90 minutes. The floodlights failed and the referee decided to abandon the match during extra time, so we had to play again. This time Partick set about us in a very businesslike way and beat us 6–0, with Mo Johnston scoring three – but it was still a Scottish Cup campaign to remember!

We were realists at Clyde. There were no great aspirations towards getting into the European Cup because we knew that was beyond us at that time. The club was simply not big enough for a sustained assault on such a target – but we were ambitious enough to want to constantly improve and better our position and our facilities. All that takes money, of course, and Clyde, like so many clubs, had to be self-generating. There was no one with a magic wand to come in and plant millions in the club's bank account and so we had to live on our wits – by developing and selling young players, or by commercial enterprises which helped to keep us apace of the rising costs of running a football club.

The cup ties against bigger clubs were a major help in keeping us afloat, and in the 1983/84 season we had a cracker against Aberdeen. It was not so much the 90 minutes of the actual game as the pre-match build-up – which had Alex Ferguson giving me what for over the telephone. But that's another story . . .

10 Fergie's Fury and then to Mexico

The highlight of our 1983/84 season was probably the 5–0 pasting of Raith Rovers which came on the last Saturday of November 1983. Prior to that result we had been struggling for a while and had been bottom of the table for almost eleven weeks.

Managers will always tell you that injury problems, new players yet to gel, bad luck, the need to spend money and various other outside sources are to blame. Sometimes those are valid points, but other times they are textbook responses to journalists' questions. What the manager really needs is an excuse. However, our season really did get off to a slow start – on the opening day we were without five key players and I would say that it was mid-October before I was able to field our strongest team.

That 5–0 victory over Raith put us on a different road and we followed it with a 1–0 win at Kilmarnock, a 4–0 win at Airdrie and a 2–0 win at home to Meadowbank. Suddenly, we were walking around with wings on our boots. We suffered only one defeat in our next six games, and there was talk of us challenging for promotion. It was premature, of course, and we eventually finished in eighth place.

Aberdeen won the Scottish Cup that year by beating Celtic 2–1 at Hampden. On the way to the final they were drawn away to us in the fourth round, and we were determined to enjoy ourselves whatever the result. I wasn't going to let Alex Ferguson have things all his own way. He is a master of kidology, but this was one time when I saw the chance to wind him up a little.

On the Thursday before the game I was telephoned by North Sound Radio in order to tape an interview from my office. While my part of the interview was being done over the phone, Fergie was live in the studio. I knew that he would be listening, so I decided to have a little fun with him. He had already done his interview but was still in the studio when the radio reporter said, 'Have you any message for your old pal, Alex Ferguson?'

I replied, 'I have two things to say to Alex. One is that we will be using a Dunlop ball on Saturday, and the other is that we haven't rolled the pitch for three weeks!'

I heard a voice spluttering at the other end and then the sound had to be cut off because – I imagine – what he was saying was fairly uncomplimentary and certainly not for tender ears. A couple of minutes after the transmission was over, my phone rang again. It was Alex.

'You'd better not be playing with that * * * * * ball, and you'd better get that * * * * * pitch rolled!' he said.

'No way, Alex,' I replied. 'We're the home team.'

A bit of good-natured banter followed before the phone was put down. I knew from the previous season's Cup Final that Aberdeen had made some criticism of the Dunlop football. Jim Leighton was in goal for them and he didn't like the flight of the ball. Alex being Alex, he condemned it in the press.

So I had made a point of obtaining three Dunlop balls for our match. You try everything, of course, to give yourselves a little bit of an advantage over the other side. It is common practice throughout the game – although I would never take it to the lengths of what could be legitimately branded as cheating. As the home side you have the advantage of deciding upon how your pitch should be treated. If you make it a bowling green you play into the hands of a good passing side – as Aberdeen was at that time. You can keep the grass a little longer and level the situation by forcing the game to be played off the ground rather more if that suits you.

As it was, we unfortunately lost 0–2, with Aberdeen's Neale Cooper and Ian Angus scoring a goal each. They deserved their victory, and by the end of the season had picked up the Premier championship as well as the Scottish Cup. Our consolation was that we had given them a run for their money and had a crowd of 5,800 to see the Aberdeen superstars, who included Gordon Strachan, Willie Miller, Alex McLeish and Jim Leighton. It was certainly a worthwhile experience for our young players to play against them.

I was always on the lookout for new young players because we were never in a situation of being able to spend large sums of money to strengthen our side. We produced many good players, one of the most gifted perhaps being Pat Nevin. He was released by Celtic Boys Club for, it was said, being too small. Personally I hardly think that was likely. We managed to sign him from Gartcosh United youth team.

When Pat came to Clyde he was a revelation. His first game was a friendly against Sheffield United, and he looked absolutely brilliant. He was still a student at Caledonian University but he was also in our first team and very impressive. He was so impressive in fact that Andy Roxburgh listened to my recommendation that he play for the Scotland Under-18 side, took a look at him and picked him. That was some achievement for the seventeen-year-old Pat Nevin when you consider that Andy had the cream of the Premier Division from which to select his Scotland players at all levels. He had young players like Paul McStay, Brian McClair, Neale Cooper, Jim McInally, Brian Gunn, Davie McPherson, Eric Black, Steve Clarke, Gary Mackay, Davie Bowman, John Philliben and others.

Andy was a bit sceptical when I told him that there was a young lad from our First Division that he could not ignore but, when he took Pat to Largs to join the rest of his squad for a trial match, he knew that he had made the right move. Pat did so well that he was in the Scotland Under-18 side that won the European Championship. Sadly, I could not be at the final between Scotland and Czechoslovakia in Helsinki, but everyone raved about Pat's performance at outside right and said that he virtually defeated the Czechs single-handedly. This was borne out by the fact that he was named European Youth Player of the Year.

That put Pat well into the spotlight, and a year later he went with Andy's Under-19 side to take part in the World Youth Championships in Mexico. I was delighted to hear that when

Andy fitness-tested his players at Colorado Springs – their pre-championship camp – there was no one fitter than Pat Nevin. I felt that was quite a compliment to our training techniques at Clyde, as well as to his natural fitness. Pat has always been a player who takes care of himself, lives well, trains hard and, in my opinion, has been a model professional throughout his career, which has so far lasted seventeen or eighteen years. As I write this, although Pat suffered a severe facial injury in January 1998, he is still playing at the top of the tree with Kilmarnock in the Scottish Premier Division.

We had Pat in the team for around two years, but it was inevitable that he would leave us because there were so many bigger clubs obviously interested in him. Ian McNeill, the assistant manager at Chelsea, came up to see us just before the Scotland Under-19s went to Mexico. He went to Pat's house in Barlanark in Glasgow and was there for hours and hours trying to persuade him to sign for Chelsea – which he eventually did for a meagre sum.

In those days there was no Bosman ruling and, even though Pat was out of contract, Clyde were entitled to receive something for the transfer. We asked for £180,000. It is rare for deals to run smoothly in football – clubs do not often reach instant agreement. Chelsea offered us £50,000, so the matter went to the first-ever international tribunal between the home countries. The meeting was held in Glasgow and Chelsea were instructed to pay us £95,000. I thought it was a paltry sum for such a highly talented youngster. I disagreed, at the tribunal, with Ken Bates, the Chelsea chairman, who was quite disparaging about the £40 per week we were paying Pat Nevin.

'You can pay players what you like, so why are you only paying him forty pounds a week?' Bates was obviously inferring that if the player was worth what we were asking we would be paying a lot more than that.

'We don't pay any of our players more than forty pounds a week,' I replied, adding that we did not pay the player what he was worth but only what we could afford. Bates then became very critical of Scottish football and I had to remind him that Chelsea had come up to Scotland to play Hearts, who were then in our First Division and had been beaten.

We were less than thrilled with the outcome of the tribunal. Not only was the £95,000 fee much too low, but it was decreed that Chelsea could pay in two instalments – half up front and the rest in a year's time.

Although Pat went for a miserly fee and what I considered to be poor wages, I'm pleased to say that he did very well for Chelsea and was instrumental in getting them out of the old Second Division of the Football League. He supplied the ammunition for Kerry Dixon to get the goals and later, when he renegotiated his contract, I think he had become much more shrewd and listened to advice. When he had first agreed to join Chelsea, Ian McNeill would not allow me or anyone else to advise him. He kept him at his house for hours until he signed. Pat learned quickly and fared much better with his next contract, and also when he moved on to join Everton.

So that was how Pat Nevin began his career with us. I was never in a position to spend big money on players and, as far as I can recall, I believe that the most I ever paid for anyone was £5,000. We were dependent upon player exchanges, free signings and finding new talent. As a further example, when we dropped back to the Second Division I had to change a few faces and did some business with my old sparring partner, Willie McLean, who was then still at Ayr United. He wanted Brian Ahern and Jim Kean and we agreed a deal in which he signed them both and in exchange we received three players and £40,000. The players were Robert Reilly, Derek McCutcheon and Billy McColl. All three became useful members of the squad and Reilly in particular did very well for us. At the same time I obtained, on a free transfer from Kilmarnock, a guy called Jimmy Docherty, a small, spritely middle-to-front player who did exceptionally well for us. Another good signing on the same basis was Jim Dempsey, who had been with Motherwell. He did a great job for us.

That is the sort of wheeling and dealing that you have to do when you are in charge of a small club, be it in England or Scotland. Queen's Park was always a fruitful recruiting ground for me, and my old friend Eddie Hunter was the coach there. I always refer to him as mild-mannered and quietly spoken because he was just the opposite, and you could hear him all round

Hampden from his place in the dugout. Eddie was attached to Queen's Park in one capacity or another for 30 years. I went to his club quite regularly and signed some super guys – players like Derek Atkins, who was an excellent goalkeeper but suffered a career setback when his leg was broken in an accidental clash with Mark Shanks of Ayr, and Ross McFarlane, who was a magnificent servant for Clyde.

As I have already mentioned, we were promoted at the first attempt after making all those changes and more than held our own in the 1983/84 season. The 1984/85 season was almost a repeat performance, since once again we finished in eighth place in the table. At one stage we stood as high as third, and we were within a shout of promotion for most of the season. A 4–1 victory over Kilmarnock was our best result, although there were some excellent games against Motherwell, with whom we drew twice and won once in our three scheduled League matches. That was pretty good really, because Motherwell were ultimately champions of the division ahead of Clydebank, whom we beat twice.

I was nearing the end of my time with Clyde, although I didn't know that at the time. There was still the 1985/86 season ahead and we prepared as normal. We got off to a good start and were undefeated in our first eight games. We were in a healthy second place in the table when Airdrie beat us 3–0 away. We began to pick up more than our share of injuries at that time, and the loss of several key players, including Derek Frye, who had been our phenomenal top scorer for several seasons, meant that we struggled to field a consistent side. We gradually slipped down the table and looked in serious trouble for several weeks until we staged a late rally and lost only three of our last ten games. That succeeded in pulling us out of the danger zone.

It was during that season that the great Jock Stein died. It was in September 1985, and the story of what happened has been told too many times for me to repeat it here – although I would not want that to appear in any way disrespectful to Jock, with whom I came into contact very many times and for whom I had the utmost respect and affection. He was a one-off, and Scotland has never seen his like before or since.

The Scottish Football Association inherited a problem when

they lost Jock. Who could replace him? The team had to beat Australia in a play-off to be sure of a place in the World Cup finals, but someone had to take charge with immediate effect. This was Alex Ferguson's cue to take the reins. He had been incredibly successful with Aberdeen, including winning the European Cup Winners' Cup, and it was no real surprise when he was asked to take the national team – at least until the World Cup campaign was at an end.

It was not the first time that Alex had been involved at national level. He had assisted Jock Stein previously while continuing as manager of Aberdeen. Such arrangements can be difficult, because there can be conflicts of interest. Every manager wants his players to be internationals, but sometimes international fixtures can come at difficult times in that there might be very important club games within days of international matches. More than one player has developed a 'groin strain' that has suddenly disappeared after an international game. When a club manager is also heavily involved in the international set-up he has more than the usual soul-searching to do.

Alex successfully steered Scotland through the play-off, drawing 0–0 in Melbourne and winning 2–0 at Hampden. Scotland was on the way to Mexico, and Alex invited me to be one of his coaching team. I was certainly delighted to be asked and willingly accepted. There was still a lot of work to be done at Clyde during the summer, but since the tournament was to run from the end of May for a month, I would still be back in time for pre-season preparations.

The 1986 World Cup tournament was exciting, albeit short-lived. Before we left there was all the usual hype and build-up, and I think some of the media began to think that the Scotland squad had the ability to walk on water. When you consider that we were drawn in a group with three very strong opponents – Denmark, West Germany and Uruguay – the reality of the situation was that we would do well to keep our heads above water, let alone walk on it! When so much expectation is built up, failure becomes a total disaster, and with it the picking over the bones to apportion blame. We did not get past the qualifying group and the criticism aimed at Alex Ferguson was very unfair, even allowing for the fact that it is always the manager who carries the can.

Against Denmark, Roy Aitken had the ball in the net but was harshly adjudged to be off-side. The Danes won 1–0, and in fact they also beat West Germany and Uruguay, so Scotland's performance was by no means a disgrace. In the next game, Gordon Strachan put Scotland ahead after eighteen minutes, but the Germans stormed back to make it 2–1 and went on to reach the final. Berti Vogts tells me a story about that game, he was assisant to Franz Beckenbauer and was sent to spy on our final training session. Alex Ferguson had decreed it to be private so that he could try out some moves and also establish the fitness of Gordon Strachan.

When Berti was refused admission he exchanged a German jersey for a Coca-Cola man's outfit and his drink's stall. He thus gained entry to the stadium and viewed the entire session. To this day he still tells the story and refers to himself as 'the Coca-Cola man'.

Our final game was against Uruguay, who had previously drawn with the Germans before being given a 6–1 hiding by Denmark. Scotland had to win – there were no other options. In an explosive first minute the Uruguayans were reduced to ten men when Batista was sent off. Everyone except those of us on the Scotland bench rubbed their hands in anticipation but, despite tremendous pressure, the Uruguayans did not crack. A goalless draw meant that Scotland was out and the criticism was in.

It had been an interesting experience and I returned to Scotland a wiser man. They say that travel broadens the mind. Travelling and being involved in football broadens the back as well. At Clyde we were wrestling with the problem of finding a home as Shawfield was no longer to be available. A ground-sharing arrangement with Partick Thistle was agreed so our home games were to be played at Firhill Park. Their manager at the time was Bertie Auld.

Every July I went on the national coaching course at Largs, and 1986 was no exception. While I was there, after the Mexico World Cup, I was approached by Andy Roxburgh, who was the Scottish Football Association's Technical Director, or Director of

Coaching. He told me that things were happening at the SFA which would affect him and, if he had his way, could also affect me. Andy was soon appointed as Scotland team manager, and a week later he contacted me to ask if I would join him as his assistant and manager of the Under-21 team.

When you are used to the day-to-day running of a football club and the fixtures being week in, week out, it can come as a bit of a culture shock to take up a post in international football. Having control of the Under-21 team meant that my involvement would be greater than just following the manager around, and so I decided that it was time for me to take up this new challenge.

That ended my career in club management to date. On the subject of management, there is one point that I would like to make about the credentials needed for such a job. When I took over at Clyde, my very first game was a friendly against Preston. Their manager was Nobby Stiles. Nobby remained as manager of Preston for about four years, during which time the club was promoted once and relegated twice. Nobby is probably most famous for the magnificent part he played in England's historic 1966 World Cup win, and I have often reflected on the fact that none of that squad of superb players was ever a great club manager. Jack Charlton did okay and was, of course, a marvellous international manager – but none of the others seriously achieved much as club managers. They were, of course, the most successful British international team to date.

Doesn't that tell us something? Just because a player reaches the top of the tree in international football, it does not necessarily mean that he will make a great manager. Therefore, when there is a clamouring for a big name to be appointed as the new manager somewhere, perhaps it might be a good idea to look at his coaching and management credentials rather than what he has achieved as a player. The qualities that are required to make a tiptop player are not necessarily the same as those required to make a first-class team manager. There are exceptions, of course, men who achieve success both as a player and as a manager. Beckenbauer, Vogts, Dalglish and Cruyff readily spring to mind. However, I don't think that top-class playing experience necessarily makes for a top-class manager. Of course, I'm bound to say that, but there are so many examples to support my viewpoint, men like Arrigo Saachi, who never played football as a professional at all.

The top countries in Europe are all now insisting on a mandatory coaching qualification before a job can be offered. This is certainly the case in Germany, where part of the course is six months of full study. It is similar in Holland as well as Spain, France, Denmark and Italy, where a coaching qualification is obligatory. UEFA are trying to extend that, and they have instigated a Pro Licence which will be standard throughout Europe and enable managers and coaches to work in any of the UEFA countries. In Scotland, with Frank Coulston at the helm, we have already started to comply with our Premier Division managers, assistant managers and coaches in the first instance. Hopefully, very soon the Pro Licence will be held by all our top managers.

There will always be a few people who argue that qualifications are meaningless and that practical experience and a playing career are what really count in order to be a top manager. I'm not going to place myself in a seat of judgement, but I would say to these people that the courses are very good, and if they were to experience one they might change their minds. At the very least they would be able to see the benefits that a coaching course provides, even for someone who is a 'natural'.

Speaking purely from my own experience, I do feel that if it were not for attending the courses and keeping up with the latest ideas and developments, I would not have been at Clyde for nine happy years, or indeed be in my current position. To the people who instigated the very notion of coaching courses – I thank you!

11 Reflections on Clyde

cannot leave the subject of Clyde without a few more recollections and observations. When I joined the club they were in the middle of the Second Division. When I left them they were in the middle of the First Division, and so I would like to think that, on the whole, I did well for the club. I had some great times at Clyde. I had some terrific young players and some very good dedicated older professionals.

The great thing about Clyde was that it was a family club with a wonderful atmosphere and the willingness of everyone concerned to pull together. It is something that I have remembered throughout my management career – that you must have a squad that is fully integrated, with no one rocking the boat or causing trouble, because that is cancerous in a football club dressing room. I have seen this throughout the years as a player and as a manager with both big and small clubs, and now, of course, as an international manager, where you deal with the biggest of players in terms of status.

I think one of the contributory factors to the club spirit at Clyde was a fair distribution of everything. I have already indicated that our wage structure meant that everyone was near enough in the same financial stratum. Everyone was treated the same in other senses too, whether a youngster just starting out on his career or a well-seasoned professional. For instance, I have always been a great believer in team photographs that included everyone. I like to get everyone involved without identifying them as either a first-team, reserve or junior player. If you wore the shirt, you were in the team, and your position in the photograph had nothing to do with your standing, either in the game or at the club.

This was a psychological ploy I used even for a World Cup qualifier against Latvia in October 1997, at Celtic Park. I told the players that if they were successful in beating Latvia, and consequently qualified for the World Cup, they should acknowledge the supporters by walking round the edge of the pitch in a dignified manner, applauding the crowd. I also insisted that the substitutes should come off the bench, take off their tracksuits so that they were not identified as substitutes, and join in, and that there should be no shirt exchanges before that lap of honour. I did not want to see any of them going round in a Latvia jersey or putting on any daft hats, as I called them. I told them that if a supporter threw a scarf or flag, they should offer to hand it back and only accept it if it seemed that it would cause offence to give it back, and after accepting it to wear it or hold it with modesty and dignity. I wanted to see them conducting themselves with the same professionalism in victory as they would have done in defeat.

The point was that the substitutes were made to feel a part of the success. The substitute goalkeeper, Neil Sullivan, walked round with Jim Leighton, our first choice, demonstrating the essence of togetherness that was a significant factor in our victory.

At Clyde, I tried to maintain that same spirit. At the end of each season, at our last home game, I used to send the players out with large cards to hold up to each part of the ground. The message was simply a thank you, but I felt that it was important to express our appreciation to the supporters and not let them feel like outsiders. They were all a part of the club to me.

We did the same with the Scotland Under-16 side when we reached the World Cup final, to thank the fans for their tremendous support during that tournament.

Other happy memories from Clyde include the board, a fine bunch of gentlemen who genuinely had the club at heart in all their decisions. I did not agree with everything, of course – but I could never say that the board were not doing their best, as they saw it, for Clyde Football Club.

William P. Dunn was the chairman who became honorary president. Tom Clark was chairman while I was there, and it was certainly a sad day when he died. Ian V. Paterson replaced him as chairman. He was a solicitor and former County Clerk of Lanark, one of the most shrewd men that you could ever hope to meet. He didn't profess to have a great inside knowledge of football, but he was a very keen supporter. He was also a very keen businessman and very shrewd in a man-management sense. I think I used to drive him to despair sometimes when I did things that were quite natural to me. If I saw a tie-up on the floor of the dressing room, I would automatically pick it up. I would also carry kit-bags and do other things that he felt were unbecoming to a manager. I just like to muck in with the rest, but he didn't feel that this was good man management. Similarly, he believed that I should not always change into a tracksuit but should watch the training from a distance. I totally disagreed.

Having said all that, I learned a lot from him – much that has been of great value since then.

When Mr Paterson retired, I was offered a place on the board myself. I had no shares, but the chairman told me that it was not necessary as the constitution of the club dictates that there must be seven directors and not all need to be shareholders. He indicated that if, or when, shares became available I could have some.

I accepted, and I well remember my first game as a director. John McBeth was the new chairman, a very well-deserved appointment because of his and his wife Frances' unstinting work for the club. That first game was at Greenock Morton. I sometimes had the habit of sitting in the stand if there was a poor view from the dugout, which happened to be the case at Greenock. I was up in the stand when a Clyde fan shouted, 'Hey, Brown, now you're a director, how about getting us a new manager?'

They never miss a trick.

We were 3–1 up at half-time and I was feeling quite pleased with myself. Obviously my new dual capacity at the club was working wonders already. Those were not my feelings at the end of the game as we contrived to lose the match 4–3, adding insult to injury by failing from the penalty spot in the last minute when Derek Frye blasted the ball over the bar. It was a rare mistake from such a deadly scorer and it just about summed up the afternoon.

Becoming a director gave me a clearer insight into the workings of a club, and in particular the financial problems surrounding any football operation. It was quite interesting, talking to Chelsea Football Club, to find that their turnover around the 1981/82 season, when we were in discussion about the Pat Nevin transfer, was £1.4 million and ours was £140,000 – exactly a tenth. I found it quite an interesting parallel.

As a board member I did see the balance sheet, and it made me conscious of the fact that Clyde was a club that wanted to stay in the black. They never wanted to risk going into the red for any reason, and it made me all the more aware of the need to develop young players and sell them on. That brings me to another aspect of being a club manager.

I feel very strongly about people assessing managers solely on match results and not looking at the other aspect of the operation – keeping the balance sheet healthy. I have gone on record in the past as saying that the best managers are not necessarily the ones with the big cheque books at the prominent clubs. I have always said that men like Allan McGraw ex-Morton and Terry Christie, who is now at Stenhousemuir and used to be at Meadowbank Thistle, are worth their weight in gold. These guys know what it means to have to balance the books, as did the Steedman brothers at Clydebank. I think at Morton, the combination of Allan McGraw and his former chairman, John Wilson, was a very good one. Their club was a perfect example to others as regards the development of young players and survival at a good standard. Similarly Clydebank, and hopefully Clyde, have been successful in staying afloat while still being reasonably competent on the football pitch.

One of the great benefits of managing a club like Clyde is that it teaches you the art of improvisation. We did not have luxury training facilities at our disposal and our Tuesday, Wednesday and Thursday training sessions had to be held on the pitch, which was not ideal if the weather was bad. In the summer we could go to nearby Richmond Park which ran alongside the River Clyde. The young players would carry our portable goals to the park and that's where we would train, watched by the passing dog-walkers. The players liked the environment of the park – except when the ball was kicked into the river. We had to hail passing rowers to retrieve the ball for us as our financial constraints were such that we could not just shrug our shoulders and wave the ball goodbye. It was a bit like our 'pitch' alongside the railway when I was a lad!

Footballs were very valuable to a club like Clyde. In fact, such was our financial position that John Watson, our physio, used to have a standard reply when players came to him for a bootlace: 'Left boot or right boot?'

It was a joke, of course, but not too far from the reality of the economics at a club like Clyde. John was an outspoken man in the dressing room. He would never allow anyone into the treatment room with their boots on – in fact he wouldn't treat anyone who had not had a bath. When I first went there he even had a swear-box – which was quite a shock to me since I had just left Motherwell, which was famed for its industrial language. When I was talking to Willie McLean a little while later he asked me how I was getting on. I told him that I was very happy and was quite struck by how polite and nicely spoken everyone was.

'No wonder they're in the f . . . . . g Second Division!' said Willie.

As I said before, you had to be resourceful in many ways, especially when you were dealing with part-time players, who could be rather more difficult than full-time players. You had a certain power of payment and selection over the full-timers, but with part-time players you only had the power of selection as most of them were in other full-time jobs and the money they earned from football was hardly of significance to them. They included some very intelligent guys, and they were not going to take what we would call 'snash' from the manager.

In a sense, dealing with part-time players is a bit like dealing with international players now. They are financially independent. You have the same kind of scenario, so you must have a discipline and a fairness that are fully understood. In football, too much kindness is often misconstrued as softness, and that applies to part-timers as well as to full-time pros.

I always think that footballers represent a complete cross-section of the community. People have this misguided notion that they are not necessarily the brightest guys in the world, and they can be quite disparaging about the intellect of players. This is particularly prevalent in Scotland where, it seems, if you went to a rugby-playing school you would automatically be far more intelligent than someone from a football-playing one. To me that is total nonsense because I have met and worked with very many footballers who not only have great intelligence but also many academic achievements on their CVs. Others may not have academic triumphs, but they have a mastery of common sense and general knowledge. Saying that footballers are unintelligent is on a par with judging an entire community as being stupid.

A lot of the part-time players I worked with were deep thinkers about the game and I valued their opinions – although I do have to admit that one of my failings is that I am an autocratic manager. I am not at all democratic in terms of selection or debates about tactics. I have always taken my responsibility to the full and, while I will always listen to someone else's ideas and thoughts with respect, I have always made up my own mind about things and been dogmatic to the point of being dictatorial.

Anyway, at Clyde we had to make do in training, and we had to keep on searching for players in the junior grades. To do that we had to keep abreast of what was going on in junior, youth and schools football. It meant that I was totally preoccupied with the game, going to match after match. In one week I attended no fewer than eleven games in the afternoons and evenings. It was an all-consuming hobby and job.

It did not stop at watching games either. As an example, Clyde had four different supporters' clubs, and I used to attend as many of their meetings as possible. The parents of schoolboys also needed time to discuss the progress of their sons.

The manager of a club like Clyde has to be a Jack-of-all-trades. In my case I had wonderful support from my two assistants. My first was Ross Mathie, whom I took from a junior side. Ross was excellent, and years later I was happy to recommend him to Andy

Roxburgh at the SFA. When he left I promoted a player, Rab Thorburn, whose commitment and involvement had greatly impressed me. Not only did he have a BSc honours degree, but he then added a Master of Business Administration degree. Rab was an outstanding bloke who had a great rapport with the players. I consider myself to have been very fortunate in having those excellent assistants, and I would urge any manager in a similar situation to make sure he is well supported to carry what can be a really heavy load.

I am sure that Alex Ferguson, currently Britain's best manager, would agree that a good grounding at a small club – as I had at Clyde and he had at East Stirlingshire and St Mirren before he went to Aberdeen – is the best possible apprenticeship. The different things that you have to do as a manager with one of the smaller clubs teach you much more about football than if you just come in at the highest level straight from playing.

I have been in charge of the national side for the last four and a half years, and I like to think that I have a catholic knowledge of Scottish football. I have coached Under-12 teams at primary school level, Under-13, 14 and 15 teams at secondary schools, the Scotland Under-16 team that reached the World Cup final, and basically every level of domestic and international football except managing a Premier Division side. Yet my most valuable time was dealing with players and jobs of all kinds while I was at Clyde.

Mrs Mary Agnew was secretary at Clyde – a redoubtable lady who worked very hard for the club and was a valuable assistant to me with her tremendous ability to keep the paperwork under control. Even at a smaller club like Clyde, there always seems to be piles of it. I did a lot of typing myself, but she was a thoroughbred on the typewriter while I was a cart-horse.

Everything was brought to the manager's attention – problems with the carpark, laundry, ball-boys, police. You name it, and I have been faced with it. That is why I have always been so grateful for all the help that was available.

I have mentioned one of our doctors but, following Dr Crorie, we had Dr John Maclean – another fine medical man. I had to make sure that there was adequate medical and physio cover all the time. To be quite frank, I could spend the rest of the book talking about my duties at Clyde. Suffice it to say that I would not have missed a moment of it for anything.

I had a broad cross-section of players at Clyde and I always tried to ensure that morale was good. I like players to socialise and become friends. That doesn't mean that they had to go out, get drunk and run riot, but to hold social occasions that included their wives and partners. With this in mind, I had a kind of social committee, comprising three players who looked after that side of football life.

Bertie Vogts, the German national manager, set up something similar with his players. He had an executive committee for his squad. We have not yet done that with the Scotland squad, although there is a players' pool committee which looks after the squad's commercial interests. It is very difficult to have a social committee when your players are spread around Europe.

We did not have that sort of problem at Clyde, of course. Our committee ran a social fund to which every player contributed a couple of pounds a week. This ensured that we had the money for our events. As an example, we might have a Saturday afternoon game against St Johnstone in Perth. After the game we would have a dinner-dance, stay over and then have a round of golf on the Sunday morning before travelling home later in the day.

I found these events to be invaluable in the social integration of the group. Players like Neil Hood and John Brogan, together with the commercial manager, John Donnelly were instrumental in organising events like that – golf days, and so on. Players who were there during my time – including much-travelled men like Steve Archibald – still tell me that their happiest days were with Clyde Football Club.

In 1978 it was Clyde's centenary year, and I was extremely proud to be manager of the club at that time. There were a great many celebratory events which involved players of both the past and the present, the supporters, and just about everybody and anybody who had been involved in any way. The club was granted a civic reception at which many former Clyde heroes appeared, including Harry Haddock, a very famous name in Scottish football, Tommy McCulloch, Tommy Ring, John

McHugh, Dick Staite, Sam Hastings, Jim McLean and a host of other great names from Clyde's past.

There were a number of players during my time who later became national and international stars but, to me, all my players were stars in that they did their best for the club. One of the most conscientious players I have ever met was Joe Filippi, and there is a little story attached to him and a game against Ayr. I signed Joe from Celtic for £3,000. He was a very good left back and he wanted to make a good impression against Ayr which was his home-town team. During the game he was a bit late in the tackle on an Ayr player. I knew it was a bad one and was not surprised when the referee, David Syme, demanded to speak to him.

'You were a bit late there, number three,' said the referee.

Joe was a very polite man, but he was also extremely quick-witted, and he replied, 'I got there as early as I could.'

The referee did not even smile. 'Name?' he snapped.

'Joseph Filippi.'

You could see that the referee was struggling with that one. Being aware that Filippi was not the most common of names, and trying to be helpful, I called out, 'Spell it, spell it!'

I heard Joe take my advice.

'Mr Syme, it's Filippi with two Ps.'

The referee jotted it down, looked the player in the eye and said, 'Well, Mr Filippi with two Ps, you're off with two Fs!'

I suppose that it doesn't always pay to be polite and helpful!

When I left Clyde in 1986 my two sons and my young daughter were fans of the club. Hugh and John were aged ten and eight. A few games after I had left, they were at a Clyde game with Kilmarnock. Clyde were playing really well and my two boys were as excited as the rest of the supporters on the terraces. One of these supporters nudged Hugh and said, 'We've turned a corner since we got rid of that Brown.'

My son replied, 'Indeed we have. You're right there, pal!'

There was no way that he was going to admit who he was.

My sons have been brought up to enjoy the game and not to take it too seriously. As a professional, I have to take it very seriously, but I like to keep hold of my sense of humour to stop myself going 'psychedelic', as I call it.

To sum up my time at Clyde, the hours spent on the training ground were of great value to me because I was not only doing my best for the club but was also continuing to learn my trade. If you are willing to admit your mistakes and to learn from them, then time spent at clubs like Clyde is time well spent.

12 In the Scotland Camp

When the offer to become assistant to Andy and coach the Under-21 team came in I was still lecturing at Craigie College, and at that same time Graeme Souness had become manager of Rangers with Walter Smith as his No. 2. I knew Walter well because he was one of the SFA staff coaches at Largs.

One morning at Largs, Walter approached me and told me that his chairman would like a private word with me. At this stage I had neither accepted nor rejected the offer from Andy Roxburgh as I was waiting to meet Ernie Walker, the secretary of the SFA. However, when Walter told me that David Holmes wanted to see me I said that I couldn't see much point because the club already had a good coaching team in place. As well as Graeme and Walter, Don MacKay was there working with the reserve team. Walter was insistent that I meet his chairman, however, and so we arranged to have a chat at Ibrox at seven o'clock in the morning in the club's Broomloan Road stand. The reason that the meeting was so early was to give me time to get back to Largs for a nine-o'clock start.

David Holmes was waiting for me and almost immediately began to put his case. He told me that the club was in the process of rebuilding throughout, and that he had made quite a study of my career. As a result, he felt that it would be appropriate to invite me to join the board of directors of Glasgow Rangers. This was a very tempting offer, and an honour, which had to be considered seriously.

I gave it a lot of thought, of course. If I accepted Rangers' offer it would take me away from the coalface of working with players, as I would be mostly involved in administrative matters concerned with aspects of club development, in particular the apprentices, of whom there were more than a hundred at the club. I would be the director responsible for that and various other development avenues.

I found Mr Holmes to be a very persuasive, enthusiastic and determined gentleman, who was obviously very excited about the future of Rangers Football Club. After our meeting he was going off for a three-week holiday, but said that upon his return he would like to have my decision, suggesting that I might like to attend the pre-season friendly against Bayern Munich and talk to him then.

Walter Smith had given me some further ideas about Rangers and told me what he knew of the plans for the future and, as you can imagine, my head was extremely full. On the one hand I had the opportunity to join the SFA as assistant manager of the national team and manager of the Under-21s, and on the other was an exciting opportunity to join one of the biggest football clubs in the world in a challenging and responsible role. Meanwhile, I was still manager of Clyde and a lecturer at Craigie College. Thank goodness for golf!

Eventually the smell of the liniment proved to be too overpowering and I realised that I could not take a position that would deny me my fair share of that unique aroma and the atmosphere that goes with it. I telephoned Campbell Ogilvie, the Rangers Director-Secretary, and asked him to inform Mr Holmes of my decision to decline the great opportunity that he had afforded me.

I accepted the position at the Scottish Football Association. I was involved with the pre-season training of Clyde and the move to Firhill because I had to work three months' notice at the college and the SFA were kind enough to allow me to work part-time for them until my notice reached its conclusion.

My first game in charge of the Under-21 side was against West Germany at Ibrox. The Germans fielded a very strong side and I knew it was going to be quite a challenge. The game was played on 9 September 1986, and I was delighted with a very resilient Scotland performance and a 1–0 victory, which was a great morale-booster for all concerned – myself included.

The team included several players who have since become household names. Henry Smith was in goal and in front of him were Robert Shannon, Joe Tortoland, Derek Ferguson, Paul Hegarty, Tommy Boyd, Steve Gray, Peter Grant, Gordon Durie, Kevin Gallacher and Ian Durrant. I also used Robert Fleck, Owen Archdeacon and Ian Ferguson, who were on the bench. The scorer? Kevin Gallacher. One might be tempted to add – who else? Kevin was as deadly a scorer then as he is now.

Just over a month later came my second game in charge. This one was very different because it was against the Republic of Ireland in Dundalk, a European Championship group match. As was customary, it was being played the day before the seniors met in their group game. I was still at college at the time, and on the day of the match I had to finish in the early afternoon, catch a flight to Dublin and then be taken by car to Dundalk to meet up with the team. The side was near enough the same as I had used against West Germany, but I put Andy Goram in goal and added Gordon Hunter, Derek Whyte and Jim Duffy.

In our group were Belgium and the Republic of Ireland, and I was keen that we should get our campaign off to a flying start at the expense of the excellent young Irish team. It was a very good game and at the end we had won 2–1, just the result that I wanted, and so, as you can imagine, I was highly delighted and considered that my journey had been well worth the effort. Shannon scored our first goal and Gallacher again hit the winner.

Having got off to such a good start, we then won the return game at Easter Park 4–1, Robert Fleck scoring a superb hat-trick and Ian Ferguson adding our other goal. Now we had to pull off a couple of good results against Belgium. The first match was in Bruges on 1 April 1987, and we were happy with the 0–0 draw. The return game took place the following season at Falkirk and we won 1–0, guaranteeing that we finished top of our group. It was Andy Walker who scored our goal.

The senior side were not faring so well in their bid to reach the European Championship finals in West Germany. In addition to

Belgium and the Republic of Ireland, we also had to face Bulgaria and Luxembourg. Victories over Belgium, Bulgaria and Luxembourg were fully warranted. But there were too many other dropped points and, although Scotland were only two points adrift of eventual group winners the Republic of Ireland, it was a defeat by the Irishmen at Hampden that made all the difference.

Our Under-21 campaign continued, and we had to play England in a quarterfinal game. The first leg was at Aberdeen in February 1988. Paul Gascoigne was among the stars in the England team but it was Watford's Gary Porter who stole the show by hitting England's winner. That left us with an uphill task in the return a month later at Nottingham Forest's City Ground. We battled, but once again it was to no avail as a goal from Manchester City's David White won the night for England, and the tie, with a 2–0 aggregate score.

I am not one for excuses. If you lose you hold up your hand to be counted just the same as if you win. However, one of the problems of running a national Under-21 side is that you never know from one game to the next which players are going to be available to you. It is not just the demands of the clubs or the injuries, but also the demands of the senior team. On the day after our first leg against England, the Scotland senior team had a friendly match against Saudi Arabia in Riyadh and I had to give up one of my best squad members, namely John Collins. I'm not saying that he would have made a vast difference because that would detract from the performance of the other players, but in a match with so much at stake you like to have all your options available to you. I was disappointed about that but I understood Andy's reasoning. He was trying to build a squad capable of reaching the 1990 World Cup and he had to use friendly matches like these to assess all his options.

I think the game in Saudi Arabia was the only one I missed during my period as assistant to Andy, so I was not a happy man at that time.

Every manager must make it a priority to surround himself with good, loyal, knowledgeable colleagues, and at Under-21 level I selected Tommy Craig. He may have earned only one international cap but he was a good, solid coach and well respected by the players. Tommy was my colleague throughout my time in charge of the Under-21 team. Our physio was my former Clyde colleague, John Watson. John had been promoted, as he had previously worked for Andy with the youth team. Our medico was Dr Craig Speirs of Greenock Morton Football Club. We later introduced a goalkeeping specialist coach in Jim Stewart, the former Rangers, Middlesbrough and St Mirren 'keeper.

The backroom staff are vital at whatever level you are playing. You have to get it right, and I believe that we had exactly the right set-up for the job during my seven and a half years in charge of the Under-21 team.

In 1992, we again won our group with only one defeat in our qualifying games against Bulgaria, Romania and Switzerland. Our quarterfinal tie was against what had now become Germany. We drew the first leg 1–1 and then had a terrific return game at Pittodrie. The Germans were 2–0 ahead before Ray McKinnon pulled one back just before half-time. Herrlich then made it 3–1 to the visitors and set the scene for a storming second half in which Gerry Creaney, Paul Lambert and Alex Rae took it in turns to score and give us a 4–3 victory and a 5–4 aggregate.

Our semifinal opponents were Sweden. The first leg was at Aberdeen where we were held to a 0–0 draw. I was not too disappointed as the Swedes had played a typically tight tactical battle to give themselves a clean sheet for the return match. I knew they could not play the same way at home and thought we might do better in Sweden. It looked, though, as if the tie was going into a stalemate situation, until nine minutes from the end when Rodlund scored the winner.

We had a very good Under-21 team at that time – Michael Watt, the goalkeeper from Aberdeen, Alan McLaren of Hearts at centre half, and Gary Smith of Aberdeen, who was also in the centre of defence. We also had Paul Lambert, who has since made quite a name for himself but was then with St Mirren, Brian O'Neil, who was with Celtic at that time, Eoin Jess and Scott Booth of Aberdeen, Alex Rae of Millwall, Gerry Creaney of Celtic and Duncan Ferguson of Dundee United. Many of those players have moved on to bigger clubs and bigger things.

Perhaps I should digress a little at this stage and explain

something about myself. Everyone looks upon me as being a quiet sort of a guy who remains cool and calm even under the most stressful of circumstances. It's a nice image to have, and if it happens to be the reality then fair enough. However, I haven't always been like that. When I was at Clyde I was quite a wild man, always raving on the touchline and treating everyone else as a bitter enemy. I received a large number of disciplinary letters from the Scottish authorities and I was always wound up like a coiled spring.

Some of that remained with me during my years with the Under-21 side. I remember that, when we were playing away to Romania in the group match to qualify for the 1992 European Championship, I had occasion to speak to Tommy Craig, just before half-time, about Gerry Creaney's first-half complaints about some aspects of the defensive display. In fairness, Gerry had scored an excellent goal to put us ahead, but we were under the hammer after that as the Romanians tried to get back on level terms. Creaney was shouting abusively at his colleagues, and I told Tommy to tell him that I would speak to him at half-time – which I did in no uncertain terms. A few years later, Gerry Creaney was featured in one of the newspapers and, when asked for his most dangerous moment, said it was being confronted by me during that half-time in Romania.

Tommy Craig said that he was going to join in but that there was nothing left to say after my ten-minute barrage. Sometimes, in anger, we don't realise how loud or vitriolic we become. It is a fact that, as a football manager, you have to have an inner hardness because players understand that, and also because it is your head that is always on the block. You have to be determined that, if the axe is going to fall, it is because you have done something wrong and not because you have allowed others to do wrong on your behalf. You have to be single-minded and autocratic. Today there seems to be a measure of democracy creeping into dressing rooms, but I am of the old school – too autocratic. What I say is what must be, and then I will stand the consequences of being proved wrong.

Luckily we had a strong squad at that time, and indeed throughout my time in charge. We were officially placed third in Europe our best ever and excellent for a country of our size.

Since the Under-21 games often coincided with the senior matches, I was able to go on spying trips for both my team and for the senior side. The Germans, for instance, tend to play the same way at all levels. In Scotland we tend to allow the coaches at the various levels to decide upon their own strategy. My missions were useful for both teams and, if we found that a country played the same tactics at all levels, it made the Under-21 games all the more interesting when they were played on the eve of the senior games.

Four years after that 1992 campaign, Tommy Craig had been promoted to manager of the Under-21 side and his assistant was Alex McLeish, who was capped 77 times by Scotland. I have a little leg-pull with Alex when I see him. I ask him how many caps he won. I already know the answer, but then I say to him that probably there were ten corners per game, and he as a central defender would come up for most of them. Even allowing for staying back for a number of those corners it still means that he had something like five hundred scoring opportunities. Then I like to ask him how many goals he scored for Scotland. I know the answer to that one as well – zero. So how come, Alex, you still like to send defenders up for corners? He has a ready response, though: 'I acted as a decoy for Kenny Dalglish!'

With Tommy in charge and Alex as his assistant, the Scotland Under-21 side once again reached the last four in the 1996 European Championship before going out by a single goal. It was another great achievement, showing the strength of the young players that we produce in Scotland, and totally vindicates the youth development programme we have. Dare I say that in England there was nowhere near the same level of success at Under-21 level over that same period of time?

The annual tournament in Toulon for Under-21 sides was something I enjoyed each year. It was a great experience for young players to get a taste of competitive football in a tournament situation, and helped to build up a squad for the European Championship games to follow. It also gave me the chance to watch other coaches in action and the opportunity to add to my own knowledge.

As an example, I watched the Brazil Under-21 team in Toulon. I know they have a very generous staffing arrangement for their teams. In World Cup finals, if they have 22 players they will most likely have 22 members of staff to take care of them. In Toulon, they had a coach just for warming up the substitutes. No sub was allowed to get into the game unless this coach was satisfied that he was ready. It was such a good system that in the Scotland set-up we have copied it. I think we were the only nation in the 1996 European Championship to employ a warm-up coach for our substitutes. I also think we were the only team to have our substitutes out on the pitch at half-time under instruction to prepare in case they were needed. Our physio, an excellent young man by the name of Philip Yeates, of Dunfermline FC, is known to everyone as Pip, and he took the responsibility of making sure that the subs were warmed up for action.

We still continue that strategy today. We have seven subs on the bench and we can use any three of them, so we have to keep all seven ready for action. Our spare goalkeeper has his own coach, Alan Hodgkinson, to keep him in readiness for action. All in all we try to keep ourselves well organised, and this stems in part from watching the tricks of the trade used by other coaches, and in particular those from the Latin American countries during my Under-21 days.

One thing I notice about the Brazilians is that they walk out hand in hand. If I asked the Scotland players to do that I know what sort of response I would be likely to get! The Latin Americans have a different view of such things, and they walk out brimming with confidence. You won't see us doing that in the World Cup, though – the disparaging remarks I would get from fans and players alike would tend to have the opposite effect to the togetherness I try constantly to achieve.

Talking of Toulon, Alan Shearer scored many fine goals for England in those tournaments, as he has for his country's senior team and his various clubs. I think I witnessed the best goal he has ever scored when I watched him in the final of the tournament against France in 1991. Shearer was already top scorer of the tournament with six goals in three games, but his winner in the final was quite sensational as he sent a scissors-kick volley into the net from twenty yards. It was a most wonderful example of striking play, and the goal was simply out of this world. Although we won two and drew one of our three games we did not make it into the final, but we did receive the tournament's Fair Play Award and we were very happy with that.

One of the big advantages in tournaments like that is that you get to know your players quite well before dealing with them in a senior situation. You can foster team spirit early on and teach the youngsters how to conduct themselves during a tournament, whether it be in a foreign country or within your own shores. One of the acid tests for young players is when you treat them to a pizza.

I know that dietitians will throw up their hands in horror, but we occasionally treat our young players to a pizza. We'll stop the team bus and they'll all pile out and pick whatever they want. That's when you find out who the 'big-time' guys are. Most pizza places have a list of 20 to 30 different types of pizza, and the majority of players are quite happy to select one off the board. The 'big-time' player will always be unable to find what he wants and have one made specially – which he feels will impress everyone else. It doesn't impress those of us who are trying to get the coach on its journey again as quickly as possible, but it does give an insight into the character of the players under your control.

Some of them get a wee bit too big for their boots. I can remember when we had trials for fifteen and sixteen-year-olds at Stirling University. Each had an individual room, and I went round at eight o'clock knocking on the doors to wake them up. I made a mistake at one door and instead of knocking and saying 'Up you get, it's eight o'clock' I said 'Breakfast, breakfast!' instead. A sleepy voice inside replied, 'Just leave it at the door!' That young man is now a well-known player at a big Glasgow club.

I will say that most young players do appreciate their opportunity and do not take anything for granted, but there is always the odd one that achieves status in his own mind long before it is bestowed upon him.

At one time you were allowed to play two over-age players in your Under-21 side, but that has now been stopped. It was a great help because it not only opened up extra options but gave you a chance to put some experience into your side and provide extra tuition for the young players. Alex McLeish was one of my over-age players, as were Stuart McCall, Andy Goram, Henry Smith, Jim Duffy, Campbell Murray and Paul Hegarty. We tried to include players who had a good sense of responsibility and I think it worked very well.

My time in charge of the Under-21 side was of great value to me. It allowed me to benefit from watching others as well as experimenting with my own ideas, and to gain further experience of coaching players for their country rather than for the more regular club fixtures. It gave me the chance to make a few mistakes which were not as costly as they would have been if I had done the same thing with the senior side.

I still think there is a strong case for more B international football. I believe there remains still a huge gap between the Under-21 side and the senior side, and a greater rise in status for B internationals would be the equivalent of having a reserves section in a club. A lot of players have a problem in making the transition, and I am convinced that the stepping-stone of B internationals would be of great value.

As well as the Under-21 side I was also in charge of the youth sides, and we had some excellent results at these levels. In 1987, not long after I was appointed, the Under-18 side qualified for their World Cup finals to be held in Chile. Ross Mathie was my assistant – and he is now the Youth Development Director for the SFA and runs the various youth teams. The medical team was Dr John Maclean and Philip Yeates, both of whom have since been promoted and are now working with me and the national team. I like the Liverpool scheme of continuity, both in coaching and in medical staff.

Peter Donald was the official in charge of our party. He is now the secretary of the Scottish Football League. Heading the delegation was John S. McDonald, a very well-known Highland League administrator, who was then chairman of the Youth International Committee of the SFA. John, or Jock as he's known is a very famous character in Scottish football. He once punched the late great Billy Bremner, and he was there when Mo Johnston and Charlie Nicholas returned to a hotel late and were disciplined. They did not recognise him, and Mo slipped a fiver into his top pocket when he opened the back door for them. Jock blew a gasket and gave them a loud dressing-down. Mo then asked him what he was going to do with the fiver.

'I am going to buy myself a large Macallan and water, thank you very much,' came Jock's reply.

In our group we had East Germany, Bahrain and Colombia. I told the players that if they did well and qualified we would have a night out at a world-famous disco, situated on the Pacific coast, called Topsy Topsy. I thought that while they were in the disco the staff could have a meal at a neighbouring restaurant.

We won our first game against East Germany with a 2–1 result and then drew 1–1 with Bahrain. We only needed to draw with Colombia and we would qualify for the quarterfinals. Sadly, at half-time we were two goals down and the Colombians were already celebrating. However, we were not about to give up easily, and when we reduced the deficit from the penalty spot I knew we could fight our way back into it – as indeed we did. The final score was 2–2 and we were through.

Among our players in that side were Alan Main, who is now goalkeeper at St Johnstone, Billy McKinlay of Blackburn, Paul Wright, now of Kilmarnock, and Scott Crabbe, the former Dundee United and Hearts striker who is now with Falkirk. Not many of the other players have come through to top-grade football, except perhaps Scott Nesbit and Brian Welsh, who were the two dominant centre-halves.

When we were flying out to Chile I met my old friend Bertie Vogts in Amsterdam and I asked him how many players he had missing. I was surprised when he told me that none were missing because it was October and both the German and British seasons were in full swing with every available player being needed at club level. Bertie explained that the president of the West German Federation had told the clubs that if their players were called up they would have to release them. I felt quite envious, because from the initial eighteen players I had selected no fewer than fifteen were not released to us. Players like John Collins, Paul

Lambert and David Robertson were forced to drop out, so we went with a reduced squad because our clubs were not forced to release their players for the three weeks of the tournament. Knowing that your opposition is at its strongest does not help your confidence.

Having qualified for the quarterfinals, we kept our word to the players and allowed them to go to this Topsy Topsy disco, but found to our horror that they would not be allowed in unless accompanied. The players all had to have partners. I asked one of the local representatives if they could find partners for all our players. They said that they would find them partners at the Catholic University of Valparaiso. We were staying in a beautiful place called Vina del Mar on the Pacific coast, and Valparaiso was the adjoining town where the games were being played. So a quest was started at the university to find eighteen girls to accompany our players.

We told the lads what was happening and gave them permission to wear their own casual clothes. They were told that their partners would be collected in small groups on the way and that they must each sit on their own so that the girls could select their partners. We thought that would be a fair arrangement for the young ladies.

Well, far from wearing jeans and so on, the players really put on the style and wore their very best suits. As for the aftershaves and colognes, the whole bus smelled like a mobile parfumerie. It was hilarious watching the faces of these guys every time the bus stopped to pick up another group of partners. Nobody, of course, wanted to be the last one selected but, in the end, it was Scott Nisbit who claimed that dubious honour, to the merriment of everyone else.

When we eventually got there it turned out to be an unusual disco. It was on three floors, and to travel upwards you were conveyed on a kind of big wheel, and to come down you slid on a mat.

Ernie Walker and Andy Roxburgh flew out to join us for our quarterfinal game in which we were facing the mighty West German team. We had been adopted by a girls' secondary school, and they had not only learned Scottish country dancing and poems for the occasion but also gave us a lot of vocal support. We were to be without them for the West German game, so Ross Mathie and I decided that we ought to enlist the support of the local school once again. It was a mixed school and we were warmly welcomed. We taught them a few Scottish songs and the inevitable 'Here we go, here we go, here we go'. They made flags and banners and gave us some great support in the stadium.

At the end of normal time the score was 1–1 and it was quite a game. We went into extra time and then lost Scott Nisbit, who was ordered off. The Argentinian referee then confounded everyone when we scored from the penalty spot through Joe McLeod, only to be told that the kick must be retaken. This time Joe failed and the game went to a penalty shoot-out which the Germans won 5–4.

It was a sad way to end the tournament, and it had happened to us twice – at this level and at Under-16 level. If you also take into consideration Gary McAllister's penalty failure in Euro' 96, you can see why I am keen to ensure that we claim our World Cup results within normal time. I don't want to leave anything to chance.

The Under-16s World Cup was held in Scotland in 1989 and, as the host country, it was up to us to maintain local interest in the competition. We did not start too well and were held to a 0–0 draw by Ghana at Hampden. We then played Bahrain and beat them. We got through our group and played East Germany in the quarterfinal at Aberdeen. We won 1–0 and faced Portugal in the semifinal. The Portuguese were coached by Carlos Queiroz, and it is interesting how many coaches of these youth teams have gone on to become managers and coaches of their senior teams, as I did.

The Portugal game at Tynecastle was watched by 28,000 with another 5,000 locked out. A Brian O'Neil goal gave us a 1–0 victory, and there we were in the final. We faced Saudi Arabia in front of a 53,000 crowd at Hampden. We went 2–0 ahead and looked to be in good shape, but the Saudis pulled one back and then we missed a penalty, which gave them renewed spirit. They scored again and we were into extra time. With no goals in the extra half-hour it was all down to penalties and, as I said before, we failed.

Nevertheless, it had been an excellent tournament and was a fitting tribute to the standard of youth football. I was very proud to have coached that team and to have been generally at the hub of football at this level. It was an excellent experience for me and, hopefully, I was able to make some small contribution to the careers of those young players who went on to even greater days.

13 Assistant Manager

One of Andy Roxburgh's early decisions was to appoint Alan Hodgkinson as goalkeeping coach. He managed to get Alan to come and coach our two chief goalkeepers of that time, Andy Goram and Jim Leighton. We also had Nicky Walker, Jonathan Gould and Campbell Money among those in the frame. Our Under-21 goalkeeping coach, Jim Stewart, worked alongside Alan Hodgkinson, and one of the reasons for the defensive success of the Scotland team is that we have had such good goalkeeper coaching provision. It also took the responsibility away from Andy and me and enabled us to concentrate on the outfield coaching.

It was a busy time as you can imagine, but there is a rule that Under-21 matches played on the eve of senior games must not be more than a hundred kilometres from the seniors' venue. That makes it much easier to get from one game to the next, and for people like me to fulfil their role. Having been a player at Rangers and Dundee, where there were many international players, I did not feel out of place when it was my turn to walk into the dressing room of the national squad. I did not feel overawed, even though I had no senior caps myself. I knew what these chaps were about and felt perfectly comfortable with them, as indeed I like to think they felt with me.

After a year or two, many of the national side were players who had been with me earlier in the Under-21 side, but of course at the beginning this was not the case. It was a very interesting time.

Andy knew his way around and he knew he had a job to do following the disappointment of the 1986 World Cup finals. He had the immediate task of getting the side through to the European Championship, unknown territory for Scotland as we had never qualified for the final stages before. He also had an eye on the 1990 World Cup and knew that he had to build a side that could keep up the momentum of Scotland's frequent appearances in the tournament.

Andy himself was a former schoolboy, youth and amateur international player for Scotland. His club experience was gained with Queen's Park, Clydebank, Partick Thistle and Falkirk. He was a striker and a deep-thinking player rather than one of those sent up front as cannon-fodder. He had been the SFA Director of Coaching for ten years before taking on the role of manager to the national side. The first couple of years of his career in charge were not easy. There was little opportunity to arrange a series of friendlies to test the water. It was straight in at the deep end to try to qualify for the European finals to be held in West Germany in 1988. The first Scotland game was at home to Bulgaria and it resulted in a disappointing 0–0 draw. Even the second-half appearance of Kenny Dalglish from the subs' bench for his final international cap failed to break the deadlock. There was little comfort in being unbeaten because in group situations you really need to capitalise on home advantage.

The next game was the one I have already mentioned. It was away to the Republic of Ireland and, once again, ended in a 0–0 draw. There was some relief when Luxembourg came visiting and we beat them 3–0. The picture was starting to look a little healthier, since we were unbeaten after three games and had not conceded a goal. All that changed when we then played our return game with the Irish Republic. I've already written about the 1–0 home defeat so I will not repeat it – it's far too painful. Andy remained cool and continued to study his players and coach them into his style. We went to Belgium for our next fixture. Remember that Belgium had reached the semifinals of the World Cup only a year earlier and still had the likes of Scifo and the Van der Elsts to lead their own assault on Europe.

At half-time we were faring quite well. Claeson had given the

Belgians the lead after eight minutes, but Paul McStay levelled five minutes later. The second half became virtually one-way traffic, though, as Claeson completed his hat-trick. Vercauteren added another and we came home on the end of a 4–1 scoreline.

By now we only had two games left, and the chances of qualifying were very remote. We would have to win both games, and some disaster would have to befall those above us. The Tartan Army were given something to cheer about because our remaining games saw a very different approach and we took revenge over Belgium with a 2–0 victory. Ally McCoist scored in the first half and Paul McStay in the second. The game was played at Hampden, so there were a lot of happy Glaswegians in town that night, no matter what scarf they wore. There was an even better result to come because in our final game we beat Bulgaria in front of their own fans when Gary Mackay replaced Paul McStay at half-time and scored the only goal of the match. We did the Republic of Ireland a big favour because that left them in top place in the group and automatic qualifiers.

All sights were now on the 1990 World Cup in Italy. Yugoslavia, France, Norway and Cyprus stood between us and a place in the finals. One particular game that is outstanding in my memory was the home game against France on a wet night at Hampden. We had researched the opposition in the usual way, Maurice Johnston helping because he was playing for Nantes. We had the added incentive of Mo wanting to put one over on the players he was seeing every day in his club life. He certainly did that because we beat the French 2–0. It was a crucial game in that we wanted to keep up the momentum that had taken us into a good position in the group after beating Norway 2–1 in Oslo, drawing at home to Yugoslavia and beating Cyprus 3–2 in Limassol. Our goals against the French? Both were scored by Mo Johnston.

We were staying at Gleneagles to prepare for the France game and there were horrendous traffic problems in Cumbernauld as we were journeying to the match. In 1989 there were no mobile phones in everybody's pockets, so it wasn't easy either to get help or to phone ahead to tell anyone of our problems. Roy Aitken did have a mobile – but it was in his case in the luggage compartment of the coach. We pulled over and Roy phoned through to Hampden to tell them that we would be arriving late. A police escort arrived and we were hurried through to the stadium. Even so, we arrived just 35 minutes before the kick-off which left little time for changing and final team talks. Players do not like to be at a ground too early, but this was carrying things a bit too far. It was an excellent performance, though, with a sense of passion and urgency lifting the players above the muddy conditions to great heights of international football.

After beating Cyprus 2–1 at home we then had to travel to Zagreb to play the strongest team in the group, Yugoslavia. Gordon Durie put us ahead in the first half and all was going well until the 54th minute when Katanec equalised. We were then seriously under the hammer and our defence went to pieces to the extent that first Steve Nicol and then Gary Gillespie scored own goals. I don't think the Yugoslavs could believe their good fortune.

There's a story attached to that game as well. As you may be aware, players are accommodated two to a room on these trips and they are told that they must not lock their doors in order that they can be checked on at any time. There was one player on that trip who nobody wanted to room with because he had a problem with flatulence – quite an overwhelming problem it was too. On the night before the game I did my rounds of the hotel, but when I came to his door I found it to be locked. I knocked and waited for a few minutes until the door was opened by the flustered-looking player who was wearing bulging boxer shorts. I asked him what was going on and checked that he was alone. Rather red-faced he told me what he had been doing. I'm not going into any detail but many a referee has been branded guilty of the same act by fans all over Britain.

The next day I was making my contribution to Andy's team talk and went through the list of Yugoslav players, which included Ivkovik, Spasic, Baljic, Stojkovic and others with similar-sounding names. Finally, I turned to the said player and added, 'There's another guy who needs taking out of the game, W . . . ovic!' The player was one of our England-based men, but I don't want to embarrass him further so I'll keep his name under wraps.

In a sense we could afford to lose to Yugoslavia, but we didn't want to have a similar result against France, who would be including Eric Cantona in their side. Andy was worried about the outcome of this game, and I think it was a masterstroke on the part of Ernie Walker of the SFA when he called Andy and me to one side at the hotel shortly before the game. I think he could see that we were both a little stressed by the situation because he gave us this morale-booster.

'You've done a fine job, guys, no matter what the result of this game tonight in Paris. I'm going to recommend that you get a new contract to the European Championship of 1992. I know the president approves so I hope you will be happy with that.'

It was not relevant to our match preparations but it certainly gave us both a great psychological lift – in particular Andy, who was, of course, in the hot seat. Ernie had done the same thing back in 1986 when we were in Mexico for the World Cup. On the morning of our final game, against Uruguay, Alex Ferguson and I were having our breakfast in the prison camp in which we were staying. The players had nicknamed the place Alcatraz because it was very remote and pretty spartan. Alex had a worried look on his face before he left the table, but he looked a much happier man when he came back. We asked if there was a problem, and Alex told us that Ernie Walker had told him that, regardless of how the game went, it was felt that he had handled the campaign very well and that it had been a useful exercise notwithstanding. They had congratulated him on the attitude of the staff and players and thanked him for all he had done.

No matter how experienced a manager is, a pat on the back at times like these can be a great morale-booster and can lighten the load, improving your approach to the game ahead. It takes a good official to recognise the need for that kind of help.

We had scored first in each of our group qualifying games up to now and we wanted to keep that momentum going. Andy told the players to keep their heads against the Frenchmen, who were in need of maximum points if they were going to stand any chance of reaching Italy.

It was interesting that although Eric Cantona played as an attacking midfielder for Montpellier, the French national coach,

Michel Platini, elected to use him as a striker. Richard Gough almost scored with a header early on in the game but all too soon we were on the defensive and Deschamps put France ahead after 25 minutes. We pulled ourselves together, though, and we were not too unhappy at half-time. We felt that we were a match for the French and could get back on terms. The second half proceeded with Scotland mostly on the offensive. When Di Meco lunged wildly at Mo Johnston, the referee had little option but to reduce the French to ten men. We continued to press but Ally McCoist was having one of those days when the ball would hit the side-netting or the paintwork off the bar, but just would not go in. Cantona suddenly found himself alone with just Jim Leighton to beat and could not resist making it 2–0. In the last minute Steve Nicol scored his second own goal in as many games, and we trooped off with a 3–0 defeat hanging round our necks – a scoreline that flattered the home side, but it was still a result, and one that did us few favours.

We had to get a result against Norway to clinch our place in Italy. There was a danger that, having leaked six goals in our last two games, we might still be suffering from the same problem, even allowing for the fact that we had scored half of those goals ourselves. There was a little extra pressure because Jim Leighton was going through a bit of a difficult time – especially since we had been forced to leave him out of the side for the Yugoslavia game as he had sustained a back problem while kicking a ball in training. He was with Alex Ferguson at Manchester United at this time, and Alex was reported as saying that Andy should assure Leighton that his place was safe in order to settle his nerves.

A journalist raised this point at a press conference and Andy parried the suggestion by pointing out that he did not pick other managers' teams and therefore he did not expect them to pick his. It was a fair point, but the next day there were newspaper headlines screaming that Andy was telling Alex to shut his mouth. Alex was soon on to Andy, and I was in the room when the phone rang. I picked it up and, before I could say anything, there was a torrent of abuse. I finally managed to interrupt and explain that it was me he was haranguing, and I tried to point out that Andy had said nothing at the press conference resembling anything like what had appeared in the newspapers. Alex was not a happy man and growled on a little more before Andy was able to take his call.

Some time later there was a need for someone to go to Old Trafford to watch some players – and guess who that someone was. Right in one – me! I had always been well received at Old Trafford before and knew quite a few of the staff, so there was no problem in arranging my seat. When I got there I was told to go to Fergie's office because 'he'll be pleased to see you'.

Oh no he won't, I thought, but I went there anyway. There were a number of people already tucking in to pre-match sandwiches. I looked around the room but could see no sign of Alex. A minute or two later I heard his footsteps and he appeared at the door. He looked straight at me and I waited for the explosion.

'Hello, Broon, how are you?' he enquired very politely. The previous matter was never mentioned and has never been spoken of since. It is another example of the Jekyll and Hyde character of one of the world's greatest club managers.

The Norway game attracted 64,000 into Hampden. We needed to draw at the very least, while the Norwegians were playing for pride only. As it was, Jim Leighton was in the side and equalled the record of 55 full caps for a Scottish goalkeeper, which was then held by Alan Rough. There were a number of our regular players missing because of injuries, but the team set about the task with a strong will. The supporters were terrific and roared the side on almost throughout the first half, even though the breakthrough goal was becoming more and more elusive.

The referee was looking at his watch and Andy and I were already well into our thoughts about what to say to the players when Maurice Malpas sent a long clearance up the field. It found Ally McCoist. Thorstvedt, the Norwegian goalkeeper, sensing the danger, rushed out of goal and Ally sent one of the finest chips from 25 yards I have ever seen – straight over his head and into the net. Hampden went wild.

The second half was fairly even with both sides hitting the woodwork but, in the last minute, Erland Johnsen let fly with a hopeful shot which dipped and swerved wickedly past Jim Leighton and into the net. It was agony to watch. Suddenly the scoreline was 1–1. We were put out of our misery a moment later when the referee ended the game. There was no misery on the terraces, though. The Tartan Army had been celebrating for some time and after the game, in the dressing room, we were able to join them in toasting the 1990 World Cup.

I mentioned earlier that when I took the youth and Under-21 sides I greatly valued the local support we were given in tournaments. Andy had the same view, and before we went to the World Cup it was decided that we should take the players to Genoa where we would be playing two of our group games, against Costa Rica and Sweden. Our other game would be in Turin against Brazil. Yes, Brazil again!

The idea was that we would travel out to Genoa to take in their local derby game against Sampdoria and be introduced to the crowd. Liverpool had other ideas. Kenny Dalglish was manager at Anfield and he did not feel inclined to allow Steve Nicol or Gary Gillespie to come on the public relations trip. Andy was not at all happy about this because he felt that it was vital for as many of the players as possible to attend. I can vouch for the fact that Andy was never a junket man. He would only make trips that he felt were necessary. As well as being a PR exercise, it was seen as a great chance for the squad to see for themselves what the ground was like and what the atmosphere would be. It also gave us another chance to have a look at the five-star Grand Hotel Bristol in Rapallo, which was to be our luxury base for the tournament.

Andy was so annoyed at the non-appearance of the Liverpool players that he dropped them both for the friendly against Argentina, who were then the reigning world champions. It was a prestigious game and everyone wanted to play in it, but Andy was not going to allow sentiment to get in the way of discipline.

The friendly was watched by about 52,000, and Scotland gave a great account of themselves against the superstars of Argentina. Maradona was not in their side, but players like Caniggia, Batista, Valdana and Monzon were very much in evidence. It was a great night for Scottish football because a Stuart McKimmie goal proved to be the only one of the night, and we were given a great morale-booster by beating the then kings of world football. For once I think the England fans were on our side as well, since they were still seething over Argentina having knocked them out of the World Cup in 1986 with that infamous 'Hand of God' goal by Maradona.

Our preparations for the 1990 World Cup could not have been better. I was working alongside Andy throughout and we went into the competition fairly confident of being able to do well, even though we had been criticised for a couple of poor performances in the other friendlies – losing to East Germany and Egypt and drawing with Poland. The latter game took our own-goal tally to four, something of which we were reminded at every opportunity.

We travelled to Malta to acclimatise and play our last warm-up match before going to Italy. We won 2–1 with goals from Alan McInally and we now felt that we were as ready as we were going to be. There were a number of worries, however. Mo Johnston had been scoring all season and was one of our main hopes for goals, but he had torn a stomach muscle and it was touch and go right to the last minute. We also found out at the last minute that Ally McCoist had been nursing a hamstring injury but had been keeping it quiet in the hope that it would go away. Alan McInally's arm had been in a sling for several weeks, and Gary Gillespie was another hamstring victim. Murdo MacLeod was another worry because he had been suffering from a bad groin strain and he actually returned to his club, Borussia Dortmund, for intensive treatment to get him fit for the tournament. There were various other niggling injuries which meant that we had rather a patched-up squad, but it was felt that we had to take a gamble.

I am the sort of person who likes to learn something every day, and I was certainly still learning each day from the activities leading up to the 1990 World Cup. Andy was very similar to me in background and in fact had once been the youngest headmaster in Scotland. We were usually on the same wavelength, but at the end of the day he was the man with his head on the block, ready to take the brickbats or the bouquets. I was merely riding shotgun, but it was a very interesting journey and a great apprenticeship, even though the thought of one day stepping into his shoes had never, at that time, entered my head.

At last our big day, Monday, 11 June 1990, arrived, and there was another setback because we were not allowed to wear our familiar blue shirts. Since Costa Rica wore red it seemed a little odd that there should be any sort of problem but, apparently, the concern was over television coverage and the fact that the Third World were still watching football on black-and-white television sets. We were considered to be the 'away' team so we were ordered to wear our second strip of white with blue-and-yellow hoops.

It is now a matter of history what happened when we played the Costa Ricans. We are still reminded quite frequently that we lost to the underdogs. It was agony to watch. The Costa Ricans were very fast and specialised in one-touch football that avoided physical confrontation. Having said that, they had just one shot throughout the first half, while Johnston and McCoist both went close at the other end.

The dressing room at half-time resembled the medical tent on a battlefield. We had several players nursing knocks, but Richard Gough was the most seriously hurt. He had aggravated a long-term foot injury and was able to take no further part in the game. He was distraught because he realised that he was going to miss more than the second half. In fact, we had to send Gough home for treatment – his World Cup was over.

Stewart McKimmie replaced him but barely had time to break into a sweat before we were a goal down. The second half was only four minutes old when Costa Rica's Cayasso was set free and cleverly shot straight into the net. After that, the wall went up in front of their goal and, despite shot after shot, we just could not score. The Argentinian referee refused what looked like a blatant handball and, when the final whistle was blown, the unthinkable had happened.

The press tore us apart and the Tartan Army let us know what they thought of it. Andy described it all as a 'bad dream', and I could not describe it any other way. That result has haunted us ever since. Nobody has ever taken into account that Costa Rica lost only 1–0 to Brazil and then beat Sweden. No excuses. We had 80 per cent of the play and should have won. It was a poor performance, but in a sense it is an insult to the Costa Ricans just to castigate Scotland and not acknowledge their ability in reaching the second round.

Our next game was against Sweden. With Brazil still to come, we just had to get a result from this one. We made a few changes, some enforced and some tactical. Morale was very low after the Costa Rican débâcle and the press overstatements. We had to work very hard to restore team spirit, and this is where I would like to pay tribute again to the Tartan Army. They had aired their views on our previous result but were in full supportive voice when they turned up for our game against Sweden. The players were bubbling by the time they left the dressing room. They were determined to silence their critics, and we worked hard in getting them focused and I undertook my usual task of dissecting the opposition. The players were given such a magnificent reception by their supporters that you could see them visibly lifted.

If the Costa Rica performance was poor, then the display against Sweden was great. Robert Fleck was a late choice for the squad. He had not been a first choice and was on holiday in Yugoslavia before getting the call to join the squad. He played very well in this, his first World Cup game, and was involved in everything. Stuart McCall headed our first goal after ten minutes when he met a Murdo MacLeod corner.

It was a battle of tactics as much as anything else, and we played our ace sub cards of Paul McStay and Ally McCoist at just the right time. Roy Aitken, our captain, also kept up the momentum, and it was his endeavour that led to our second goal. Roy latched on to the end of a great piercing pass from Fleck, the goalkeeper parried his fierce shot, and as Roy went for the rebound he was fouled by a defender. Mo Johnston converted the penalty and even a late goal from Sweden did nothing to detract from the result and a performance that we felt must have given our next opponents, Brazil, something to think about.

We moved camp to St Vincent and made our preparations. A draw would benefit both teams but there was no way that we were going to shut up shop, even against the Brazilians. We adopted a sweeper system because it suited the occasion, but we were seeking maximum points if possible. Brazil were described by the media as 'subdued', and it is true that they did not seem as zestful as usual. However, their skilful passing was not below par and we knew that we were in for a game of the highest standard.

There were nine minutes left when Brazil struck. Jim Leighton made a good save, but the ball bobbled in the mud. The loose ball was picked up by Muller, who had no hesitation in sending it into the net. A little later, Mo Johnston had a great chance to equalise from six yards out – but he fluffed it. Devastated, he lay prostrate in the mud, symbolic of how we all felt.

The game ended and we were out. Yet again, Scotland had failed to get past the first round. Andy had little to say except that he felt sorry for the supporters, who had all been brilliant. The media raised the usual questions over Andy's future, but there was never any serious thought of changing the set-up. I felt the same as everybody else – extremely disappointed – but I was already looking at another quest.

Scotland had never before appeared in the finals of the European Championship, but I genuinely believed that we had the capacity to change all that.

14 Europe and Beyond

The dust of the World Cup disappointment still hadn't settled when the campaign for Europe began. In our qualifying group were Switzerland, Romania, Bulgaria and San Marino – who were expected to be the whipping-boys. We knew that the others were not going to be push-overs by any means, and I was soon on my travels to spy out the opposition.

The Scottish public were in mourning for our World Cup appearance when we began the trail to Sweden 92. I think they must have been waiting to see how we would shape up because only 12,801 turned up at Hampden to see our opening game against Romania. Our visitors were well organised, as we expect from the eastern European countries. Our players were a little nervous and took time to settle – too long in fact because, in the thirteenth minute, Catamaru put Romania ahead. Our players protested that there had been an infringement but their claims went unheeded. I looked across at Andy Roxburgh but his face was as expressionless as usual. His mind was already into the next phase of the game.

Far from making matters worse, the goal actually spurred the Scotland side on and, just before half-time, our efforts were rewarded when John Robertson scored the equaliser. You could sense the relief all over Hampden, and at half-time the players were in a much better mood. Around midway through the second half Ally McCoist scored a fine goal to make the final score 2–1, which got us off to a flying start.

A month later Switzerland were the visitors to Hampden and

the score was the same. It was John Robertson who broke the ice once again, late in the first half with a penalty. Gary McAllister, with his first goal for Scotland made it 2–0 early in the second half, and even when the Swiss pulled one back there was never any serious danger that we would let it slip. The Scots went home happy. The Hampden crowd had topped 27,000, and the feel-good factor was creeping back.

We were off to Sofia for our next group game. Bulgaria had beaten Romania 3–0 away, so we knew that this was going to be our toughest test thus far. We were not expecting to get off to a flying start, but in fact we did when Ally McCoist put us ahead in the ninth minute. The Bulgarian fans were silenced, but the Tartan Army became even noisier, and it was certainly looking like we were in with another chance of victory. However, a second-half lapse let the Bulgarians through, and in the end we had to settle for a draw. I have to say that when the home side attacked they were very threatening indeed, and it was a credit to our defence, and in particular Andy Goram in goal, that we came away with a point.

We were at home for our next game, and it was the return with the Bulgarians. We were at the top of the group and good value for that position. The game was not exactly a bundle of fun for the spectators. The defences dominated and there were rare scoring opportunities – until the second half when John Collins replaced Gordon Strachan with ten minutes left. Then, within a very short space of time, he headed home a delightful cross from Brian McClair. The place erupted and we were on our way again. The party was pooped, though, by a bizarre late goal in which the Scottish defenders, to a man, stood appealing for off-side while the Bulgarian substitute, Kostadinov, gently placed the ball into an empty net. There was barely time to restart the game and we were all a bit shellshocked, although words were spoken in the dressing room about one of the very basics of the game – namely, playing to the whistle. Probably the player was off-side, but it is the referee who has to make that decision and not the players or anyone else.

San Marino came next, and that was a game both to forget and to remember. The part to forget was the fact that we only won

2–0, while other sides had fired six or seven past the minnows of the group. Our first goal didn't come until well into the second half when Gordon Strachan put us ahead from the penalty spot after Pat Nevin had been fouled. A few minutes later it was a cross from Gordon which helped Gordon Durie make it 2–0. It was an adequate, but not a great, performance in heavy rain on a pitch that became more of a bog as the game wore on. For me, the aspect to remember and savour was the role of the Tartan Army, who once again did us proud. There were only 3,512 people on the terraces, and I am convinced that 3,500 of them were from Scotland. Despite the conditions and the lacklustre performance from both sides, the supporters made it seem like a home game.

By the time we travelled to Switzerland for our next group game we had slipped from the top place, replaced by the Swiss who had beaten San Marino 7–0. We were stunned when the Swiss raced into a 2–0 lead in the first half, and Andy had a few words to say at half-time. We had paid the home team too much respect. Gordon Durie led the charge in the second half and scored a goal within two minutes. We battled away, and with seven minutes left, Ally McCoist popped up for another of his vintage goals, and we were more than happy to come away from Berne with a 2–2 draw.

We were away again for our next game and had to face Romania. We were now at a crucial stage in these qualifying games and every goal counted. The 30,000 home crowd played their part in cheering on their side, and we were grateful that we had done our defensive homework because the Romanians worked hard to break us down and threatened to run riot if we caved in. We were doing fine, even though we were under intense pressure. Unfortunately, Gordon Durie lost his head momentarily in the 73rd minute and gave away a penalty when he handled in his own area. It was one of those things that can happen to anyone. Gheorghe Hagi, the Romanian superstar, scored from the spot and his side then shut up shop for the rest of the game.

It was a blow to our qualifying hopes and we knew that we had to go for gold against San Marino in our final group game. The crowd of 35,170 at Hampden was almost exactly ten times the

…in of the St John's
…mar School football
… sitting in the middle
… front row

In 1957 at Ibrox

My father watches me train in Orchard Street

Kilmarnock v. Dundee in 1962

Dundee FC, Scottish champions in 1962

The legendary Hammy and the Hamsters

Motherwell FC in 1975

April 1978, celebrating as Clyde win the Second Division championship

Clyde FC 1978/79

Italia '90. A few of the lads get feisty as Andy looks on

Training with McCall, Ferguson, Johnston and Collins in 1992

The Scotland U21 squad in 1992

Who's the guy in the middle? Walter Smith and me in the crowd at USA '94

Scotland in 1996

We've qualified! October 1997 at Celtic Park after the game against Latvia

crowd that had witnessed our previous encounter. The Tartan Army were in party mood because they knew that we were in with a very good chance of qualifying for the European Championships for the first time ever. Bulgaria and Romania still had to play each other but nobody was prepared to think in terms of Scotland not making it after coming this far.

Within ten minutes Paul McStay had opened the scoring. Richard Gough added his name to the score sheet and then Gordon Durie made it 3-0 by half-time. We told the lads to keep plugging away but not to change the tempo at all, and Ally McCoist made it 4-0 midway through the second half. I think the fans wanted a goal riot, but it is never that easy and, in the end, we had to settle for 4-0 and wait for the final group game a week later in which we hoped that Bulgaria would do us a favour against Romania. Hagi, uncharacteristically, missed a penalty, but Popescu gave the Romanians a 1-0 half-time lead. Time stood still in the second half until Dirakov made himself a Scottish hero by scoring the equaliser. The score remained at 1-1, and we were through to the European Championships for the first time.

Meanwhile, the coaching at Largs continued apace and became much improved. Some of the improvements came before the 1990 World Cup when the pitches were dug up for renovation. That year, for the first time since I joined the coaching staff in 1969, we had to go to St Andrews, where we took advantage of the excellent facilities of the university. They certainly did their best for us and made us very welcome.

In my coaching group was an international player who had been enjoying a remarkable career but was now apparently coming close to the end of his playing days and doing his best to obtain the highest possible coaching qualifications. He was none other than Gordon Strachan. He sailed through his A Licence award, and it is obvious that he did indeed put into practice the things he learned when you look at the excellent job he is doing at Coventry.

So, Andy Roxburgh had become the first manager to take Scotland into the European Championship tournament. It was no more than he deserved because he was always a very hard-working guy, always very methodical, and a great talker. He put a lot into motivating his players. After the World Cup defeat by Costa Rica, for instance, he restored morale by showing a video of great Scottish sporting achievements.

He also used to pick themes for his team talks. I remember him asking the players if they would like to win another cap. It was his way of putting it into their heads that their international careers lasted as long as the quality of their performances. Unfortunately, when he came to Alex McLeish, he came upon a player who was just about to earn his 50th cap, a place in the Hall of Fame, and a ticket for life to every Scotland home international. So when Andy asked Alex if he would like another cap, Alex was quick to nod his head. I couldn't resist a joke and said, 'Well, you'd better weigh in with a bit of cash, then.' All the players laughed, but Andy didn't and he had a word with me later about 'ruining' his team talk.

To get ready for Sweden we played several friendly games. We beat Northern Ireland 1–0, and then we drew 1–1 with Finland before going to the USA, where we won 1–0 in terrific heat in the Mile High Stadium in Denver. We then beat Canada 3–1 in Toronto before flying back to Europe and a 0–0 draw in Norway – our final preparatory game before the European Championship. A lot of people still think that this kind of travelling taxes the players before a major competition, but believe me it has quite the opposite effect. It gives them the chance to play a few games together and focus on the job ahead and, at the same time, distance themselves from the domestic season they have just completed. Because the guys are together all the time it also helps to build team spirit and cements their friendship and loyalty to the squad.

Our group for Sweden could hardly have been more difficult. We had to play Holland, the defending champions, Germany, the world champions, and the CIS – who had only just changed their name from USSR and had come through their qualifying matches undefeated. However, we were undaunted and in buoyant mood as we took the pitch to play Holland in the Ullevi Stadium. The scoreline tells everyone that Holland won 1–0, but it does not give a full and true account of the story. Holland were very impressive in the first half with Van Basten, Gullit, Rijkaard and Wouters on top form. For Scotland, Gary McAllister, Paul McStay and Stuart McCall were also in good form, and at half-time there was still no score.

In the second half we exerted some pressure of our own, and while the first half belonged to the Dutch, the second half was unquestionably under Scottish dominance. It was really against the run of play that Dennis Bergkamp scored the only goal of the game and sent us from the pitch beaten but unbowed. We won many friends with the quality of our play, the determination and the character shown – not only by the players but by the Tartan Army, who had been magnificent representatives for Scotland.

On to the next game and Germany. Once again the Scotland side fought bravely and gave the Germans a severe fright. But for the brilliance of Illgner in the German goal, I am sure we could have been two goals ahead in the first ten minutes. As it was, the Germans composed themselves and took the initiative through Riedle to make it 1–0 at half-time. We suffered a cruel blow early in the second half when Effenberg's shot hit the boot of Maurice Malpas and soared into the air. Andy Goram, trying to change direction, slipped and could only watch helplessly as the ball sailed into the net. To their credit, the players did not give up, and when the final whistle went the Germans smiled more with relief that with delight.

We were thus eliminated from the competition and had not yet scored a goal. We still had to play against the CIS and really wanted to wave goodbye to Sweden with a flourish. Our performance was probably the least impressive of our three games – but the result was excellent. After six minutes, Paul McStay fired in a 25-yard shot through a ruck of defenders which Kharin, the CIS goalkeeper, did not see until it hit a post, ricocheted to the back of his head and bounced into the net. Just over ten minutes later Brian McClair tried a long-range drive. It took a slight deflection and went in, which made Brian particularly happy as it was his first goal for Scotland in 26 appearances. When Pat Nevin was tripped during the second half, Gary McAllister made no mistake with the penalty and at the end of the game we had won 3–0.

The Scottish supporters were out in force and the players went to them to show their appreciation for the tremendous backing they had received and for the fact that the Tartan Army had become the characters of the championship – a lot of fun and well behaved.

There hardly seemed time to breathe before the World Cup qualifiers were underway. Once again there were some tough games to come as we were drawn in the same group as Italy, Portugal, Switzerland, Malta and Estonia.

The first match was away to Switzerland in Berne. It would be an understatement to say that it was a disaster. It was in fact a total disaster. Not only did we lose, but Richard Gough was himself sent off for an instinctive hand ball. Our campaign was certainly off to a bad start with a defeat and the prospect of having one of our most experienced players suspended.

Our first home game was against Portugal at Ibrox, and they proved to be a handful. They were fast and very tricky and we were under pressure for much of the game. We just did not seem able to get into the game, and were grateful at the end for our first point from the 0-0 scoreline. The Portuguese were a little disgruntled at having two penalty appeals turned down, but that's football for you.

Less than a month later we were at home again, and this time it was Italy who were the visitors to Ibrox. Franco Baresi came out of retirement to boost the Italian campaign, and they were the favourites to win the group. They were also favourites to win at Ibrox, but I found them less than convincing. The usually solid Italian defence was nervous and at half-time we felt that the points were there for the taking. Despite several good opportunities, the ball simply would not go into the net and again we ended with a 0–0 result. It was beginning to be a worry. We had two points from our three games and had scored only one goal.

It was three months before our next game in February 1993. Once again we were at home, this time to Malta. A lot of people decry the Maltese, but they are not an easy team to beat, especially on their own ground. When they visited Ibrox they were out for damage limitation. Ally McCoist put us ahead after fifteen minutes, but it was not until midway through the second half that he made it 2–0. Pat Nevin added a third near the end.

At last we had a victory, and some goals, and our record suddenly looked a little more respectable, with a goal difference in our favour and one defeat in four games. The prospect of a trip to America for the 1994 World Cup had not entirely faded.

We knew it was going to be a tough job getting a result from Portugal in Lisbon in April 1993, but we felt that it was not an entirely hopeless task. If we pulled something off, we were still in with a shout for the World Cup finals. It was obviously a very important game for us.

Leading up to the game there was quite a bit of hassle because we had a large representation from Glasgow Rangers at the time. In fairness, Rangers were doing very well, both in Europe and at home, during this time. They had gone something like ten games without defeat in Europe, including that wonderful tie against Leeds United which they won both home and away. They were certainly in exceptional form and you cannot ignore players who are part of a success like that. The McCoist–Hateley partnership was outstanding.

In the Scotland squad we had Goram, Gough, McPherson, McCall, McCoist and Durrant. The Scotland game was sandwiched between European Cup games against Marseille, so there was a lot of pressure on those Rangers players to peak several times in quick succession. In hindsight, it is easy to see why there was not full concentration on the Scotland match from those players, who were in the middle of a very tense and important European tie.

I'm not making excuses for the players involved, they don't need my help, but you have to be fair and say that the timing could not have been much worse. I don't go along with what Richard Gough later said, blaming our defeat in Portugal purely on tactics. It's a question of 'Well, he would say that, wouldn't he?'

Gough said that we had been told that Rui Barros, the little midfielder with Monaco and Portugal, would not be playing. I can confirm that. The information came as the result of a conversation I had in the car when I was travelling back from the Under-21 game. In the vehicle with me was Bobby Robson. He told me that he didn't want to be disloyal to Portugal, which I can believe because Bobby Robson has always been an outstanding gentleman, but he marked my card to the effect that the Portuguese choice for that midfield position would be Figo. He didn't volunteer the information. I had to ask him.

I reported back to Andy what Bobby had said. What later crept into the newspapers was that we had taken the advice of a taxi driver. The idiots who misreported it had no idea that my 'cabbie' was an official of the Portuguese Football Federation and that my 'informant' was Bobby Robson.

We had prepared for a team that included Figo instead of Barros, and didn't realise our mistake until it was too late. I asked Carlos Queiroz, the manager of Portugal, whom I knew, what had happened to make him pick Barros.

'He failed a urine test yesterday, and again this morning – but at four o'clock this afternoon he was OK,' said Queiros. He went on to explain that Barros had been taking antibiotics for a heavy cold and that he had not wanted to risk any misunderstandings. As a result, the Portugal manager had prepared his team without Barros but had drafted him in later in the day.

I can assure you that Andy Roxburgh sat the whole Scottish team down, more than an hour before the kick-off, told them that Barros would be playing, and made arrangements for dealing with him. The point is that there is no doubt whatsoever that the team was fully informed of the situation. I was there – I know.

Nevertheless, the newspaper headlines read that a taxi driver had supplied Scotland's tactics for the game, which was, of course, absolute nonsense.

Within a few minutes of the game starting, Barros made his presence felt by scoring at the near post. They quickly settled and the rest of the story is now history. Cadete scored twice, Futre got one, and Barros scored another to make the final score an embarrassing 5–0. Scotland simply did not perform. Nothing went right and we were pretty dejected, I can tell you. Worse than all that, this was also the game in which Ally McCoist broke his leg. It was a shock to us all. We were 3–0 down when it happened and Ally was carried off.

He was examined in the dressing room and the general opinion was that the leg was broken. However, you can't keep a man like

Ally McCoist down for long. He remained cheerful and refused to blame anyone for what had happened. When the game ended, his teammates rushed to the dressing room to see how he was. He was lying on a table with his leg in a splint, waiting to be X-rayed properly.

'How are you doing, Alistair?' someone asked.

'Och, it could be worse,' replied McCoist, with a grin. 'We could have lost five–nil!'

Needless to say, Ally didn't know the final score at that stage. When he flew back to Scotland, Andy travelled with him, journeyed on with him to the hospital and stayed with him until the results of the X-ray were available. I have known other managers who would not even bother phoning to see how a player was.

That injury was a major blow to Ally's career at that stage because he had been in such incredible form. He is also such a great character that it was sad to see him invalided. Happily, he bounced back and I had the privilege – and the benefit – of selecting him for his Scotland comeback.

After that hammering from Portugal we had to pick ourselves up, because we still had two more World Cup games to play before we could say that the season was over. On 19 May, just three weeks after that last game, we were away to Estonia. We could not afford to lose this one, not only from the point of view of the World Cup place, but also for general confidence.

Estonia proved to be a tough nut to crack, but Kevin Gallacher demonstrated once again what an excellent player he is when he scored just before half-time. You could see the tension lift and the dressing room was very lively during the interval. John Collins made it 2–0 about a quarter of an hour after the restart, and then Scott Booth scored our third with ten minutes left. The journey back home was much happier.

Two weeks later we met Estonia again, this time at Pittodrie. As has been proved more recently, you can never underestimate teams like Estonia. They are the underdogs most of the time and have nothing to lose. They are also greatly underrated, and that puts a lot of pressure on their opponents, who always carry the burden as favourites to win the game. That great club and country servant, Brian McClair, put us at ease with a goal after sixteen minutes. Pat Nevin made it 2–0 before half-time, but then we lost our sense of direction somehow and when Bragin pulled one back after about twelve minutes of the second half, things looked as if they were drifting. With just under twenty minutes left we were awarded a penalty which Pat Nevin converted. The score was 3–1, but it was not a vintage performance, and we were all concerned about our remaining group fixtures.

We were back at Pittodrie on 8 September to play Switzerland. They had beaten us 3–1 a year earlier in the first fixture of the group. Roy Hodgson was in charge of the Swiss, and he had developed a very good side. They had beaten Italy at home and drawn with them away, so we knew that they were possibly the greatest threat to our ambitions. We had to win – it was as simple as that.

After a very tense first half, John Collins gave us the lead with a great goal in the 50th minute. The celebrations started – but too soon, as it happened. The referee awarded the Swiss a penalty and Bergy put the ball past Bryan Gunn. The last twenty minutes dragged by with little hint of another goal, and when the final whistle went we knew we were out of the World Cup.

I looked at Andy's face and his expression matched my own. He had been in charge for 61 games, equalling Jock Stein's record. He had earned much applause and recognition for his Scotland squad, but now it looked as if it was time to reconsider his future.

A few days later Andy resigned. The SFA International committee did discuss it with him with a view to changing his mind, but he explained that he felt that his team had died during that game against Portugal. He had made up his mind and that was that. I believe, though I do not know for certain, that Andy had many offers on the table – and indeed he has since become UEFA's co-ordinator of coaching, a very responsible job and one that I know he enjoys immensely. As technical director of UEFA he is responsible for 51 countries, and I have attended many of the courses he organises and presents for coaches. All the top coaches attend, and Andy Roxburgh is well respected by all of them.

Having failed to get Andy to change his mind, the committee

called a press conference which Andy agreed to attend in order to formally announce his resignation. At that same press conference it was to be announced that I was being temporarily put in charge. Looking at it from my point of view, it was not the greatest compliment I have ever been paid. I had taken the Scotland Under-16 team the furthest it had ever gone, the Scotland Under-20 team the furthest it had ever gone, and the Scotland Under-21 team the same. The committee knew my record but with sometimes five to six weeks between meetings I had to be patient. I did not complain because that is not my way, but I was a little disappointed at the delay.

I was left to get on with the job, with little attention being paid by anyone to my track record. As well as my successes with Scotland I had won two championships with Clyde and had a very good pedigree in the transfer market. I was not exactly a novice to the job, but I felt uncertain about my future.

15 So There I Was . . .

So there I was, holding my head in my hands with my whole past life flashing before me, wondering if I would not have been better off pursuing my career in education rather then subjecting myself to this torture. The Olympic Stadium in Rome is a huge place, but there is absolutely nowhere to hide when something goes wrong. Remember that we were playing for nothing but pride because we could not qualify for the World Cup even if we had scored a hatful against Italy that night. I had to forget all about what had happened before, and the fact that everyone was calling for a former football star to take over as manager of Scotland. I was partially ignored in all the speculation – which showed exactly how the media thought of me. I was not there to prove any points to anyone, just to get the best result possible for the players and my country. The rest was up to everyone else.

There were more than 80,000 fans in the Olympic Stadium and Italy had to win their last two qualifying games to guarantee a place in the World Cup of 1994. The scene was set for us to be sent home with our tails between our legs. We had lost our previous game in Portugal 5–0. Andy Roxburgh, after the match, simply said, 'A team died out there!' It is not easy to lift players after a result like that. If they have lost by the odd goal they are often more determined to do better next time – but a heavy defeat can be a wipeout in more senses than one.

I was thrust into position when Andy Roxburgh resigned and the SFA were in no rush to replace him – mainly because they wanted to make sure of making the right move for the right man. So, there I was, the temporary manager of Scotland. It was not the most flattering position for me to be in, but I had been asked to hold the fort while the SFA committee were deliberating and that is exactly what I had planned to do. I had no idea what would happen when the new man took over, but I suspected that I would probably be visiting the Jobcentre to see if anyone wanted a football-mad teacher with a dodgy knee.

I prepared the team as thoroughly as possible with the assistance of Murdo MacLeod, himself a former Scotland international. Part of the preparations for a match involve taking a good look at the opposition. In big business it is common practice to study your competitors, and I believe that the same should apply in football. Never dismiss your opponents as irrelevant. No matter what the game, or who is opposing you, you still have to win, and you have to do so by defeating that opposition. You need to know them in order to achieve that.

The preparation doesn't end the day before the game. It is important to watch even the warm-up of the other side, and I did exactly that. The Italians worked very hard on their warm-up for this important game. They were on a rubber-floored indoor pitch about the size of two goal areas put together. They were put through their paces very thoroughly and very strenuously. I saw the sweat dripping off the ponytail of Roberto Baggio and running down his back, soaking his T-shirt.

When they took the pitch just before the kick-off, they were very loose and alert for the game. I stood at the side of the dugout on the running track that went around the pitch and watched what was going on. When the whistle went for the start of the game they tore into us like a team that had already been playing for a quarter of an hour. Within four minutes they had taken the lead. A well-worked throw-in saw the ball go to Baggio. He ran a few yards and sent the ball straight to Donadoni, who wasted no time in putting it past Bryan Gunn. We were caught completely cold as Rome went crazy, with the Italians taking another step nearer to the World Cup finals.

To their credit, the Scotland players did not allow their shoulders to sag. In a sense it would have been understandable if they had. In your previous game you are beaten 5–0 and now, in your next game, you are a goal down within minutes. I thought at the time that Bryan was a bit unfortunate to allow Donadoni's long shot to go past him.

We were restricted for the next twelve minutes to rare attacks as the Italians decided to make a romp of it. In the sixteenth minute Roberto Baggio, playing in an inside right position just off the front, sent a beautiful ball to Casiraghi. He got there just before our centre-back, Brian Irvine, and angled his shot across the goalkeeper and into the net. So just imagine that it is your first international in charge and you are two goals down within such a short space of time. There is still an hour and 14 minutes to play against one of the best teams in the world, on their ground and in front of 80,000 Italian supporters.

I felt a kind of numbness and bewilderment for the first and only time. I wondered why I had involved myself in this situation at all. Fortunately we settled down very quickly after that and played with some composure. We had nothing to lose and, once again, I have to praise the players for keeping their heads. They drew strength from their situation and contained the Italians for some time. I watched them growing in stature all the time. Even the home fans were beginning to quieten down just a little. Then Kevin Gallacher pounced on an opportunity and sent the ball over the head of Pagliuca in the Italian goal. Suddenly it was 2–1 and we were back in the game. It certainly silenced that very volatile Italian crowd.

At half-time we tried to pick things up a bit and inspire more of the same from the players. They were quite cheerful and couldn't wait to get out for the second half. Gordon Durie and Gary McAllister were winding everyone up as well. I don't know how things were in the Italian dressing room, but there was no lack of spirit in ours at that time.

Perhaps this is the right time for me to explain that I had shocked a lot of people by leaving out Paul McStay. Paul, of course, was, and still is, a legend in modern Scottish football, and had been capped for his country more than 70 times. Dropping him from the starting line-up was leaving myself wide open to the most abusive criticism that you can imagine – though not from the player himself, I hasten to point out.

I have a policy about handling players. On the Monday before the game we were leaving the Gleddoch House Hotel, which had been our base before flying to Italy. I took Paul McStay to one side and told him that I didn't think he had been playing particularly well lately and that I would not be naming him in the starting line-up. I also said that I knew how much he wanted to play against Italy in Rome and that, if it was appropriate, I would send him on to the pitch from the subs' bench at some stage of the game. I told him that I could not guarantee doing that and we would have to wait and see how things went. I wanted him to realise that he was still an important member of the squad. I simply wanted to reassure him that I had not forgotten him and that he was still a very valuable player to me.

Earlier, there had been much press talk about who would be given the captaincy for the game. Although I was only in temporary charge, I had decisions to make and the authority to make them. Would I choose Paul McStay or Gary McAllister as captain? That was the question the media wanted answering. I try to give the press a story every day, because I know they have a job to do, but I was being pushed to name my captain before I was ready to do so. You can imagine the headlines when I told the press that Paul would not be playing other than on the subs' bench. Gary had obviously got the job and I was, of course, in a no-win situation. If I had picked Paul I would have been told that it was time for a fresh start – if I didn't, then I was making a big mistake by not keeping to a stable captaincy. Those are the sorts of things that you learn to live with when you have responsibility – and especially so when you are in the spotlight as manager of Scotland.

Well, at half-time I thought about bringing him on, but I decided against it. I decided it would be better to leave well alone. Sure enough, the second half kicked off and we were playing really well. We were seriously unlucky not to equalise when Gordon Durie fired in a tremendous shot that had 'goal' written all over it before it hit the shoulder of his teammate Ian Durrant and ricocheted just wide. We had come desperately close to making it two goals each and it was clear that the Italians were becoming worried. Their football was not flowing as well as it

had during the first quarter of an hour of the game. I did bring
Paul McStay into the game with about twenty minutes left, and
he played his part in keeping our tails up.

As inevitably happens in games like this, the matter was finally
settled when the Italians had a breakaway as we were piling more
pressure on them. They raced away down the right with a good
fluid move which ended with Eranio – who now plays for Derby
County – collecting the ball just inside the area and making the
score 3–1. You could see the relief among the Italian players and
hear the same from the mass of supporters. It was an excellent
goal, but it did feel a little cruel after so much effort had been put
in by the Scotland team.

So, we lost my first international and I think the media were
left a little bemused. Some representatives would very much have
liked to have been vitriolically critical, but they could not really
fault the performance.

The only thing that annoyed me was when one well-known
newspaper sarcastically wrote that the Italians had not even
bothered to come out on to the pitch to warm up before the game.
It shows just how ill informed that writer was because I had
watched their rigorous work-out indoors before the game with
my own eyes. It was suggested that the Italians treated us with
disdain, almost contempt, by not bothering to come out on to the
pitch. Because our journalists had not witnessed what I had seen,
they reported that the Italians had opened the scoring without
even breaking into a sweat.

Believe me, those Italian players, and their coaches, gave us a
lot of respect both before and after the game.

Anyway, that was my first game in charge. I returned to
Scotland amid the whirlpool of speculation about who was going
to be the new manager. All the newspapers were listing likely
candidates. Names like Dalglish, Ferguson, McQueen, Bremner,
Jordan, Strachan, Miller and Souness were widely touted, with
each newspaper picking its own favourite. Brown was still not
getting much of a mention, although there were a few reporters
wanting to ask me who I thought would be the best man for the
job. Only a few asked me if I fancied it.

Mind you, I really wasn't sure if I did fancy it. I hadn't

really given the prospect much thought. I had been too busy getting the trip to Rome organised and being at the match to think of much else. With the game over I felt much better. We had done well even though we had been defeated. I still hadn't gone as far as thinking about having the job myself, but I had gained some satisfaction from the fact that the players had come off the pitch with their heads high – and that meant a lot to me.

There were many lessons I had learned from that first game, and I had also renewed my acquaintance with the Tartan Army. I must tell you a few things about those great Scotland supporters who will follow the team anywhere and everywhere – sometimes even without a ticket for the game.

I have been a Tartan Army man myself. It was at the time I was playing for Falkirk, and the club decided to take us south by bus as a treat to see the game against England on 10 April 1965. We arrived in London on the morning of the game and the club secretary, Charlie Taylor, handed us a ticket each and a ten-bob note to buy a meal. You could get a pretty decent meal for ten bob in those days.

A group of us, including Doug Baillie now of the *Sunday Post* and John Lambie, who was later to become manager of Hamilton, Partick Thistle and Falkirk, headed for the centre of London to have our meal. We found a pretty top-notch restaurant and the food was very good. The only problem was that the service was very slow and we had limited time because we still had to get to Wembley. In the end we hit the panic button and didn't wait for our sweet but left the restaurant.

The game at Wembley was a cracker. The final score was 2–2 and we watched Ian St John and Denis Law get a goal each. My old pal Billy McNeill was there in the heart of the defence as usual, and I think even the England fans would admit that they were a little bit lucky that day not to have been well beaten. Our fans were superb. Unless you have travelled with them, you might not realise that they are the most passionate, noisy bunch of guys you could ever muster together. At matches they are tremendous, and they always bring the place to life wherever they go. You rarely see them engaged in battle, either. They go to support their country and to have a good time while they are doing it. Their idea of a good time does not include being baton-charged and thrown into a cell for a few days.

There are known characters among them too, and one of these made his presence felt on that trip to Rome. We were staying at the Sheraton Hotel, about fifteen miles outside the city. It was the eve of the game and the players had all gone to bed. I was having a drink and a chat with the other members of the Scotland entourage. I suppose it must have been about half past ten or eleven o'clock. Suddenly we heard a bit of a commotion in the hotel foyer. We were in the lounge but could still hear the noise quite distinctly. There were four of what we might call 'the lads' in their kilts and T-shirts, and they were carrying cans of 'refreshment' in this very posh hotel.

The hotel staff were excellent and they treated us very well, and while 'the lads' were not intent on causing any harm, they were certainly disrupting the atmosphere and causing some alarm to many of the other guests. They found us in the lounge and they all wanted to come and shake my hand and wish us all the best for the match. Of course, they didn't do all this in a whisper, as you may imagine. In truth, they were also looking for tickets. They had made the journey to Italy on spec, hoping that they might be able to get some tickets when they arrived in Rome.

One guy I recognised was John Grigor. Now John is a very conscientious Scotland supporter. He is a member of our travel club, which has more than 12,000 members, and he is also a great organiser of bus trips. I have seen him at games all over the world wherever Scotland have been playing. He would hire a submarine to get there if he had to.

On this particular night, John and his pals had imbibed a few too many. I jumped out of my seat and went over to them, shook hands, talked to them a little and ushered them back out of the hotel and into the carpark. They departed quietly enough after that, and I guess they found some tickets somewhere. I didn't have any for them – I rarely do. They did embarrass us because they had taken a bit too much liquor on board, but I'm sure they were the first to realise it afterwards.

To all members of the Tartan Army I would say to you that

your support is appreciated much more than I can ever hope to explain. You are an important part of the squad wherever we go. However, please remember that we have to try to keep some kind of a peaceful atmosphere at our hotels – especially on the eve of a big match. Most managers will tell you stories of the opposition supporters trying to give you a bad night's sleep before a game. We can do without our own supporters doing the same – even with the best of intentions. Get a good night's sleep yourselves so that you are match-fit for when we need you – at the game!

We arrived home amid speculation about the new manager, as I have mentioned, but still there was one newspaper trying to get something else going. I was told that a newspaper had offered Paul McStay quite a large sum of money to vent his anger about my decision not only to have him on the bench at the start of the game, but also to relieve him of the captaincy.

It says a lot for Paul's character that he refused the newspaper's offer. For my money that is a great tribute to the man's tremendous loyalty. A lesser person might well have taken the money and given the newspaper what it wanted to hear. Paul didn't, and I admired him for his honesty, integrity and loyalty.

The decision I took with regard to Paul had been an honest one and I had been open and quite frank with him in telling him of my decision. I hadn't asked someone else to tell him or even kept my mouth shut and let a team sheet do the talking. Of course, the matter was not totally forgotten by the Celtic fans, who worshipped Paul!

Some months later I went to watch Celtic play in a European tie against Cologne at home. I parked my car in the school carpark, which is adjacent to Celtic Park, and I had to walk into the stadium. It was like running the gauntlet. Sometimes the supporters just want to shout your name, but on this occasion I was called by various names as I walked through the crowd – some of whom had even climbed up on the railings to make sure that I heard their voices. They had not forgiven me for my Paul McStay decision. I was shouted at and spat upon. When I got into the ground I sat next to Kevin Kelly, one of the directors. In front of the directors' box there was this huge chap wearing a Celtic scarf. As soon as he saw me he turned round and gave me some terrible abuse: 'You should be at Ibrox, watching that Durrant and that Ferguson in the Rangers reserves. What are you doing here watching us?'

I had already had one supporter tap me on the shoulder and say, 'By the way Craig, Paul's wearing No. 8!' . . . so I was getting a bit fed up with all this. You can never show it, though. In situations like that you just have to take it. Anyway, when this other guy was hurling abuse at me, Mr Kelly turned to me and said, 'I'm glad you're here. Otherwise it would have been me and the other directors getting all that.'

My embarrassment was increased when, about three minutes from the end, the very loud Celtic Park Tannoy came into play. There was the usual ding-dong, ding-dong, but instead of an Avon lady at the door there was a very clear voice saying, 'Ladies and gentlemen, tonight's sponsor's choice for man of the match is Paul McStay of Celtic!' The crowd roared its approval and I received another torrent from this guy in front of the directors' box. Paul had given me the best possible response to my not putting him on from the start in the Italy game by turning in a blinding performance for his club as I sat in the stand. The relationship between the Celtic fans and the board was not very good at that time, so I think my presence had served to take some of the pressure off them. No wonder the directors always welcomed me back to Celtic Park!

For the record, I have always had the highest regard for Paul McStay and his exemplary playing style. I don't think he has ever committed a dirty foul in his entire life, and he has always trained well, worked hard and played at the top of his game. He was a magnificent midfield player for Celtic and for his country, always contributing his best and scoring some great goals into the bargain, and he deserves the greatest respect possible. I will be eternally grateful to him for his attitude towards my decision at that first game in charge. I hold him in as much repect as I possibly could anyone, and I hope to a degree that it is mutual. What a role model he has been, and still is when he works with our youth international teams.

The Paul McStay incident throws up another interesting point.

How do you tell players that they are dropped – especially international players with great reputations? Do you hope that they will find out by some devious method? Do you phone them in advance and hope that you will not have to face them? I decided that there was only one way for me – the way that I had seen other managers, whom I have respected, tell players that they are out of the side for a particular game.

One thing I didn't want was a repeat of something I had witnessed in 1990 when we were preparing for the World Cup in Italy. We were staying in the Hotel Bristol and we were on the training ground in Rapallo. Andy Roxburgh elected to tell Ally McCoist what was happening. I do think it is the best policy to tell players your decisions in a football context rather than in the office. As a manager at club level I always used to have end-of-season talks with my players on the training field. Some I would have to tell that they were being released, while others would be offered new terms. Either way, I always thought it was better for both parties if it was done on a man-to-man basis in a football environment.

I have already mentioned that when I was given a free transfer I received the information written on a piece of paper in a very impersonal manner. I know how I felt about that. I have always tried to be as courteous as possible to players and others, whatever their situation or status.

To go back to Andy and McCoist, we were at the training ground and most of us were already on the bus waiting to go. What was delaying us was a discussion between Andy and Ally after the manager had told the player that he would not be playing. I think that perhaps Andy could have handled it differently. That is not being disloyal to Andy, it is just my own opinion. When you try to talk to a player in the hotel, you cannot go to his room because he usually has a room-mate. He could come to your room but that is a bit too formal for me, and therefore it can be difficult to find somewhere private enough to break the news. It's tricky – but you have to learn to handle it if you are going to be in charge of players. I have also learned that you have to talk straight to players. They don't want to be mollycoddled or listen to a lot of excuses. Talk straight to them and let them know exactly where they stand. Be honest and truthful – it is much better that way. I never say that another player is a better player than the one I am talking to. I always say that, for this occasion, I think that player so-and-so is a more appropriate choice.

Another aspect to take into consideration is the role of the press in these things. If you are straight with your player and he is an honourable person, then he will not let you down. It is advisable, I have found, to talk to the player about what is going to be said to the press. I usually tell them that I am going to say such and such a thing, and then ask the player if he would agree with taking that line. We can then discuss it until we arrive at a uniform response, so that we don't find ourselves falling out over a newspaper discrepancy in our story.

So, there I was, back from Italy with a defeat under my belt and some abuse ringing in my ears. I did not know what the future held and could only read the newspapers the same as everyone else to see if there were any new developments in the supposed quest to find a really big name to take on the mantle of Scotland manager. My first match as caretaker had been a great experience and, as always, I had learned a great deal too.

We still had one more game to play in the World Cup qualifiers – away to Malta just over a month after the Italy game. I expected that I would probably still be in charge for that one because the SFA were not rushing to name my replacement. I had no idea that the Italy game would be my first and last as caretaker manager.

16 The Job's Mine

Before the Malta game the speculation about who would be named as manager was still going on, as you would expect, and there were times when I thought that perhaps I had become invisible because my name seemed to just disappear from the scene. I was determined that, even if I was in charge for just a month or so, I was going to make the most of the experience. I decided to make a temporary appointment of an assistant, and the man I chose was Alex Miller.

Alex is someone I respect greatly. We had been on many courses together and I had no doubts that he knew his stuff and would be a great asset. He was a guy with a huge knowledge of the game and its personalities. I knew that we could work together because he was a man of integrity and knew what hard work was all about. I made an informal phone call to him to ask how he felt about the possibility of joining me in the Scotland set-up – possibly for just one game, because I had no idea what was likely to happen after that. Alex spoke to his chairman, Douglas Cromb, and then agreed to the arrangement, and we both began work on the preparations for our trip to Malta.

We were due to leave for Malta on the Monday, with the match being played two days later. At the hotel, on the day before the game, I was called to the room of the chairman of the SFA international committee, Yule Craig, former chairman of St Mirren. He was a man who commanded respect and he certainly got it from me because I knew that his heart was in the game and he wanted the best for whatever he was involved in. Alex Miller and my pal Alex Smith had both been managers of St Mirren while he was in charge and had nothing but good things to say about the man.

I went to his room knowing that whatever dealings I was to have with him would be honourable, and therefore I was in no way apprehensive when I knocked on his door. He called me in and I sat down with him and Chief Executive Jim Farry. He smiled and came straight to the point.

'How would you like to stay in charge of the team up to and including Euro 96?'

I have to admit that, although I knew we would be discussing some aspect of the job, I was totally unprepared for this. I was pleased, of course. It felt the same as if I had been picked to play for my country. We sat and talked it over for a while, agreed terms and shook hands.

The official announcement had still to be made and so I couldn't share the news with anyone at that stage. The players were talking all the time about who the new boss was likely to be, and of course this fuelled further speculation in the newspapers. It was not until the players were changing for the match that the then president of the SFA, Bill Dickie, vice-chairman at Motherwell, announced to everyone present that I had been appointed. There was spontaneous clapping in the dressing room. Gary McAllister came straight over to me and said: 'You've come a long way since you were teaching at Belvedere!'

'And you've come a long way since you were a pupil at Keir Hardie Primary School,' I replied. Gary was the first person to shake my hand. The other players subsequently joined in the congratulations and handshaking – and then they went out and won the game 2–0!

The team for that Malta game was Leighton, McLaren, Hendry, McKinnon, Irvine, Durrant, McAllister, McKinlay, Nevin, Ferguson and Gallacher, and we used Boyd and Booth as our substitutes. Billy McKinlay and Colin Hendry scored a goal in each half – it was Colin's first goal for his country. The Ta Quali stadium had a crowd of 8,000 and the date was 19 November 1993. That's for the benefit of all you statisticians.

We finished fourth in our group of six, having won four and drawn four of our ten fixtures. It could have been much worse but, there again, it could have been much better too. Italy and Switzerland were the qualifiers from the group. I was pleased with our performance and I like to go back to Malta because I have friends there – wonderful people like Father Hillary, former technical director, Philip Psaila, a recent national coach, and Joe Mifsud, the president of the Malta FA – and because it now has a special place in my memory. We have been back since for a friendly match where we won 3–2.

It was useful to me to have players in the squad with whom I had worked before at club level. Pat Nevin was an excellent example. He was a player with tremendous skill, a good brain, and the desire to please. Ian Ferguson was another – a very misunderstood player in my opinion. Ian is a quiet teetotal guy who changes into a Mr Hyde character on the football field, where he becomes an aggressive, snorting and snarling kind of player. You would never believe that he was the same person. These two players I knew well, both from my club days and also from the Under-21 team, where many served their international apprenticeships.

Before beginning our campaign to reach Euro 96, we had a number of friendly matches in which to experiment and get settled in to a new way of football life. I had taken a conscious decision to play the way I had been playing the Under-21 side – a way that had already proved itself successful. In 1992, for instance, against Germany, I had favoured a 3-5-2 system and I liked it. It was never 5-3-2, always 3-5-2. I do not use the term wing-back and never have done, but I suppose that it is not a bad description of how I used my wide midfield players.

I adapted this system from watching the Germans, whom I consider to be the most efficient in Europe. In those early days I used Stewart McKimmie and Tom Boyd as wide midfielders. I told them that their priority was defence but that they must have a midfield mentality and attack where needed. The system gave us a five-man defence when we needed it, and wingers when we were on the attack.

Some of our most excellent players were midfielders –

McAllister, McCall, Lambert and Collins among them – and we needed to play to their strengths. It was our best department, and we did not want to have that sort of talent sitting on the sidelines if we could find a way of harnessing it and using it in a suitable system. Our central defenders were men who played in that position every week with their clubs, including Craig Levein of Hearts, who was the man I had as the original free defender. It was a great tragedy that Craig had to give up the game, because he told me that he was very happy with the role I had given him. He felt that it used his particular abilities to the full. He was certainly a very skilful player who could adapt to every position. No wonder he enjoyed himself so much. With Craig hurt, I decided to give Colin Calderwood a chance. I had watched him and admired his style for some time, and Lou Macari, his former manager at Swindon Town also chipped in a recommendation – so Calderwood got his chance and took it very well indeed.

Alan McLaren was another great talent whom I had admired since seeing his performances in the Under-21 side. He was being tipped by Walter Smith as the Rangers captain of the future, and I also tipped him to become Scotland's captain one day.

Regrettably Alan has also had his share of injury, but hopefully we have not heard the last of him by any means. He was in my squad in those early days, as was a man I have already mentioned and can only mention again as Mr Reliability – Colin Hendry. What a player!

All in all we had problems with central defenders because of various injuries, and it was expressed to me by more than one person that Richard Gough should be recalled. I had other ideas, though and, even though Richard had stated in public that he would be available to play for Scotland now that Andy was no longer manager, I decided he would not be playing in the team.

Of course, we had problems with our striking positions too. The stars in my time were of course Maurice Johnston and Ally McCoist, who had formed a very good partnership. Johnston had dropped out but we still had McCoist, although he was not then available because he was still recovering from a broken leg. We tried various people in various permutations. I used Duncan

Shearer, Andy Walker, John McGinlay, Kevin Gallacher, Darren Jackson, Gordon Durie, John Spencer and others, but it was difficult to find a regular scoring partnership. That brought some criticism in the early days that we were well able to defend but that we couldn't score goals. I couldn't really argue with that because the scorelines were there for all to see, and we were not scoring as many as we should have been, even though each of those players were, in my opinion, of the highest standard.

So the structure was modelled on the German examples, and I think subsequent achievements have proved that it was the right decision. Alex Miller went along with me, even though the system was alien to what he was using at club level. In his typical professional manner he soon adapted and coached it the way I wanted it to be coached. Even today, Alex usually prefers to use a 4-4-2 system with his club work, but he is happy to support me with the international set-up and coach it my way.

Of course, there has been a lot of criticism of Scottish goalkeepers over the years. I think that it is totally unjustified. The guy wearing the No. 1 jersey is probably the most important on the pitch because he has not only to be the last line of defence but also has to give confidence to the entire side. In our Scotland set-up we have Alan Hodgkinson as goalkeeping coach and, for my money, he is one of the best in Europe. I am sure that our excellent defensive record in recent years is a testimony to his coaching. Yes, he is an Englishman, and he was capped by his country five times, as well as having a career spanning more than six hundred senior games with Sheffield United. He has probably never been more appreciated than he is now as part of the international scene with Scotland. Alan certainly not only knows his business but also has the capability of teaching others in a way that they can both understand and relate to. Nobody jokes about Scottish goalkeepers any more. These days we have the reputation of being a difficult team to beat and that is, in no small way, because of the quality of our 'keepers.

Alan not only takes charge of our goalkeepers but also takes responsibility along with Tom Stewart for coaching the coaches of goalkeepers, and is involved with the judging of those coaches for their diplomas.

As you can see, I was gradually getting my staff together and had a fair basis of assessment of the players at my disposal. There were also players who were often brought to my attention who had Scottish parentage but had not actually been born in Scotland. We have a good system to make us aware of such players and to keep an eye on their progress.

I thought we needed someone with greater international experience because neither Alex Miller nor I had been capped at senior level and we felt that was a deficiency in our set-up. Tommy Craig had been my colleague in caring for the Under-21s, but even Tommy – great player though he was – had only been capped once by Scotland. To compensate for our inexperience as international players we brought other coaches in to help. Willie Miller was one. He was then manager of Aberdeen and had been capped 65 times. Another was his former Aberdeen teammate Alex McLeish, who had 77 caps to his credit. Murdo MacLeod I have already mentioned and he was still with us. Tommy Burns came in as well, and like Andy before me I put him in charge of the 'B' international side. I invited other managers to join us as guests for our away matches, which gave them an insight into what we were trying to do. Walter Smith, Jim Jeffries, Alex Totten, Bobby Williamson and Lou Macari are just some who accepted the invitation. It also provided us with extra brains for our think-tank, because I have always had a listening ear and will consider any advice that anyone has to offer. Besides these things, it helped to develop an understanding and a good relationship between the national coaches and the club managers. I believe that it has resulted in an excellent comradeship between managers at all levels in Scotland.

The staffing situation was an important one and I gave it a high priority in my first moves as the new manager – I still do. The medical team too had to be of the highest quality. International sportsmen are rather like thoroughbred horses – they should have only the best. You never see top racehorses roaming over pieces of balding common land scavenging for food and grabbing a little bit of exercise only now and then. They have the very best in treatment, training, diet and facilities – and that is how international footballers have to be treated.

With our World Cup commitments finished we were now in the business of being sparring partners to those countries who had made it to the USA. We also had the draw for the European Championship to look forward to and the added incentive that the finals were going to be held in England – probably the shortest possible journey for the Tartan Army to have to make to accompany us. The draw for the qualifying round was made in Manchester on 22 January 1994. For me personally it was an exciting moment because I was there for the first time as manager of my country and, as such, I was rubbing shoulders with some of the biggest names in European soccer. One thing I could guarantee was that we would not be coming out of the same hat as England because Terry Venables and his men had the luxury of not having to qualify since they were the host country.

There were a few complaints about the way the draw was handled – mostly from those media representatives who struggled to get into the place. The draw was being televised live from the theatre of the Granada Tour – the visitor centre attached to Granada Television. Not everyone from the media was able to fit into the venue, and so an overflow room with a video screen accommodated the rest, and I think it was from there that most of the moans originated. Some of those not in the actual theatre probably felt that they had been slighted.

The stage-managed draw threw up some interesting match prospects, but I was concerned only with where we would land. As it was we fell into Group 8, the last on the list. In that same pen were Russia, Greece, Finland, the Faroe Islands and San Marino. As the names come out you don't really take in what is being said. It is only when you look at the list later, several times, that you start to realise the implications.

Russia and Greece had both qualified for the World Cup, which meant that they were certain to provide us with stiff opposition if we were to qualify for Euro 96. Finland have never been push-overs, the Faeroe Islands meant a demanding journey, and San Marino had given England a shock just a couple of months earlier when they had scored in nine seconds. No, nothing could be taken for granted in this group. We had to finish in one of the top two places and that was not going to be a simple task.

The European Championship was then forgotten for a while as the full force of international publicity focused on the World Cup, covering it from every possible angle months before it actually began. In Scotland, though, we continued with our rebuilding programme.

The rebuilding included the first stage of the overhaul of Hampden Park, and we were to be hosts to Holland in a match to mark the reopening of the great stadium, which had been out of commission for two years as it was given a £12 million face-lift. Like most Scotsmen I have always loved Hampden. The place is now being given another face-lift preparatory to becoming the headquarters of Scottish football, to include the offices of the Scottish Football Association. It looks magnificent now, but then it has always looked magnificent to me. Anyway, on 23 March 1994 Holland arrived to help with the celebrations.

We prepared for the game the same as we would for a competitive match. Holland had qualified for the World Cup from the same group as Norway, which meant that they had played a part in eliminating Graham Taylor's England with a 2–2 draw at Wembley and a 2–0 victory in Rotterdam. The Dutch players were keen to prove that they were worth their place in Dick Advocaat's squad, so we knew they would not be coming along just for a kickabout. I wanted to start my preparations for the forthcoming European qualifiers, but I decided against any dramatic changes to the squad. Gary McAllister remained as captain, a job he was well suited to.

The Dutch were a class act with players like Dennis Bergkamp, Ed de Goey, Frank Rijkaard, Bryan Roy, Marc Overmars, Aron Winter and Frank de Boer in their side, along with other great names. Bryan Roy scored the only goal of the game about midway through the first half, and probably, to an independent onlooker, Holland had control of the game. However, the Scotland players gave a good account of themselves and I was encouraged by what I saw. I took advantage of it being a friendly to use four substitutes, and I learned a lot from seeing my players in action against another of the best teams in the world. Holland had lost only one of their ten World Cup games and had averaged virtually three goals a game. I was not unhappy with that final 1–0 scoreline, and the 36,809 in Hampden Park that night were well aware that they had seen a creditable performance.

It was my first home game as manager of Scotland and I would have liked to have recorded a victory, but it was still early days and I did not mind forgoing the luxury of victory in a friendly in order to prepare for victories at a later date. A month later we were on the road again – this time to Austria for another friendly. The Austrians had failed to qualify for the World Cup so they were keen to save face in front of their own fans – and 35,000 of them turned up to watch them do it.

There was a cold edge to that Wednesday evening in Vienna. Our hosts were quietly confident but then so was I, and I hoped that I had instilled some of that confidence into my players. I had decided that it was time to give John McGinlay the chance to wear a Scotland shirt. He had been playing well at club level and you can never have too many striking options, so I included John in the squad and told him that he would almost certainly get his chance.

It can be very difficult to decide whether to put a new player straight into the side from the start of a match and be prepared to substitute him later, or to keep him on the bench and use him at an appropriate time in the game. Every player is an individual and you have to know what decision will get the best out of him. McGinlay was old enough and mature enough to be given a place in the starting line, and so that is exactly what we did.

Austria went on the rampage from the start and threw everything at us. It probably worked to our advantage because, if you can soak all that up at the start and wear the opposition down both physically and mentally, you will get stronger as they become weaker. In the twelfth minute it began to look as if we had made a mistake in our thinking. Austria took the lead through Hutter and we had a hill to climb, as they say. We fought back manfully and I was very pleased with the work-rate and the leadership of Gary McAllister, who refused to let any of the players have anything less than a totally positive outlook.

The hard work was rewarded in the 34th minute when John McGinlay announced his arrival with an excellent equalising goal. I was very pleased with him. You can't get much better than scoring on your international debut. The Austrians were taken aback by the effort put into our comeback and they seemed to have little answer to it. Their attacks floundered time and time again on our rock-like defence. Then, on the hour, the unthinkable – if you were Austrian – happened when Billy McKinlay made it 2–1.

With a quarter of an hour left I sent Duncan Shearer on to replace John McGinlay. I wanted to give Duncan his debut and see how he coped at international level. The Austrians did their best to get back on terms but our defence held and they became more and more depressed as the game wore on. When the final whistle blew, we had won 2–1 and I had gained my second victory as manager of Scotland.

We owed Holland a return visit and the fixture was scheduled for Utrecht on 27 May 1994, Holland's last game before the World Cup opened on 17 June. Once again, there were no half-measures from the Dutch. Jan Wouters was back as captain and Ruud Gullit was also back in the side along with Ronald de Boer. Brian Roy had inflicted the damage on us in the match at Hampden Park but we were going to do our best to keep an eye on him this time.

The home fans were keen to give their men a good send-off before they went to the USA, and they were certainly given something to cheer on the quarter-hour when Brian Roy slipped the leash we had put on him and put Holland into the lead. I was pleased that we did not buckle but kept our game going for the rest of the first half. The Dutch supporters had been expecting a slaughter but, in spite of tremendous home pressure, it was not happening.

I gave instructions at half-time that we were to stick to our game and not allow the Dutch any more freedom than they had already had. The game had just passed the hour mark when Peter Van Vossen struck to make it 2–0. Once again, though, we kept our heads and did not allow our shoulders to sag. We were having our moments at the other end but, with no disrespect to those players who were taking part, we were definitely missing the extra golden touch of Ally McCoist, who was an expert at turning a half-chance into a goal.

I have always had great admiration for the Dutch and their

football and they were not at all flattered by the scoreline when they were gifted an own goal from Brian Irvine in the 71st minute. I waited five minutes and then sent Duncan Shearer on for the last quarter of an hour. The fresh legs were just what we needed, and within five minutes Duncan, from a great pass by Eoin Jess, had pulled one back for us with his first senior goal for his country.

The last ten minutes or so were cut and thrust but there was no further change in the scoreline. In the history books it will show that Holland beat Scotland 3–1 on that night in May 1994, but it was a brave performance from the Scottish players. We had actually scored two of the four goals in the game – and that told me that we were able to mix freely with the best and give as good as we got. It also told me that we should never take on a match long after the end of the season when the players were out of training. This knowledge was used later when we had to play vital qualifying matches in the Faroes and in Minsk.

By the time the season had come to an end, all eyes were glued to the World Cup – mine included. I was particularly keen to watch our European Championship rivals, Russia and Greece, as they took on the best of the world in their attempts to win the crown. The Greeks were largely unimpressive. They had some dangerous-looking players, but they did not perform as a unit as well as most other sides, and it was no surprise to me that they were among the first to go home.

Greece lost each of their group games against Nigeria, Bulgaria and Argentina to finish bottom of the mini-table with ten goals against and none scored. Back home in Greece there was a massive amount of criticism, and some of the Greek players were apprehensive about going home to a welcome that was to be less than a hero's. That is the pressure in football. One minute you are a hero for reaching the World Cup finals, and the next you are almost Public Enemy No. 1 for not being successful.

The Russians were in Group B with Brazil, Sweden and Cameroon. They also had a difficult task and were beaten by both Brazil and Sweden. They did take some consolation from recording the biggest score of the tournament when they beat Cameroon 6–1, but it was too late to get them past the group stage and they, like Greece, caught the early plane home.

I was always brought up to take a good look at the opposition, whether it was at club level or internationally, and the World Cup tournament gave me plenty of chance to observe these two nations, against whom we had to pit our wits in the European Championship qualifying group. I watched Greece and I watched Russia, and I knew that they were capable sides. But I also saw Holland win their group and then beat the Republic of Ireland 2–0 in the next round before going out at the quarterfinal stage after a tremendous tussle with Brazil, who won the game 3–2. Brazil had been 2–0 ahead and then Holland had fought back to draw level before that final killer goal from Branco. Brazil went on to win the World Cup, but Holland had given them a run for their money and it made me remember our performance against that same Dutch side.

As I contemplated these events and considered that I had now won two and lost three of my first five games in charge of Scotland, my thoughts turned again to Euro 96. We would soon be starting our campaign for a place in the finals. It was not going to be an easy passage, but the more I thought about it the more confident I began to feel. My agreement was to be manager of Scotland up to and including the European Championship, and I was determined to do my best and make the most of this great opportunity.

17 The Euro Challenge

There could not have been a much greater incentive for getting to the European Championship than the fact that it was being held in England. Scotland's chances of ever staging the tournament, or even part of it, seem very remote because we are probably not considered big enough or wealthy enough. The next best thing is to take part in the tournament when it is being staged in England. We missed out on the 1966 World Cup, but we were determined to take part in Euro 96.

Our qualifying group was a tricky one. Greece had qualified for the 1994 World Cup and therefore it would have been a mistake to dismiss them lightly. San Marino and the Faeroe Islands were no longer the push-overs that they had previously been labelled. Finland were a team of excellent players and very unpredictable, and then, of course, there were the mighty Russians.

As part of our preparation, I travelled to Casablanca to see Finland in action against Morocco. It was a very revealing experience because my cab driver asked if I would like to see some street or beach football and, when I agreed, he showed me what must have been thousands of youngsters playing. Their enthusiasm was tremendous, and showed that you don't have to go to Brazil to find tomorrow's stars playing in the streets.

The campaign began in September 1994, and a trip to Finland. I was able to field a fairly strong side, as could be expected so early in the season. There was no Ally McCoist because he was still recovering from a broken leg, but Duncan Shearer was a reliable striker and I decided to give him the chance to get us off to a flying start. Within 29 minutes Duncan had put us ahead after a magnificent move that involved 21 passes. We were on our way. John Collins scored our second after the break and we left Helsinki with maximum points and a lot of smiles. A month later we were back at Hampden Park for the visit of the Faeroe Islands. I have a lot of respect for countries like the Faeroes. They never have any major successes but they are more than happy just to be involved. They love their football and they are always very good-natured and hospitable. If anything, they are perfect examples of what this great game is all about.

At Hampden we beat them 5–1. John McGinlay scored after four minutes, Scott Booth made it 2–0 half an hour later, and John Collins struck just before half-time. It was Billy McKinlay who made it 4–0 in the 61st minute. He had only been on the pitch for a few minutes after replacing Colin Hendry, who had taken a knock. John Collins made it 5–0 but then we went to sleep in defence and allowed Muller to pull one back. I was not happy about that because we had been sound in defence and to me every goal counts, whether it is for or against.

When the Russians visited Hampden for our next qualifying game we were well aware that this was likely to be one of the most crucial games in our quest to reach the finals. Even though the break-up of the old Soviet Union had rendered some players unavailable to Oleg Romantsev, the Russian coach, he was still able to select a formidable side.

I had been to the 1994 World Cup just to watch our European opponents Russia and Greece, and I saw the Russians give an impressive display against Brazil. Amazingly, when I sat down in that 70,000-seat stadium in San Francisco, I was next to an all-American guy complete with baseball cap, reflector sunglasses, denims, the whole works. I had been sitting there for some time before I realised that this 'all-American' guy was actually Walter Smith, the Rangers manager. I had not recognised a man whom I had known for years. Mind you, I don't think his own players would have recognised him either. I was not alone because, after the game, we bumped into Alex Ferguson and, as a joke, I introduced Walter as an American pal of mine. Alex didn't recognise him either.

At Hampden, Scott Booth put us ahead after nineteen minutes, having received a wonderful pass from Gary McAllister. Radchenko equalised six minutes later and the game became a stalemate. The Russians were obviously happier with the result than we were. I was disappointed that the territorial advantage had not turned into goals. I was not displeased with the defence, who had contained Andrei Kanchelskis and his teammates very well. However, we could and should have won.

Greece were having a good run at this time. They had won each of their three games and had scored eleven goals with only one reply. Admittedly, they had played what had been described as the 'weaker' teams in the group, but you still have to score goals and win games.

It was a harsh penalty decision against Colin Hendry which settled the match in Athens. The game was just eighteen minutes old, and no matter how hard we tried we could not get level. Hendry was alleged to have tripped Alexandris, the Greek winger, but it was a highly debatable decision. Later in the game we lost Andy Goram with an injury and I had to send Jim Leighton on to replace him. It was quite a turning point for Andy Goram because he took no further part in the group games and made only two brief appearances for Rangers during the rest of their season.

We were becoming quite concerned now because our next match was to be against the Russians in Moscow. The game was not scheduled until March, but I went early in the New Year to Moscow to check a few things and was telephoned there by Iain Ferguson, who was then sports reporter on the *Daily Record*. He had some really good, relevant news for me as he revealed that, in his newspaper's poll, only 8 per cent of supporters wanted me to be the Scotland manager. Kenny Dalglish had polled 28 per cent with 21 per cent going to Alex Ferguson. Gordon Strachan was third and I believe I came after him.

I suppose I was expected to make some peevish remark in response, but I was not going to fall for that one. You can twist statistics any way you like, so I just said how interesting it was that, when you looked at the percentage polled by Alex Ferguson, it showed that 79 per cent did not want Scotland to be in the charge of the best manager in Britain. Needless to say my words did not appear in the newspaper – there was just a piece about my lack of popularity. You are supposed to ignore these things and just soldier on, which you do, of course, but it does not help you to feel good about your work.

I was in Russia with Willie McDougall, who is our security guy, and we were well looked after by the Russian representative, Sergei Kussainov who was actually their top referee. On the way back we were held up at the airport where there were massive queues in the passenger area. Our embarrassed host took us past the queues and we found ourselves at the front, forming a new queue. When members of other queues decided to join us they were waved away, and you can imagine that there were more than a few people disgruntled by the whole affair. Our host explained that we were VIPs. A lady with a London accent became even more indignant. 'VIPs indeed! Who are you anyway?'

Quick as a flash, Willie answered her, 'Glasgow police – and this is my prisoner!'

'Oh my God!' cried the woman, and she vanished into the crowd, convinced that she had just confronted a hardened international criminal rather than a football manager.

Willie is very conscientious on these trips. He leaves no stone unturned. He does not just look at the facilities for the players but those for the supporters also, to make sure that they have the best facilities possible.

My own brief is to check on the size of the pitch, the type of grass, the dressing rooms, training facilities, and of course our accommodation. At the hotel I check the air-conditioning, the quality and size of the beds and the linen used, and the catering. If necessary we take our own chef, Tom Kirkpatrick, but in Moscow that was not needed at all. Everything was very good indeed.

The game took place at the end of March. Our Under-21 team had played the night before and won their game, and that gave us a lift. Our chief enemy was the weather. Moscow was still in the icy grip of winter at that time, and we had the coldest training sessions I can ever remember, with snow as well as freezing temperatures. George Scanlon, the linguist who has acted as interpreter for Andrei Kanchelskis among many others, was with us, and I think he was feeling the cold along with the rest of us.

Tom Boyd was given the job of keeping Andrei Kanchelskis quiet for the 90 minutes and he did a great job – very positive. In fact he did his job so well that there was a real possibility of him scoring a couple of goals himself. It was 0–0 at half-time and remained that way for the rest of the game. I was very pleased with the performance. Some might say that we could even have won it, but not many teams go to Moscow in those conditions and get a result.

One of the things I have learned in my job is that you never underestimate San Marino. Our next game was away to them at the end of April 1995. There is no point in denying that we struggled, and it took a special bit of magic from John Collins to get our show on the road. We seemed to be labouring against a team that did not have a great reputation but, believe me, San Marino are a very difficult side to beat on their own ground. It was them who frightened England to death with the fastest goal in World Cup history a few years ago.

John Collins turned it on in the nineteenth minute, though, when he took possession and went on a run that was a slalom through an obstacle of challenges. His finishing touch was to round the goalkeeper, Benedettini, and put the ball in the net. It was a magnificent goal. We struggled to add to it, though – until about five minutes from the end when Colin Calderwood met a cross from Gary McAllister and gave us a 2–0 scoreline with his first goal for his country.

We were relieved when that game was over. I don't think our supporters were too impressed with the performance, but it was a victory nevertheless, and we knew there would be better days against higher-profile opposition.

Our season ended in June with our next European qualifier, this time away to the Faroe Islands. Before that, we flew to Japan to take part in the Kirin Cup. We had just two games to play, but it gave us the chance to keep a squad together and introduce some of the younger players to senior international football. We drew 0–0 with Japan in Hiroshima in a game that remarkably saw two players sent off, including our own John Spencer. A few days later we played Ecuador and beat them 2–1, with goals in the second half from Robertson and Crawford.

The Kirin Cup trip was criticised by some, who felt that it was a long way to go just before a crucial European game. However, we had done our homework and knew what we were getting into. The facilities out there were excellent and we were able to train every day. A fitness expert, Roger Spry, travelled with us. Far from being a taxing event, it was more like going to a training camp. Wales had been there in the past and we made some enquiries about their experiences. So we were well informed before we decided to accept the invitation to go to Japan, and I am convinced that it did us a lot of good.

We had only a brief respite before travelling to the Faeroes. It can be a tricky flight, mostly because the landing strip is a little on the short side and the pilot has to get his approach just right. Sometimes they have to circle several times before going into a descent that is not unlike a white-knuckle ride at a theme park. For the uninitiated, when you play away to the Faeroe Islands you land on one island, live on another, and play on a third, so it is quite an experience. The hospitality is excellent because the people are always pleased to see you, and I must say that, after that flight in, we were more than pleased to see them as well!

The game was the old story. We were 2–0 ahead at half-time, thanks to a Billy McKinlay goal in the 25th minute followed by one from John McGinlay four minutes later. There were no further goals, which gave rise to a few critical comments once again. I understood the sentiments, but it did not matter if we had scored two or ten because under UEFA rules the goal difference against these smaller nations would not count in the final group reckoning.

We said our goodbyes for the summer and I went on my travels again. I had coaching engagements in Canada and America, and a UEFA commitment in Geneva as well as the courses at Largs. While I was in Minneapolis I saw the future of football in the United States. I attended a youth tournament for the USA Cup, which involved 675 teams and 43 football pitches. Anyone who believes that soccer will never get off the ground in the United States had better think again. There is a coming generation who love the game and, more importantly, have a lot of talent.

Greece were our visitors at Hampden just after the season started, and for one player at least it was going to be a fairytale evening. It had been more than two years since Ally McCoist had broken his leg against Portugal. He had experienced a number of setbacks but now, at last, he had been able to prove his fitness, and I was delighted to welcome him back to the squad.

I could not take the risk of putting Ally into the starting line-up, but he was on the bench. We had a setback when both Colin Hendry and Alan McLaren failed fitness tests, but I called up Tosh McKinlay and he fitted in perfectly.

We managed to meet at 11 a.m. for a training session at Hampden and when I arrived I was met by Andy Goram, who told me that he didn't feel fit enough or mentally attuned to the game. There was a suggestion that the real problem was that the game fell between two vital Rangers matches – but that has never been confirmed.

I spoke to Andy and put it to him that since he would probably be playing in the forthcoming Rangers European Cup game, it would not look too good for him to drop out of our match unless he went and explained it to the press himself. I was quite firm and told him that I was not prepared to make his excuses for him.

We spoke to Alan Hodgkinson and he tried to persuade Andy to do a little training, but really we both knew that there was little use in trying to cajole a player whose mind was simply not on the game because we would be going out at a disadvantage. There are those players who want to be talked into playing, their supposed injury being simply an excuse for the need to feel wanted as you persuade them to play. I've never found that at international level, but it certainly happens at club level. My policy is that I will never beg any player to play.

Anyway, we held a press conference and the media guys were quite shocked when Andy talked to them. I was not left with a serious problem in the goalkeeping department because I had the ever-reliable Jim Leighton with us. The press kept pushing me for the real reason for Andy's sudden withdrawal. I explained that I knew no more than they did, and that I was not a psychologist who could look inside Andy's head.

Predictably, the following day's tabloid headline was 'You Need A Shrink Andy – Says Brown'.

I was a bit upset about that because I had said nothing of the sort. Knowing Andy's character, I had no doubts that he would laugh it off, but I was worried about his family as I did not want them to be offended.

A few days later I was talking to Walter Smith on the phone and he told me what had happened in the Rangers dressing room. Ally McCoist and Ian Durant had obtained a straitjacket and had hung it on Andy's peg. Walter thought it was hilarious, but I was a little concerned. Fortunately the story faded away in the end.

Greece had little room for manoeuvre up front as our defenders kept control. We were having a few problems in attack ourselves. We were creating chances but it seemed we could not get the all-important goal. At half-time I told the players not to get over-anxious, keep plugging away and the goal would come.

With nineteen minutes left I sent on John Robertson and Ally McCoist. Ally was thrilled because he had missed fifteen internationals as a result of his injury. Now, at last, he was back in the shirt. Within 60 seconds he had headed a terrific goal from a John Collins cross. Hampden erupted as we all came to our feet. What a spectacular comeback! Never mind Roy of the Rovers – we had Ally of the Rangers!

That goal was the only one necessary. We beat Greece 1–0 and went joint top of the group alongside Russia. We had an excellent chance of reaching Euro 96.

Before the Finland game, their coach, Jukka Ikalainen, was reported to have said that we were likely to qualify on luck and, of course, I was expected by the newspapers to respond to this. I just said that we would show whether or not we were lucky by putting the ball into their net. Once again, this was taken as fighting talk when it appeared in print. I'm pleased to say that most of us coaches know each other well enough to understand what has really been said without all the embroidery. Very often, supporters are surprised to see opposition coaches enjoying a joke together when, according to the media, we are supposed to be stabbing each other in the back. The truth is that there is a great camaraderie among coaches – much the same as you would find on Death Row!

Again, we had a few injury problems before we faced Finland. Duncan Shearer was unable to play and Darren Jackson was a worry. I recalled Scott Booth, and it was fitting that he celebrated his recall with an excellent goal after ten minutes. It was the only goal of a game that was businesslike rather than exciting.

Our final game was to be at home to San Marino, but before that we had a friendly in Sweden. On the same day Russia were playing Greece, and if the Russians won then we were guaranteed qualification.

Sure enough, Russia won a very tense battle 2–1 and, as the news filtered through to us in Stockholm, we were beaten 2–0 by the Swedes. It did not seem too much of a disaster. We used the game to experiment with players, while Sweden, who had not qualified, were playing for pride. One worry was seeing Gary McAllister carried off with what appeared to be a severe ankle injury, which fortunately turned out to be not too bad.

I think everyone wanted to play in our final game at Hampden against San Marino, and certainly the Tartan Army made the occasion a real party.

There was only ever going to be one result but, to their credit, the San Marinese gave the game their best shot. Eoin Jess scored our first on the half-hour and Scott Booth made it 2–0 moments before half-time. The second half was three minutes old when I decided to send Ally McCoist on. Within a minute he struck again and made it 3–0. Pat Nevin made it 4–0 and then we were given an own goal by Francini to make it 5–0.

The supporters applauded the players and the players applauded the supporters. They had come a long way together in the ten qualifying games, and the road to England lay ahead – but for now it was party time!

There was excitement at having qualified for Euro 96, but it was nothing compared to the buzz that ran through Scotland when the group draw was made and we fell into the same frame as England, Holland and Switzerland. I was at the draw ceremony and I could not believe my ears. I was almost lost for words when interviewed for television. Of course, the England coach, Terry Venables, more than made up for my inadequacy.

The draw not only brought our two nations together to resume the traditional clash that had been shelved since 1989, but also put us into the category of underdogs. The bookmakers rated only Turkey below us of the sixteen competing countries. That did not bother us at all. We were in the tournament by the front door and we had every hope of making our presence felt.

There was also talk of how great the financial incentives were for the Scotland players. I found that distasteful because the players who pull on the Scotland jersey do so for pride. In my twelve years as assistant manager, and in my current position, I have never once heard money mentioned. These guys are all well-paid club professionals. They do not need financial incentives to play for their country.

Our warm-up programme included a friendly against Australia at Hampden in March 1996. They were a difficult side to break down, but Ally McCoist scored in the second half and that was the only goal needed. A month later we travelled to Denmark and were beaten 2–0. I have never been concerned about defeats in these games. They are all about experimentation.

In May we set up camp in the United States and played two games. In New Britain we lost 2–1 to the USA. Gordon Durie scored for us but the Americans netted in each half. A few days later, in Miami, we lost 1–0 to Colombia with Faustino Asprilla getting the all-important goal after he had come on as a substitute. The important point was that the squad had been prepared properly, not just in playing but socially as well.

Our first Euro 96 game was at Villa Park, and there was a terrific atmosphere at the stadium when we arrived. Holland were our opponents, and they were among the favourites to win the competition. We were determined to at least contain them and the 0–0 scoreline verifies that we were successful.

The Dutch came at us like an express train immediately the game started. Andy Goram made a wonderful reflex save from Seedorf. Stuart McCall brilliantly tackled the same player when he was in a likely scoring position and John Collins cleared from the goal line. That was the frantic start to the game. I think it did us good to be woken up so early. That flurry of activity had the same effect as a bucket of cold water in the face.

We had our moments in attack. John Collins had a fierce dipping shot punched away by Van der Saar and, in the last minute, Gordon Durie almost snatched a winner. As it was, the Scotland team had played its heart out and suddenly the rest of

Europe realised that we were not there just to make up the numbers.

Of course, the big game was against England at Wembley. We were very keyed up for this one, perhaps too much, but it meant a lot to us. On the way to Wembley there was a great atmosphere on the team coach, and that was echoed by the fans inside the stadium.

The first half was almost like a sparring round, and I felt that we had the better of the exchanges. There were no goals, and at half-time I told the players to keep up their work-rate on the tiring turf and keep plugging away. I was very disappointed when Alan Shearer found space to head home in the 52nd minute, but we did not let our shoulders droop and only a wonder save by David Seaman prevented Gordon Durie from equalising.

When Tony Adams brought Gordon Durie down in the goal area, time stood still for a while. We were awarded a penalty and you could have heard a pin drop as Gary McAllister stepped up to take the kick. Another great save from Seaman denied him, and I could not help but remember the penalty that Gary had scored in the 1992 tournament in our 3–0 win over the CIS. I would willingly have exchanged them.

With eleven minutes left, Paul Gascoigne came to life and scored a superb solo goal to make the final score 2–0. We were disappointed but had nothing to be ashamed of. We had forced eight corners to England's two and that was basically the story, except that they had the points and we didn't.

I was very conscious of the fact that we had not scored in either game. There was still a chance that we could create a little bit of history and go into the next round. We needed England to give Holland a beating and ourselves to beat Switzerland.

Ally McCoist gave us the first bit of magic with a great goal after 37 minutes. He ran to the bench and we celebrated together, along with the Tartan Army. News reached us that England were winning 4–0. If it stayed like that we would go through. The magic spell was broken when Patrick Kluivert scored a late goal for Holland and improved their goal tally sufficiently for them to finish in second place in the group. We savoured our victory over Switzerland, where we had fourteen shots on target and our ten corners, but, at the end of the day, we were packing our bags. The dedication and commitment shown by all the players was summed up by the actions of John Collins. John's transfer to Monaco had led to a problem with his insurance. To ensure that he could play he had to pay the premium himself; a substantial amount of money which far outweighed his playing fees and left him well out of pocket.

The European Championship had been exciting and a wonderful event for us, but now it was time to look ahead to a new challenge. When the 1996/97 season dawned, we would be on a different road. One that could lead to France and the 1998 World Cup.

18 The Road to France

Austria, Sweden, Latvia, Belarus and Estonia stood between us and a place in the World Cup finals in France in the summer of 1998. Only the top country would definitely go through, and there were various permutations and possibilities for those placed second in their groups. One would also go through, while the other eight would have to play off for the four remaining places.

Our road to France began with a journey to Vienna. It was expected that Austria would be one of the toughest opponents in our group, though to me they all looked difficult. There is no such thing as an easy game or an easy opponent. I recalled Duncan Ferguson to the side, but I did not want to make any drastic changes to the squad that had performed so well in our European campaign. The Austrians were lively, as you would expect from a home team playing their first World Cup match of a new challenge.

Our defence held and we were very pleased to come away from one of the two strongest teams in our group with a point and without conceding a goal. There were even times when I thought we might sneak a goal, but when the whistle went at 0–0 I felt that we had done a professional job and that was all that could be asked.

Our next task was to travel to Riga to meet Latvia. The trouble with so many of these recently emerged countries is that they are still an unknown quantity and can give you quite a shock if you are expecting them to be just also-rans. We made no such mistake in our match preparations and worked towards the fixture just as we would if we were playing Germany, Holland or any of the other leading lights of world football.

Again we gave an assured performance. John Collins scored for us in the eighteenth minute and we kept plugging away for the next hour until Darren Jackson made it 2–0 in the second half. The score remained that way and, once again, we returned home like businessmen who have just done a successful deal. I have always tried to coach patience and the realisation that there are 90 minutes in which to play. I think our performances during the World Cup demonstrated that patience a number of times, and this game was one of those times. The players set about their task in a methodical manner, kept their heads and were rewarded for their professionalism.

With those two games under our belt, we were in good spirits when we travelled to Estonia for our next game just a few days later.

The visit to Tallinn proved to be a complete farce and a waste of time. We had been there before in other qualifying matches, but there was nothing quite like this one. In fact, there has probably never been one like it in the history of the World Cup.

The argument was over floodlights. We had seen the floodlights and knew that they were just not up to standard. The FIFA officials agreed with us and we were told that the kick-off would be brought forward. There had been some earlier controversy about what time the game was to be played. We were happy to play at whatever time we were told. But the notion of playing such an important game under temporary floodlights, which did not illuminate the pitch adequately, was not only ridiculous but also against FIFA World Cup rules.

We turned up at the revised kick-off time. When it became obvious that Estonia were not going to be there, we sought further guidance from FIFA and were told to prepare for the game and kick off. If Estonia were not there, the referee had instructions to start the game and end it as soon as the ball was in play.

We followed the directive, as did the match officials. Later we were told that Estonia had appealed and that the game would have to be replayed. Thus the team that had complied with FIFA rules appeared to be penalised, while the team that didn't had a second chance. It was a bizarre situation made all the more ridiculous because there were those who blamed us for not wanting to play under lights that looked more like the sort that illuminate motorway roadworks.

It was even more galling when it was also suggested that we wanted the game cancelled because Gary McAllister was suspended. Since our next game was against Sweden we would have preferred him to have missed the Estonia game. As it was, we were without him for a key game, so that misinformed argument is easily nullified. It does annoy me when people sit at their desks passing judgement without having any first-hand knowledge of the facts.

We returned home and then took on Sweden at Ibrox on 10 November 1996, before a crowd of 50,000. What a game it turned out to be! The Swedes brought their strongest side and went for maximum points. Their early enthusiasm proved to be a mistake because a gap opened up in their defence and, after eight minutes, John McGinlay put us ahead with a superbly-worked goal. After that, it was time for our defenders to shine as Sweden threw everything at us. Jim Leighton was in great form and dealt with anything that broke through our tight defence. The minutes ticked away and in the end McGinlay's goal proved to be enough. Ibrox celebrated, and I felt a great deal of pleasure when I saw that we were top of the group.

The Estonia game was finally replayed in Monaco in February 1997. There is no doubt that we were below par, and I wonder if the players found it hard to get to grips with the game, feeling that they should not have been required to play it. The final score was 0–0 – the least said the better.

We had not seen the last of Estonia because, a month later, we played them at Kilmarnock in our group return match. It was an unspectacular match, but again a competent and professional performance. Tom Boyd scored a first-half goal and our pressure in the second half forced Meet of Estonia to concede an own goal. We were happy at 2–0.

Now we had to play one of our chief rivals again. After our

draw at the start, Austria had won their next two games, including a victory over Sweden in Stockholm. Celtic Park was packed for their visit in April 1997, and our supporters were in good voice.

The game lived up to expectations. Austria had come looking for victory, but so had we. It was a great night for Kevin Gallacher, as he played out of his skin to get us the points. He scored a brilliant goal in the 25th minute which would have taken the roof off the stadium had there been one. In the 77th minute he repeated his performance and, at the final whistle, we were 2–0 victors and seven points clear in the table.

I was very pleased for Kevin because he was another player I had known from his Under-21 team days, and he had battled back from severe injuries to regain his place in the Scotland side.

We needed that cushion at the top because we had played more games than the others and we were yet to play away to Sweden – which was, in fact, our next date, just a few weeks after the Austria game. At this stage we had not conceded a goal in the qualifying games, but we knew that our defence would have to be in top form against Sweden.

Everything went according to plan until a minute before half-time when Kennet Andersson gave Sweden the lead, to the delight of the majority of the 40,000 crowd. Back in the dressing room we had to repair the psychological damage of going a goal down, but I have to say that there is always a strong will in the Scotland camp and our heads are never bowed for more than a passing moment.

We battled away in the second half and gave as good as we received, but there was a brief spell of shakiness in our defence, and Andersson was in for a second goal. We bounced back again and pushed the Swedes for most of the remainder of the game. Kevin Gallacher finally scored another of his excellent goals and we came close to the equaliser several times. Eventually we ran out of time and settled for the 2–1 defeat, our first of the competition.

There was just one more World Cup game after the end of the season, and that meant a trip to Minsk to play Belarus. The game was fairly uneventful except that everyone worked extremely hard and we came away with a 1–0 victory, thanks to a finely executed penalty by Gary McAllister. We were all delighted when we flew home. We had terrific support from the players who made the trip but did not take part in the game. Possibly they deserve even more credit than those who did play.

I remember putting Billy Dodds on with just a few minutes to go. He was desperate to get into the game, preferably from the start. I expect 90 minutes' work from substitutes, even if they are only on for ten minutes. Billy Dodds is just the sort of player for that work-rate. Gordon Durie and Gary McAllister were both extremely tired, and Paul Lambert and Kevin Gallacher were also absolutely exhausted. All the players had answered the call and had not been found wanting.

The performance was warmly applauded by the five hundred or so members of the Tartan Army who had made the trip to Minsk. I had been to a Sweden away match and noted that they had taken only about a dozen fans. It says something for the loyalty, dedication and passion of the Scotland fans that there is almost always a large presence whenever and wherever we are playing away.

After the summer break we had to prepare for the run-in with games against Belarus and Latvia. The matches were scheduled to be played at Aberdeen's Pittodrie Stadium and Hibernian's Easter Road ground. I felt that, since these two games were so important, they ought to be played in Glasgow. I spoke to the SFA president, Mr McGinn, who was with Jim Farry, the chief executive, and put my case. They agreed to discuss it, and then came back to me to ask if I would settle for just one venue change. I said that I didn't mind the Belarus game being played at Aberdeen, but that the all-important final fixture against Latvia should be switched to Glasgow.

Eventually I was told that the Latvia game would have to remain at Easter Road because the agreement had been signed and that was the end of it. I was disappointed, of course, since I firmly believed that the final game should have as many Scotland supporters present as possible.

As it was, the Belarus game was scheduled for the Saturday on which the funeral of Princess Diana was to take place, and the game was subsequently postponed for 24 hours, as I will describe later.

We were training at the ground of Highland League side Cove Rangers, thanks to the co-operation of Alan McRay, an SFA council member and owner of Cove Rangers. Because of the death of the princess, most of the players were making arrangements to visit churches and so on, but we still had to train.

Before the game there was a very moving moment when a piper played a lament on the pitch while everyone stood in silence. The players were a little subdued, but they seemed very determined as they carried out what is a tradition in the Scotland dressing room – shaking hands. For as long as I can remember, everyone has shaken hands with everyone else before an international. There is often a lot of shouting too, but not on that day.

Just to give you some idea of what it is like inside the dressing room before an international match, picture a scene with guys changing, some changed already, others stretching and warming up a little, some joking to keep their nerves under control, some starting to shout. If Colin Calderwood is there, you will find him shouting at himself and slapping himself really hard. There are those who prefer to be quiet.

I do not believe in last-minute team talks, but Alex Miller, Alan Hodgkinson and I will go round the players individually, offering a word or two of encouragement, or a reminder of some previously discussed point. We have a habit of putting charts of set pieces on the wall, and we might take a player to one just to give him a little reminder of a move or a position.

We like the substitutes to look immaculate. They can decide for themselves if they are going to wear tracksuits or jackets, but they must all wear the same and be uniform in their appearance. In my time, the number of substitutes has grown from two to seven, so there is less space in the dressing room and more players to speak to.

From about half an hour before the game I don't like people who are not directly involved in the game anywhere near the dressing room. That includes players who are not playing. We encourage players who have been injured and might otherwise have taken part to look in and wish their colleagues well – but not after my half-hour curfew.

I admired the tremendous attitude of Colin Hendry, who was injured and could not play in the Belarus game, when he flew to

Aberdeen just to watch the match and flew straight back afterwards. A great example of his support for the national team.

Gary McAllister and John Collins were in charge of set pieces during the game, and before the Belarus match I reminded them of a move that had been highly successful against Latvia, resulting in John scoring a terrific goal from a free kick. I said that Belarus would have seen that and would not allow the same situation to arise. These were famous last words because, early in the game, we did get a replica situation. This time it was McAllister who had the shot. The goalkeeper parried but the ever-alert Kevin Gallacher was there to follow up and put us ahead.

The tension drained out of the team and the crowd immediately, and everyone began to enjoy themselves. At half-time McAllister and Collins came to me very pointedly and said, 'Aye, that ones not going to work, is it?' – reminding me of my advice before the game. It was rare that they went against my instructions, but on that occasion I was glad that they had.

Gary indicated that he had had a recurrence of his knee trouble, so we watched him for a few minutes into the second half before sending on David Hopkin to replace him. What a fairytale it was for him. I had seen him in a Crystal Palace League match against Queens Park Rangers, and he had been highly recommended to me by Dave Bassett, who was then his manager. I was impressed by him, and he certainly lived up to all the praise Dave Bassett had heaped upon him. I had seen him before several times, but never playing as well as this.

He made his debut by replacing McAllister and he scored two goals. It was sensational stuff and I was delighted, both for him and for the team. Kevin Gallacher scored another between David's goals and we were having a good time. It might seem strange, but I became concerned when we were 3–0 ahead and conceded a penalty. Petr Katchoaro scored from the spot and ruined one of our many clean sheets. It was only the third goal that had been scored against us in the nine games that we had played – but every goal lost is like a flesh wound.

I was, and I am, proud of our defensive record. In our Euro 96 campaign we conceded only three goals in our ten qualifying matches, and in this World Cup campaign we had done the same.

There are not many teams with such a record. In all competitive games since I became manager we have conceded just eight goals and lost three games. I think that is why we were seeded for the European Championship draw for the 2000 competition.

All eyes were now on the Latvia game, our last of the competition. We knew that we would stand a good chance of getting through as the best runners-up if we beat Latvia. Public pressure demanded a change of venue, and the SFA quickly amended their plans. I wrote to my old friend, Lex Gold, the chairman of Hibernian, thanking him for releasing us from having to play the game at his Easter Road ground.

There was great anticipation when we played Latvia at Celtic Park on 11 October 1997. It was a sell-out, of course, and covered live by Channel 5 television. I was very happy to remember the request of Janis Mezeckis, the general secretary of Latvia, who asked me for a Scotland jersey for his son. Later, he told me how delighted his son had been to receive it.

As everyone knows, we won the game 2–0 with an excellent goal from Kevin Gallacher and a very well-earned one by Gordon Durie. We were delighted with the result and we also had a secret celebration laid on for Dr Stewart Hillis, our medical man, who had just gained a professorship. Win, lose or draw, we had arranged to take him for a meal that evening.

At the same time, Spain were playing the Faeroe Islands in an evening match and, had there been a shock result, our standing would have been affected, so we were eager to hear the result.

We went to a restaurant in Cumbernauld. Professor Stewart Hillis thought he was just going for a meal with his colleague, Stewart MacMillan, and it came as quite a nice surprise when all the Scotland backroom staff showed up dressed in our team uniform. I'd had a silver salver engraved, which I presented to him. We were delighted to have a professor among our backroom staff.

Around this time, I received a letter from Paisley University, which now includes the Craigie College campus. The letter informed me of a possible honorary doctorate, and I felt highly honoured and flattered to have such an award bestowed upon me. I shall receive it at a degree ceremony after the World Cup.

The news came through that Spain had proved their superiority over the Faeroes – we were definitely finalists in the 1998 World Cup. The next morning there was a press conference at Glasgow Airport because I, and several others from the Scottish FA, were about to fly out to France to look at possible accommodation. I had refused to entertain such a trip until I knew that we were definitely going to France as finalists – but now it was time to start on the next phase of our quest for the World Cup.

While in France, we took the opportunity to go and see our Under-18 team in action in a tournament, and we were delighted to watch them beat Denmark 5–0. It was a very good result because the Danes are one of the strongest sides in Europe. The Scotland performance was excellent and we were especially pleased to see the new generation of Scots on their way to becoming senior internationals in some style.

We later played a friendly against France in which they narrowly beat us, but it served, I believe, to give us a further taste of what to expect in the summer of 1998.

Since then I have hardly stopped travelling. I am at home so little that our milkman thinks I'm a burglar when he sees me. But the reward for all this is the honour of carrying the hopes of my country into the 1998 World Cup finals. Believe me, it has all been worthwhile.

19 The Draw

We don't want Brazil!

That was one of my statements before the World Cup draw took place in Marseille. I expect every manager or coach said exactly the same thing. Having Brazil in your group would virtually mean that you would be playing for second place. To be honest, I was not in particular dread of anybody, because you have to respect each and every country that has qualified for the finals of the World Cup. The hosts will have the full backing of their supporters, so there is no way that they can be taken for granted. The champions are keen to hang on to their crown so they will be no push-over – and all the other countries had to fight for their places too. Given the choice, though, I would not have selected Brazil to be among the countries in our group.

The French were keen to make a spectacular event of the draw and among the attractions was a 'Europe against the Rest of the World' game which experienced its own hiccups. The sides were to be made up of representatives of the various countries taking part in the World Cup finals. Gary McAllister was our obvious first choice, but he had been forced to withdraw because of injury. Darren Jackson was next on the list but the Celtic coach, Wim Jansen, did not want him to play because he wanted him in his squad for a game against Kilmarnock at the weekend.

I must say that Gordon Strachan, Gary McAllister's manager at Coventry, was keen that Gary should take part. Gordon had himself twice played in such a game and knew what an honour it was for the player, his club and his country. Coventry had even arranged for a private jet to fly him back, but Gary was simply not able to take part because of his injury. I was instructed by FIFA to find a striker replacement for Gary, and I thought of Ally McCoist or Gordon Durie, but both of them were also carrying injuries and Walter Smith suggested that it would be unwise for either of them to play. I told FIFA that I would try for Darren Jackson.

All this was happening on the Tuesday before the World Cup draw which was scheduled for Thursday, 4 December at the Stade Velodrome – which was also where the game would be played. FIFA jumped the gun and sent a fax to Celtic with instructions to the player advising him on travel and meeting arrangements. Celtic, naturally, were a little surprised, and Wim Jansen put the brakes on. I did not blame him for that – I only wish that FIFA had waited until I had spoken to them again before taking it upon themselves to contact Celtic. It would have saved a minor misunderstanding.

When I met Gordon Durie at Hampden during the launch of the Scottish Gas sponsorship of the Scottish international team, he indicated to me that his injury had responded to treatment and that he felt fit. I contacted Walter Smith again that Tuesday evening and asked if Gordon might be available after all. The Rangers manager confirmed that Durie had improved and that he would be prepared to let him take part rather than have no Scottish representation in the side. It helped that Rangers did not have a fixture until the Sunday. I contacted Gordon, who was thrilled at the opportunity. He postponed a charity appearance and the day was saved – but it had been a near thing.

I know some people might say that it was not worth the trouble but, if you were an established international player like Gordon who had the chance to be honoured by Europe, you would think it was well worth it. Also, I'm sure that nobody would want Scotland not to be represented in an historic match that would have been played with or without a Scotsman in the side. I was tempted to put on a pair of boots myself . . . well, no, not really!

On the following morning I was up early at my home in Ayr to drive to the airport to meet up with my colleagues for the flight to France. The party included Jim Farry, the Scottish Football Association chief executive, David Findlay, our assistant administration head of the department, Willie McDougall, our chief security officer, Jack McGinn, president of the SFA, Doug Smith, chairman of the International Committee, and Maurice Brannan, manager of Scotball Travel, which is affiliated to the SFA. We met at Glasgow Airport at 8.40 in time for a 9.30 flight to Gatwick, where we were due to pick up a flight to Marseille.

I had a look around the duty-free shops and then realised that the England party was also there to catch the same flight, so I went and sat in the lounge with Glenn Hoddle. We had a few laughs about the prospect of us being drawn in the same group – a prospect on which the press had already used up quite a few columns. David Davis, who looks after PR for the English FA, was also there, and we enjoyed a bit of good-natured banter before boarding our plane.

The plane was full of journalists, and it struck me that the World Cup finals had almost already started even before we arrived in Marseille. The flight didn't take too long and I talked with one or two members of the press, including Paddy Barclay, a well-known Scottish journalist. After disembarking we shared a bus with the English contingent as we were taken to our hotel, the Mercury. Even I began to feel the pangs of anticipation as the draw loomed ever nearer.

There were several other delegations at the hotel, and there was also quite a press pack. Among those I spoke to was Archie MacPherson, who was commentating on the Europe versus the Rest of the World game, and I was able to mark his card about the Gordon Durie situation. I have mentioned Archie before – we go back a long way. As well as updating him on the football news, I was able to tell him how his sister was doing, because I had been in Bahrain just a week earlier for the Awali Caledonian Society's St Andrew's Night celebrations. I had been a guest of Archie's brother-in-law Bob Ferguson and his wife Mary – Archie's sister. They had treated me very well indeed in Bahrain, and I wanted Archie to know how much I had appreciated it.

After checking in at the hotel and changing, our next stop was the Palais du Pharo for a reception and a meal. There were many famous faces there, of course, including all the powers that be at FIFA. In charge of the proceedings was Claude Simonet, the president of the French Football Federation. With him on the stage were Michel Platini and Fernand Sastre, the joint presidents of the French World Cup organising committee. The mayor of Marseille, Jean-Claude Gaudin, was our host. The speeches, which included a few words from Joao Havelange, president of FIFA, were not too long-winded, and then we were shown to our tables for the meal.

I hope you can picture how it was. There was a sea of people, and every now and then you would pick out a familiar or famous face. Everyone was being very friendly and diplomatic – but some of that diplomacy went out of the *fenêtre* when we were shown to a table that we were obviously intended to share with the England delegation. Upon it was written 'Great Britain'. For some time there has been a move by some of our European friends to have the home nations lumped together and, just for a moment, we wondered if someone was trying to tell us something. We also discovered that there were not enough chairs to go round. The mystery was solved when someone realised that there was another table with *Ecosse* on it. So we went to our Scotland table and left the English with their Great Britain table.

As usually happens at these events, I kept bumping into people I knew – fellow coaches and their assistants. The fraternity among national coaches is very good – probably because we understand each other's problems. Our table was visited by Warren Mersereau, who was in charge of Umbro US and is now one of the top executives of Adidas in Amsterdam. Warren is a wonderful guy whose support of Scotland goes back a long way. He takes his kids to Scotland games as often as possible and brought them to the final qualifying game against Latvia, at which he was jumping up and down as much, if not more, than they were. So you see, Scotland has fans in high places. Werner Kern, also of Adidas, was with Warren, and it was good to see them both among the many other high-profile personalities.

Warren told me that his ten-year-old son, Davis, was thrilled not just by the game and the result, but also because he came away with the autographs of both Ally McCoist and Rod Stewart.

Bertie Vogts, the German coach, and I had sat together on the bus taking us to this function, and he had been singing the praises of Paul Lambert, who had been playing with European champions Borussia Dortmund. Bertie told me that if Paul had been German he would have had no hesitation in naming him in his squad for the World Cup. High praise indeed.

After the meal Bertie and I talked again, and he told me some of his preparatory plans. His squad was to stay in Nice throughout the tournament and would travel from there. Before the tournament, during the mid-season break in Germany, he planned to take his players to Saudi Arabia for a game or two. He also told me that his goalkeeper, Kopke, would be the German player in the European squad for the celebration match. I hope this gives some insight into the fact that managers and coaches are not always at each other's throats at these competitions.

We all have a job to do and there is always some kidology before a game, but in general there is a strong feeling of camaraderie.

The Dutch coach, Guus Hiddink, congratulated us on qualifying and praised us on our performance in the friendly against France, as did Bo Johansson, the coach of Denmark, with whom I travelled back to the hotel. We discussed the form and recent performances of some of his players who were involved in the Scottish Premier League, and I was able to confirm some of his thoughts about them. He told me that Denmark too would be based in the south of France, at a complex near Marseille.

Before the day ended I was interviewed by the BBC and then had a further discussion with my Scottish Football Association colleagues. It had been a long day and I was quite happy to get to bed!

When I awoke next morning my mind focused immediately on the day ahead. By the time I got to bed again we would know exactly what kind of a passage we were going to experience in our bid to be the first Scotland squad to get past the early round of the World Cup.

The rest of the Scotland delegation was also up and about early, and by nine o'clock we were breakfasted and on our way to look at a possible hotel complex near Avignon, which we were hoping would provide us with the ideal base for our World Cup challenge. We were met by the mayor of St Remy, which is near Avignon, and he could not have been more welcoming, especially when we told him that it was almost certain that this would be our choice as a base.

I had already been to St Remy, and I was happy with the facilities that would be available to us. My colleagues were equally impressed, and we were able to confirm that we would definitely be taking Scotland to St Remy. I was glad to get that settled in my mind, and I think the mayor and his colleagues were even more delighted. They were genuinely nice people and I knew that they would all do their best to take care of us while respecting our need for privacy.

We returned to our hotel in Marseille and prepared to go to the Stade Velodrome for the match in which Gordon Durie was playing. If anyone is thinking that we were away on some kind of holiday, let me assure you that we were extremely busy. In addition to that, it was very cold indeed, and we were all forced to wear heavy coats. If I had been choosing a holiday destination, it would have been somewhere a little warmer than Marseille in December.

At the stadium I sat near Berti Vogts and Bo Johansson, and also the French coach, Aimé Jacquet, with whom I had a few words. At one end of the ground the stage was set for the draw to take place a little later. The rest of the stadium was filled to capacity.

The game itself was quite entertaining. Ronaldo was in good form and seemed to be at the centre of all the Rest of the World's attacking play. Europe opened the scoring after just two minutes when Romania's Marius Lacatus planted the ball in the net. However, the Rest of the World side took over from that moment. Antony de Avila of Colombia scored the equaliser in the seventeenth minute, latching on to a through ball from Ronaldo, who himself put his side ahead six minutes later, and then set up two goals for the Argentinian, Gabriel Batistuta, before hitting another goal himself just before half-time.

With the Rest of the World leading 5–1 at the interval there was not much time to talk about anything else as we sampled the

Marseille hospitality. The security had been stringent earlier in the day, but I must say that, when we all left our seats for the hospitality suite, everyone had to pass through the crowds, and it struck me that this showed a certain lapse in the arrangements. I wasn't bothered too much for myself because nobody would know who I was anyway, but men like Joao Havelange are high-profile people who are not universally popular and therefore could be the target for an assault. This was very possible as he too had to jostle with the half-time crowd, pushing towards the hospitality suite.

Gordon Durie made his appearance when the second half began. He had replaced Patrick Kluivert of Holland. I was surprised to see Gordon playing in a midfield role but he acquitted himself well. Europe pulled a goal back through the Frenchman Zinedane Zidane, and that pleased the home fans. There were no more goals and the game ended with everyone still speaking to each other. England's representative, Paul Ince, had played well so Glenn Hoddle was as happy as I was, although I was still puzzled that FIFA had chosen to play Gordon Durie in midfield after asking me to supply a striker.

Not long after the game had ended it was time for the draw – and all the pomp and circumstance normally associated with such occasions. The draw was controlled by FIFA's general secretary, Sepp Blatter, with the eyes of all the world upon that windy stage in Marseille. There were several personalities introduced to take part in the draw, with the players who had just participated in the game also being reintroduced as they took their places on the stage. The various national coaches were introduced. As one who has never liked being in the spotlight, I hated that moment – but it is part of the job and you have to make the best of it.

Finally, the draw got under way and the moment of truth had arrived. Brazil were in Group A and everyone wanted to avoid them – me included, as I have already stated. Naturally, we were also drawn in Group A, along with Norway and Morocco. I felt that it was a great honour that we should be involved in the opening game of the 1998 World Cup – even though it did mean that we were to be pitched against Brazil.

I was asked for my comments by the television contingent

immediately after the draw and I had to repeat myself when I said that we had wanted to avoid Brazil but, having had no choice in the matter, we would do our best to upset them. We've played against them three times in past World Cup tournaments and have never succeeded in beating them – but that will count for nothing when we meet them again in France. If we had beaten them on each occasion in the past, it would still count for nothing. Our quest will be to restrict the damage, get the points if we can, and then concentrate on taking at least second place by virtue of successes against Norway and Morocco. That plan has not changed.

When you are involved in a draw like that, you do not have too much time to consider the other groups – but I felt that England did not have a bad draw. A successful first round against Romania, Colombia and Tunisia is very much on the cards for them, and I am sure that Glenn Hoddle would much prefer to be in his Group G than in our Group A. At least we were not drawn in the same group.

There were more press interviews to follow for all concerned, and I was reminded that we had drawn 0–0 against Brazil in the 1974 World Cup. I am never quite sure how to respond to points like that because – and I don't want to seem disrespectful to the people who were involved in that game – it has no relevance whatsoever to a match nearly a quarter of a century later. It is rare for two teams to record the same result twice in a season, let alone in international matches which have generations of players between the fixtures.

Back at the hotel we discussed the matter and work started on arranging warm-up friendly matches. Everyone does this at gatherings of this type. National coaches very often get their heads together to suggest the fixtures and then hand over to the admin men to make the necessary arrangements. I was no different, and had already met with Steve Samson and set the wheels in motion for us to visit the USA, who were also keen for some friendly matches before the World Cup.

I finally slumped into bed at goodness knows what hour and reflected on a very full, interesting and exciting day. I didn't have much of a problem getting to sleep, although I did keep seeing those famous Brazilian shirts flashing in front of my eyes.

The next day I was on my travels again – but not back to Scotland as yet. Knowing that we would be playing in Bordeaux against Norway, I went there to check out the hotel facilities. We would be based as arranged in St Remy, but we still had to have other hotels near to the grounds for the actual matches. Our base would be for match preparations. I realised that we would probably be flying to the games from our base, and I like to check out the facilities and travel arrangements personally. Maurice Brannan came with me to Bordeaux because he has the professional travel expertise and he also wanted to check out the arrangements.

On the same flight was Alfred Ludwig, the general secretary of the Austrian Football Federation. He was also going to sort out his team's arrangements for the World Cup. Austria will be near Bordeaux even though they will not be playing a game there. That's the way it goes in tournaments like this. You cannot leave your arrangements too late, but there is no way of knowing how far you will have to travel for your matches. I'm delighted that Austria qualified. We had taken four points out of six from them in our qualifying group but their attitude did not change. They never fail to demonstrate the spirit of friendship that international sport should foster.

Michel Laffont was our contact at Bordeaux as he is the co-ordinator of the Bordeaux site. He had the enviable job of being appointed by the French Football Federation to look after the visiting teams. We made our first choice of hotel and hoped that confirmation would follow within a few days. Just in case, we took the trouble to check out alternatives – you never know when things may go wrong.

Having achieved all that, we travelled on to Paris for another hotel inspection. Since we were to play our first game at St Denis – and it was to be such a high-profile game – I wanted to ensure that everything would be first class, and I did not want any delays in the arrangements. We found suitable alternatives, and now things were beginning to take shape.

We now had the potential of hotels and facilities in Bordeaux, Paris, Lyons or St Etienne, and I was happy to travel home to Scotland, an older and wiser man but with still more questions ringing in my ears about our game against Brazil. It was the Sunday when I arrived back, and I took off to see Rangers play Hibernian and win 1–0 – but it is a day I shall never forget for a very different reason.

I was shocked to hear on the radio about the sudden death of Billy Bremner. I received numerous press telephone calls requesting tributes to Billy and I was pleased to talk about him – although I wish the circumstances had been different. I had previously had the privilege of writing the foreword for Billy's book on Scottish football heroes. That it was a privilege I appreciated even more when I heard the gravely sad news about his death. What a great player and what a great man. He was a one-off, never seen before or since.

It was a very sad day, and I shall always remember it as the day when Scotland lost a national hero.

That evening I was in Dundee for a charity dinner to help raise funds for St Joseph's Junior Football Club. My good friend Jim Leishman was MC, and Tommy Docherty and Willie Allan were speakers. Of course, Tommy was recalling his days in charge of Scotland and remembered the time he had travelled down to see Billy Bremner to ask him to be captain. He also spoke about the time in 1972 when Scotland were invited to take the place of England in a tournament in Brazil. The countries involved were all previous World Cup winners and, when England could not go, we were the next choice. Scotland made it to the semifinals – which was no mean feat. Tommy turned to me and said: 'You've no need to worry about Brazil, Craig!' It was typical of him to be both topical and supportive, as he always has been.

I was sitting near John McCormack, the manager of Dundee – one of my old clubs – and his superb youth coach, Kenny Cameron, and we had quite a blether with Tommy Doc. It was a very enjoyable evening but, as you can imagine, by now I was pretty tired as I had been going non-stop since the Tuesday, with only a few hours' sleep in each of the hotel rooms along the way.

The next day I was on my travels yet again. This time it was to London to take part in a sports chat show for BBC Television. The show was presented by John Inverdale, and Alan Hansen was also on the show – so the Scots were back in town.

The following morning I flew to Aberdeen to help put together a video of the Scotland qualifying matches. Brian Hendry was overseeing the project, which was to supply the visual material I required for a coaching stint in America a few weeks later.

That same evening I took in the Aberdeen–Celtic game. Next morning I was back in my office in the Scottish Football Association headquarters for more meetings and the inevitable paperwork.

In little more than a week I had given countless interviews, toured a vast area of France, taken in three football matches, visited any number of hotels, and performed a multitude of other functions. That's what life is like when you are the national coach for Scotland. I am not complaining. For me, it is the best job in the world, and I am enjoying every minute of it. It is not every job that gives you the chance to take on the mighty Brazil in the opening game of the World Cup.

Before the draw I said that I did not want us to be in their group. Now, I can hardly wait.

20 People, Places and Post-Mortems

Everyone asks me about Richard Gough and why I never picked him for Scotland. In as dignified a way as possible I shall now discuss the situation. Things have been said by many people concerned except me. There have been statements, biased reports and all kinds of speculative assertions.

One of the first things I was asked, and certainly the 'big issue' when I was first appointed as manager of Scotland, was whether or not I would pick Richard after he had refused to play international football for Andy Roxburgh. There were suggestions that loyalty to Andy would stop me from recalling him. Yes, I was loyal to Andy, and I am still loyal to him, but what had happened between him and Richard had no bearing whatsoever on my decision to leave him out of my plans.

Having been a part of the set-up that Richard very publicly disowned, I was in the privileged position of having seen the international set-up at close quarters over a number of years. I decided that I must look to the future and that it would not be in the interests of the Scotland team and of my style of management to recall Richard to the side.

Richard had certainly carved a very fine image with the media and the fans and I am aware of his playing performances with Dundee United, with Tottenham and with Rangers, as well as the impression he made during his short playing spell in Kansas City. However, taking all things into consideration, I made the decision not to select him.

My decision did not please Rangers fans, nor certain members of the media, but my thinking was based solely on what I felt was the right choice for Scotland. That is my job, after all. I think the results have vindicated my decision because we have emerged with an excellent defensive trio drawn from four or five very good players.

We have Colin Hendry, for instance, who has been immense in the heart of the defence, and also Colin Calderwood, who has performed extremely well. I believe that Alan McLaren was destined to become a star and quite likely a future Scotland captain, but he has been sidelined by a knee injury that has seriously interrupted his career. We are all hoping that he will come back better and stronger than ever. Tommy Boyd has been first class when called upon to play in that area, and the recent emergence of Christian Dailly, Derek Whyte and Matt Elliot has proved that there is no problem with the Scotland defensive set-up.

I have been questioned about Richard Gough fairly non-stop since I was appointed. One of the questions I received came in the form of a letter from a Rangers supporter. I responded, thinking that my reply would be read out to the supporter's friends and fellow Rangers supporters. I did not expect to see it reproduced in a newspaper. I replied factually to the letter without giving any opinion, and simply pointed out the record of Scotland under Andy Roxburgh – both with Gough in the side, and without him. The writer had told me that Gough was indispensable to Rangers and to Scotland. Gough's record with Rangers was, as I emphasised, nothing to do with me. The Scotland record without him spoke for itself.

I would not want to appear to be knocking members of the media at every given opportunity. On the whole they do a fine job and I know the difficulties they face, having been in their position myself for a time. However, I do wish that they would show a little less favouritism and not get everyone involved in discussing players who have not been selected rather than featuring those who have. There are many players who have given everything for their country and yet hardly get a mention, while pages are devoted to players bemoaning the fact that they have not been picked. I am drawn into the conversation and the next day all kinds of quotes and counter-quotes are being flung about, making it appear that the players and the management are at each other's throats, which is rarely the case. I often have cause to kick myself for allowing myself to respond to questions about players who have not been selected rather than championing those who have.

There is very little I can add to what I have already said about the Gough situation.

One well-known Scottish journalist, Jim Rodger – sadly no longer with us – actually met me solely to ask whether I was going to pick Gough or not.

We arranged to meet in the Marriott Hotel in Glasgow, and when I got there Jim was sitting with a cup of tea. I never did see him drink anything stronger. I sat down with him and he said quietly:

'Son, I've known you a long time and you've got a major problem. Your problem is concerning the captain of Rangers.'

Jim highlighted the issue much more than I had – once I have taken a decision I put it behind me and do not become introspective about it. In preparation for our meeting he had written a list of six pluses and six minuses concerning the selection of Richard Gough.

'Take this and have a good look at it, son, and then make up your own mind. It is a very important decision and, whatever you decide, you know I will fully support you. If you need any advice, come to me!'

I still have that piece of paper, and it raised some interesting points about Gough's following among the Rangers supporters and his friends in the press – as well as posing the key question about who could be left out to accommodate him. Those were the plus points, I think. On the minus side, Jim pointed out that Gough himself had taken the decision not to play again for his country. It was his firm choice.

That there were six points in both columns was interesting in itself because, to select someone to play for your team, you need to have a weightier argument more in favour than against.

I would not want anyone to get the false impression that I select a team on the advice of journalists, cab drivers or anyone else. I was obviously not entirely alone in my opinion and, at the end of the day, my view as manager is the one that matters. I am no philosopher, but when you start to get on a little bit in years, you realise that there is no point in worrying about decisions you have made – or indeed games that you have lost. You do your best and there is no point in being a martyr to anxiety afterwards. I can assure everyone that I have never lost a moment's sleep over any decision that I've made or a defeat that I've suffered. I stand or fall by what happens when it happens. I would like to say, though, that while I did not seek advice from Jim Rodger – or DScoop, as he was affectionately known – I have been well advised from time to time by him and other members of the press, and I like to think that I always have a listening ear.

To conclude the Richard Gough affair, earlier in 1998 I attended a Rangers game and found myself sitting in front of Richard. He warmly congratulated me on our qualifying for the World Cup. There was no hint of bitterness or resentment. He assured me that his good wishes were genuine, but I had no need of such assurance – I could see that they were heartfelt.

Richard Gough is not the only player who has not been in the frame for a while. I expect loyalty and respect from players, not because of who I am but because of the position I hold in the country they are representing.

David Robertson surprised me when we were waiting for our luggage at the airport carousel after returning from Greece and our European Championship qualifier. Tommy Craig was there as well and will, I know, confirm everything that was said.

I spoke to David and asked him to be patient and said that his turn would come. He had been capped three times but was not, at that stage, a regular in the side. He was only 26 and had a good few years ahead of him. I had taken him to Greece in the squad but had not used him in the game. I reminded him that Andy Goram had remained patient for years before he became first-choice goalkeeper for Scotland. My words were designed to encourage him, but he responded by telling me that he did not really want to be travelling anywhere if he was not going to be in the team.

'Are you really saying that I have to pre-select the team for your benefit?' I asked. David just looked at me and nodded his head. I took the decision there and then that, if he was going to attach conditions to his selection, I was not interested. I know there are many players who would crawl over broken glass to play for their country, and I did not appreciate David's rather negative approach. I'm afraid that situation has not changed either. Other players have served us well in that department. I have mentioned Tommy Boyd, but what about Tosh McKinlay? I remember that he left the building site of his new home to travel all the way to the Faeroe Islands just to sit on the bench. He never took part in the actual game but he was thrilled to bits at being a part of the Scotland set-up. That is the sort of attitude we want in the Scotland camp.

More recently we have had the case of Duncan Ferguson. Duncan announced that he did not want to play for his country. I have known Duncan for years, and have had him under my management as a youth player right through to senior international level. I even had to send him home from an Under-21 squad once, but I put that down to the impetuosity of youth. If Duncan Ferguson or anyone else decides that they do not want to play for Scotland, I respect their decision. They have made their choice and life goes on without them. After the initial announcement you would think it would become old news, and yet I still get reporters asking me about Duncan Ferguson's situation in my plans for Scotland.

I do not feel the need to dwell on players who do not want to play. My attention is on the players who do want to wear their country's shirt. I believe that we have an excellent squad of players now, with guys who really want to play for their country. If I feel that there are those who are just cap-collectors, or have doubts about why they are there, I have to seriously consider their position and, in some cases, eliminate then altogether from my plans. We must have a happy squad of players who really want to be there and give of their best for the privilege of playing for their country. Those who have eliminated themselves must live with their actions and decisions.

Ally McCoist is one of the greatest servants ever to pull on a Scotland jersey. He is so popular with everyone, even people who do not like football. He has been a great goalscorer, one of those players you wish could go on for ever because you never get tired of seeing him. He has won award after award for his scoring feats, and holds a Scottish Premier Division record that will probably never be broken.

Alistair has become more than a top footballer, though – he is a superstar. Who else could get on stage at a Wet, Wet, Wet concert and almost steal the show? His success on *A Question of Sport* led to him getting his own chat show on BBC Scotland, and he is destined to continue being a star long after he has hung up his boots.

McCoist is one of those players that you just love to have around. In the dressing room he is always full of life and a lot of fun. He plays terrible jokes on people but is just as enthusiastic when the joke is turned on him. Never trust him if he is quiet, because you can guarantee he is plotting something, and you could well be his next victim. He is also very quick-witted and never short of a smart reply.

Early in the 1997/98 season, Walter Smith had a go at him for putting on weight. Walter told him that he didn't care how many goals he had scored for Rangers, if he didn't lose weight he would not be considered. He was really angry and was laying into the whole team after an indifferent performance, saving his most scathing attack until the end, when he blasted McCoist. Walter stormed out and slammed the door, but not before he heard McCoist say, 'Where the hell does he think he's going to get a Biafran to score him thirty goals a season?'

Another McCoist story involves the time that Rangers were playing Ajax in a Champions League away match. He was unfit and did not make the journey. Instead he was invited to be one of the commentary team for the television coverage. That morning he was in the treatment room at Ibrox with three of the Rangers apprentices. They were surprised to see him there, having expected him to travel with the team even if he was not playing.

'I'm going to be seeing the game at the television studio,' Ally told them. 'I'm an expert and I'll be giving my opinions. If you look in tonight you'll see me on the screen.'

One of the lads asked him what he would say.

'That depends on the match,' said Ally, who then decided to

have a bit of fun with these young lads. 'Why? What do you want me to say?'

They laughed, but Ally pressed them and told them to pick something for him to say, and then go to the pub to watch the TV and make a few shillings by betting on him coming out with those words. The lads decided to take him up on it, and one of them, seeing a pools coupon in the room, said, 'There's one for you, Ally – say the word "coupon".'

'That's not really about football,' protested Ally, but the lad insisted. A second one looked at the diagram of a human body on the wall and told McCoist he must use the word 'tibia'. Not to be outdone, the third one picked the word 'piriformis', which is a muscle around the backside.

Ally squirmed a little, but the lads jibed that he had boasted he could say anything on television so he decided to do his best, but insisted that the boy write 'piriformis' down on a piece of paper which he tore from the *Daily Record* – or the *Daily Ranger*, as he likes to call it.

Later, in the studio, the presenter, Jim White, asked him how he thought the game would go.

'Well, this is going "tibia" difficult game for Rangers, but if they win it will be a real "coupon"-buster,' said Ally, delighted that he had already managed to squeeze in two of his designated words. The third word was a real struggle, however. Eventually, about halfway through the first half, Rangers were two goals down, Paul Gascoigne had been ordered off, and there was an air of depression around the studio. He was asked for a comment and Ally recalls that he was tempted to say, 'This is the worst Rangers "piriformis" I've seen all season!'

The McCoist stories and pranks go on and on. The well-known referee Brian McGinlay was caught for having too little blood in his alcohol stream. He had been stopped by the police while driving, and the story made the *Evening Times* headlines the night before he was due to referee a Rangers game.

When he turned up at Ibrox he was expecting to have his leg pulled, but no one mentioned the incident. Neither of his linesmen said anything, and Brian was beginning to think that nobody had seen the newspaper. He went down to the Rangers dressing room to check their boots. (Just to digress a moment, I think that checking the boots is one of the most futile exercises that referees undertake. I remember that at Motherwell we had a player called Harry Hood, who boasted that in the fourteen years of his senior career he had never had his boots inspected. Like many players he was superstitious about his boots being touched by the referee, and he went to extraordinary lengths to avoid it. He would hide them, hide himself, tell the referee he'd already seen them, anything to avoid the inspection.) Anyway, after Brian had looked at a couple of pairs of boots, Ally McCoist piped up and said, 'You had a long walk today, big man, eh?'

That was when the referee realised that his transgressions were indeed common knowledge. If he needed confirmation, it came five minutes after the start of the game. He gave off-side against Ian Ferguson, who voiced his disapproval at the decision. McCoist ran over and said, 'Fergie, you're wasting your time with him. If he cannae see a big white car with a blue light on top of it, how can he tell if you're off-side?'

That is typical of Alistair. There are many tales about him, nearly all true. He is a tremendous player and a great character.

The Shanklys are among the best-known names in British football. Bob Shankly eventually became general manager at Stirling Albion. This is a comparatively new role in football. David Pleat has that position at Tottenham, Billy McNeill at Hibs and my brother, Jock, is in a similar capacity at Celtic, but it was Stirling Albion who created the role some years ago. In the late seventies, Bob was the man for Stirling.

The team manager was a young guy by the name of Alex Smith, who will be the first to admit that he learned more in his short time with Shankly than in the rest of his career to date. One very good story that Alex told me about his time at Stirling was to do with fitness. The old school of managers like Bill Shankly and his colleagues at Liverpool, Reuben Bennett and the rest, hated players to be unfit or injured. When they were injured, the players would very often be snubbed, ignored until they were fit again.

Bob Shankly was no different, as I found out during my time with him. He would take it very badly if a player could not be considered for selection. You would be frightened to tell the manager if you were hurt, let alone venture into the treatment room.

There was a guy called Rab Duffin, a very good inside forward who played for Stirling. He had been out for some time with a shoulder injury, and during one particular evening training session at Annfield, Stirling's ground before they moved to their plush new stadium, there were a number of players participating. Bob Shankly saw Rab Duffin pressing himself against a wall. The player was embarrassed at the general manager seeing him not training with the other players but having his own work-out. Bob grunted something, which was his way if he came across a player not training to the full because of a fitness problem.

'I'm doing exercises, boss,' Rab said, not wishing to appear to be taking it easy. Shankly replied with another grunt of apparent disapproval. Rab tried his best and continued, 'In fact, I feel like Christ.' This was a reference to his exercise, in which his arms and legs were outstretched against the wall.

Shankly's response was both quick and clear. 'Well, son, you might feel like Christ, you might even look like Christ – but Christ was back with us in three days . . . you've been out for six weeks!'

That was Alex Smith's favourite Shankly story and I hope I haven't ruined it for him.

One of my own favourites is the time when there was a problem with mice at Dundee. Mouse-traps proved to be useless so Lawrie Smith, our physio, was sent to get a cat. Sure enough the cat took up residence and did a fine job devastating the Dundee mouse population. However, the cat was a bit lazy and used to love to curl up in the boot room where it was always warm.

One morning Alex Hamilton came in early, probably because he had not been home from the night before. He went to the boot room and there was the cat snoring across his boots. Very gently Alex put his toe under the cat and flicked it a little way into the air so that it landed safely on all four feet. He did not realise that Bob Shankly was standing in the doorway behind him.

'Hammy,' said Shankly, 'when you've done as much for this club as that cat, then you can put your boot behind him!'

As you can see, the Shanklys' reputation for bluntness and wit is not without foundation.

Talking of Bob Shankly, he had a way of elevating his players to the opposition while keeping them humble within their own company. Just to give you an example, at the start of one of my seasons at Dundee we were having the usual team photograph taken and Bob was organising where everyone was to be in the photo. If you had not re-signed for the season than you could not be in the photo at all. Those that were in could tell how they stood in the manager's estimation by where he positioned them. If you were in the middle you knew that you were in good standing with the manager. I can remember Doug Houston and myself waiting and waiting while he gave thought to where he wanted everyone. Fortunately, we were among those placed early on. It was usually the young lads who were left until last, and Bob would have them positioned at the very ends of the rows with such encouraging words as, 'A pair of scissors'll get rid of you two.'

I learned a lot from Bill Shankly, even though I never played for him. I had copies of the Shankly Tapes, and I used to play them over and over again, listening to every pearl of wisdom that dropped from the great man's lips. I considered that he had everything that a manager should have, and I looked upon him as a wonderful source of management sense.

One of the things Bill Shankly said on those tapes was that the first time a manager walks into the ground and doesn't change into his training kit, the rot has begun to set in. I have always kept that in mind and, when I became a manager, I made sure that I lived by that little gem. I still do it today as team manager of Scotland. I don't do anything until I have changed into training kit. Even though some of the training is started by a Philip Yeates warm-up and activities by Alex Miller, I am still there directing things.

I have not always seen eye to eye with referees, as I've already explained. I defy anyone in football to say that they have never had a cross word with a referee at some stage in their lives. We all know that it is a waste of time because the referee always has the final word and the protection of the authorities – but we still lose our heads from time to time and say our piece.

One referee I fell out with was Donald McVicar from Stonehouse. This was during my days as manager of Clyde. He was a good referee and a very nice chap, and I still see him occasionally. At this particular game I was getting angrier and angrier, and I think he soon realised that I was reaching boiling point because he took the heat out of the situation. At the end of the game, when I was complaining to him, he put his hand on my shoulder and calmly said, 'Craig, the tide goes out and the tide comes in.'

It was one of the most pertinent phrases I have ever heard, especially from a referee who could so easily have exacerbated the situation instead of calming it down. I have never forgotten it.

John Spencer is one of the game's great characters and has proved his worth at all levels. I think one of his favourite goals was one that he would not have scored if I had had the choice. It is a story against myself, but I'll tell it anyway.

We were playing Switzerland away from home in an Under-21 match and I had Spenny on the bench. I told him to prepare himself because we were losing our way a bit. John Watson, our physio, put him through his paces and then told me that he was ready to go. I was just about to send him on when the Swiss conceded a corner kick. I make it a practice not to put a substitute on at such a point – and especially since we had not been practising set pieces with Spenny – so the last thing I wanted was to send him into the game at that moment. Also, with his lack of height, I did not see much point in taking off a player who might just get his head to the ball and replacing him with Spenny.

The referee took the decision for me and signalled for us to send Spenny on. We were all ready so I couldn't say that I had changed my mind. You can imagine what happened. The corner came over, a fiercely driven ball, straight into the area, and, of course, John Spencer's head was in just the right place at just the right time and he nodded the ball home brilliantly. He had heard me trying to avoid sending him on so, after the game, he delighted in telling everyone about the goal he was not supposed to have scored. I was very pleased that he did, though.

The John Spencer saga does not end there. Spenny was one of those guys who liked to wear his baseball cap round the wrong way, but he didn't appreciate it when Alan Hodgkinson, our goalkeeping coach, started calling him Norman Wisdom. Personally, I would have thought it was a compliment, but Spenny didn't like it one bit.

When we were staying at Sanary on the Cote d'Azur for the Under-21 tournament in Toulon, we told the lads that if they did well we would take them to the disco in the neighbouring village of Bandol. We kept our word and took them in the team bus. They went into the disco while the backroom staff and I went to a restaurant nearby. Dr John Maclean went to the disco with them to make sure things were all right. Suddenly, while we were eating, he burst into the restaurant and said, 'Come quickly, you've got to see this!'

We didn't know what to expect, but what we found was John Spencer breakdancing in the middle of the floor with about 1,500 youngsters clapping and cheering him on.

On another occasion we decided to take the Under-21 side to Aix-en-Provence to watch the England Under-21 side play a tournament game against the Russians. We went for a meal in an outdoor café after the game. It was beginning to get a little chilly, especially for the players, who were in their T-shirts. The French coach-driver was in the café with us, plying himself with rather more glasses of wine than I would have done had I been driving. He was in no hurry to finish his meal, but we thought we might just impart some sense of urgency by heading for the coach, which was parked some distance away across a park. Andy Roxburgh had flown over to watch one or two of the games and so it was Andy, Tommy Craig and I who took the lead and arrived at the coach first. When we got there we found that it was locked and there was no way we could get in.

We began to chat, and were vaguely aware of the arrival of John Spencer and Alex Rae, the first of the players. Within a moment they were inside the bus and Spenny was sitting in the driving seat. We were amazed because we had tried every possible door.

'How did you get in?' I asked, to which Spenny replied, 'Alex is from Dennistoun!'

Without wishing to cause any offence to residents of that area, there was no need for further explanation. A simple thing like a locked coach door was not going to keep Alex out in the cold. You could always guarantee that Spenny would never be too far from any mischief like that.

A word about Tommy Burns, who was a very fine player in his day, and also a gentleman and a singer. Yes, a singer! To give you some idea of what Tommy is like, I have to go back to two incidents in 1988, when we were playing against England at Wembley. We trained there, and it was the first time I had ever set foot on the pitch. I soon realised why it was so energy-sapping. You really have to put some force into your passing, so your legs are asked to use up much more energy than usual.

We were staying in an hotel in Windsor, and Andy used to like to organise some sort of entertainment for the players. We were having a singsong which had developed into a sort of talent contest. Ally McCoist was the star turn with his rap number – at least, he was until Tommy Burns burst into 'Mack the Knife'. He brought the place down and showed that he had another talent which he kept in hiding.

There was also another side of his character which was revealed when he was told to prepare to take the field in the game. He left the subs' bench and warmed up. As he waited to get into the game, he turned to Andy and me and said, 'Thank you for making my life's ambition become real.'

He had always wanted to play against England at Wembley.

Another moment to remember was before the 1992 European Championship in Sweden. We played in Denver in the Mile High Stadium. The conditions were very difficult, not only because of the heat but also because of the altitude. The air was very thin, and you could very easily get out of breath by just walking around, let alone running.

After the game we were due to fly to Toronto but, because of the lack of air in Denver, the weight on the aircraft was too great for the plane to take off. The captain asked if six people would volunteer to leave the plane. They would be able to travel on the very next flight and would also receive $300 in compensation. We could not split our party, although there were one or two people on the coaching staff who would have been quite keen to subsidise their salaries with the extra cash.

A well-known Scottish journalist, Doug Baillie, the former giant Airdrie, Rangers, Third Lanark and Falkirk player who is a correspondent for the *Sunday Post*, immediately volunteered to leave the plane. He said, 'Now you'll only need two of us to get off!' It gave us all a laugh. In fact, five other media men also volunteered, and presumably they made good use of the extra money, although they soon caught up with us in Toronto.

It was a bit worrying that, even with the lightened load, the aeroplane seemed to take a long time before it took off. I think it was the longest I have been on a runway. We seemed to be speeding along the tarmac for ever before we finally managed to get airborne.

Just for the record, that game in Denver was won by an excellent Pat Nevin goal in which he combined with his pal Brian McClair. I have often thought that their play together reflects the great friendship they have off the field. There is a sociological message there which underlines the need for players to have a good relationship if they are to work together during a game.

While we were in Canada some of the lads clubbed together and took a helicopter ride over Niagara Falls which, I understand, they enjoyed very much, considering it to be a memory that they will cherish all their lives. We also went as guests to see the Blue Jays baseball team in action at the famous Skydrome Stadium – and that was quite an experience too.

They say that travel broadens the mind and there is no doubt that it does, but incidents and events when you are travelling as a squad also cement the relationship between players. When they have shared wonderful experiences, as they do, players often become pals for life.

I must mention Jim Farry, the chief executive of the Scottish Football Association. He is often given a very bad press because of decisions he has to make that cannot possibly please everyone. I have seen and heard him being maligned by people who are not in possession of the full facts, so I think it is only fair to set some matters straight in connection with him.

His negotiating skills are quite incredible. He and Yule Craig, chairman of the International Committee, when given an indication of the fixtures we want, are very, very adept at the negotiating table, and I am sure their expertise before a ball is even kicked has undoubtedly helped us qualify for the various tournaments.

My philosophy has always been to play one of our major rivals away from home first, if at all possible. This means that if you win the game you are off to a flyer, if you draw you are still in contention and, if you lose, you can still redress the situation when you play at home. If you play at home against a rival early on and lose, it leaves you with a real mountain to climb.

A lot of countries think in terms of the finances generated by playing their stronger rivals and try to get a home game with them early on so that they can benefit from the bigger crowds. If their campaign proceeds well they will continue to get big crowds against lesser opposition, and if it fizzles out they have had the monetary icing on the cake anyway.

We have been a bit more positive than that. Our sole aim is to qualify, and the financial spin-offs are well down our list of priorities. If possible, I have asked our negotiators to leave us with a couple of home games at the end of our campaign, preferably against the weaker nations. Similarly, I try to get an away fixture or two during the summer against weaker opposition. Their pitches are usually in better condition than ours, and we are away from home at a time when home interest in football is taking a sabbatical in the wake of the stresses and emotions of a rigorous season.

That formula started when Andy was in charge, and I reinforced it. It is usually the skills of Jim Farry which enable that ideal programme to become reality.

One of my fondest fun memories goes back to the 1992 European Championship in Sweden. The support from the Scotland fans was just amazing, and we wanted to make a gesture to thank them. This was after we had played our first two games, and before the 3–0 victory over the CIS. We knew that many fans were staying in tents on a campsite so, after training, we decided to pay them a surprise visit.

We probably arrived at around midday. Many of them were still asleep, but the word went round like wildfire and it was quite a sight to see hundreds of bleary-eyed Scots tumbling out of their tents in various stages of dress – and undress – to acknowledge the team. The visit was greatly appreciated by both the players and the supporters, and was a credit to its instigator, Andy Roxburgh.

During 1995 I was asked to give a talk to managers of oilfields in the North Sea. A professor at Robert Gordon's College in Aberdeen is one of our travel club members, and he approached me to ask if I would give a talk about motivation.

I would not for one minute suggest that I am the best motivator in the world, but I manage to get the team together and inject the right sort of spirit. I was being questioned on this, and I explained that the motivation must come from within. In the Scotland squad, for instance, the motivation required is different from that needed at club level because it is a much higher-profile platform. Most of all I like to appeal to the fact that the players are Scottish and should take pride in wearing the shirt.

There are some who criticise the use of players who are not actually born in the country, especially since we are now down to the grandparent rule. That rule is the same for everyone, and I don't see why we should penalise ourselves and not use players with a Scottish heritage just because their place of birth was not within the boundaries of the country. I very often find that those players who have Scottish parents or grandparents are even more motivated to play for Scotland than those who are born in the country.

The criterion now is that if a player has a British passport, and a bloodline reaching back to a grandparent, he can play for whichever country picks him first. For instance, if a player is born in Cornwall with Welsh parents and a grandmother from Kilmarnock, he could play for any one of the three home countries. There is no question of rule-bending. That is the rule, just as it is the rule that it is permissible to head the ball back to your goalkeeper, but not to kick it back. Selecting players who fall within the rules is an excellent option.

Players like Stuart McCall, Neil Sullivan and Matt Elliott are typical of those players from outside Scotland. Try telling them that they are not entitled to wear the Scotland jersey – but don't stand too close! Their passion for Scotland is as fervent as that of anyone with a Glasgow accent.

I was explaining this at the talk I gave to those oil managers and reminded them that money is no motivator. It can be a form of bait to get someone to take a job, but it will not motivate them once they have started the job. You don't find Scotland internationals talking in terms of money – it has no bearing on their motivation for being there.

The day after my talk one of the tabloids featured the headline 'I Failed – Says Brown!' It went on to suggest that I was saying that I had failed to motivate the players. The story alleged that I had said this while giving the talk. It was complete nonsense, of course, and I had video proof of exactly what I had said and in what context I'd said it. I was telephoned by the professor, who was absolutely distraught at the story, and asked if she could help redress the matter in any way.

Usually I treat such things with a pinch of salt, but I thought this story was out of order. I did contact the newspaper in question and later received an apology from the editor – although there was never a retraction printed in his newspaper. It just goes to show that even at private functions you have to be very careful that you are not misquoted.

In order to get to this function on the oil-rig, I had to fly by helicopter. It was a very interesting experience to fly from Aberdeen to the Shetlands and then out to the rig. I travelled with a group of guys who were quite laid back about the whole thing because they had done the same journey many times, but for me it was a totally new experience. Before the final stage of the journey I was issued with a survival outfit, which is rather like a shell suit. I was also given a helmet and goggles as well as some instructions, and off we went in the helicopter.

While everyone else was either sleeping or reading, I couldn't help but look out of the windows. Those rig platforms look very small, very vulnerable and very, very rusty from above, and I was beginning to wonder if these were not some kind of mini-rig – until we landed at our chosen destination.

The platform did not look any less rusty when I stood on it with the wind howling and the waves crashing into the air. I wondered if all my insurances were up to date. Then I went inside and it was like entering a different world. I have seen five-star hotels that did not match up to this. I was barely inside when a Tannoy announcement said, 'Come to the cinema this evening at eight thirty to hear the Scotland manager, Craig Brown, talking about why he hasn't picked Richard Gough!' I nearly turned round and walked out again at that stage, and it did not get any better. I was still wearing my survival gear as two guys walked past me. Upon hearing the announcement, one said to the other, 'They should have sacked that b . . . . . . months ago!' They nodded to me as they went past, obviously not recognising me beneath all the gear. I did give them a second look in case they were executives of the SFA!

Later, in the cinema, they were sitting up near the front. I looked at them and said, 'Hi, I'm the b . . . . . . who should have been sacked months ago!' We had a good laugh about it and the evening went very well.

It is experiences like that, though, which help you to keep your feet on the ground – so to speak!

I am not one of those people who like to make themselves readily available for after-dinner speaking. Some have made a second career out of it – but not me. I restrict my speeches to special occasions – charities, testimonials and events of that sort. I know that there are many others in my position who are not given to be entertainers, and 'He wasn't very good' or 'I didn't think much of him' doesn't do your confidence much good. People tend not to take into consideration that you haven't asked to be there, much less to stand and talk when you have so many other commitments that you should be getting on with.

As well as after-dinner speaking and visiting oil rigs, I have often been invited to talk in prisons. I'm not sure if someone is trying to tell me something. I do enjoy these visits, because the guys – and the women – inside those establishments really know their football. They glean every scrap of available information from their newspapers, radios and televisions, and they ask very significant questions. They also appreciate the fact that you have made the effort to go and see them. I know they are all in prison for a reason but, if one of my visits helps just one guy to want to stay out of trouble so that he can be free to go and watch football instead of getting it second-hand, then that has to be good enough, doesn't it?

We were staying in Connecticut, preparing for a summer game against the USA as part of our preparations for Euro 96. Rod Stewart was in concert at the famous Madison Square Garden in New York, and he contacted us to make arrangements to come and watch the game. We thought it might be a good idea to invite him to come and train with us, because it would be great for the team's morale.

Rod is a huge football fan and in particular follows Scotland – as indeed Scotland follows him and his career. He has a full-size football pitch alongside his house and runs his own team as well. He has been a close pal of Gordon Strachan for some years, and I remembered when we were in Los Angeles prior to the 1986 World Cup he had invited us to his house, and it was good to be able to repay his kind hospitality.

Rod arrived in a stretch limo and we had a huge problem with all the press, who were obviously keen to get their photos and stories. We asked the Scottish press in particular to take it easy. We wanted to train, he wanted to take part, and he was happy to pose for a few photos if we would then be allowed to get on with it. The press guys were very helpful and did their job professionally without causing too much hassle for us.

The popular image of Rod Stewart is one of arrogance, flamboyance and mild conceit. I found him to be a very humble and down-to-earth guy who called me Mr Brown, and Alex Mr Miller. He never presumed anything and asked, 'Is it all right if I warm up with you, Mr Brown?' He was a real gentleman and enjoyed his training session with us.

Rod was also kind enough to supply us with 32 tickets for his concert at Madison Square Garden so that we could all go. They were seats near the front, too. We had a few moans before we left the hotel because the coach was late arriving. I think we are spoiled by the treatment we receive from Douglas Park of Park's of Hamilton, who provide the coach for the national team. He is always conscious of our every need, including punctuality. Mick Riley is our regular driver, and his Celtic tattoo gives you some idea of where his heart lies. If we travel anywhere near Ibrox, Ally McCoist suggests that if Mick has a couple of days to spare he should go and visit the Rangers trophy room. Mick is used to the ribbing and takes it all in his stride. He is an excellent driver who again takes very good care of us.

The American bus, however, was late, and we had to dash to the concert, cancelling a plan to get something to eat on the way. We arrived a few minutes late, and it was amazing to see the number of people who had been unable to get in. They were a complete cross-section of all ages, giving some idea of the universal popularity of Rod Stewart.

Hugh Allan, our physio, had taken along a Scotland shirt to give to Rod if there was an opportunity. He did not have to wait long. As soon as Rod knew we were there he summoned us up to the stage, which was in the centre of this huge venue. One by one we were called up. Hugh gave Rod the jersey, which he immediately put on, and then he went into a number which we clapped along to. I looked around the vast arena at the thousands of people singing, dancing and clapping along with Rod, and I thought, Hammy and the Hamsters were never quite like this!

Afterwards Rod had arranged some hospitality for us in his dressing room, where we chatted to him for some time and met his lovely family. He said that he'd try to see some of our World Cup qualifying matches, and indeed he did, along with his pal Ricky Simpson, who is also a great gentleman and has been very helpful to me on my European fact-finding missions.

The game that Rod was able to fit into his busy schedule was our penultimate World Cup match against Belarus at Aberdeen. It was scheduled for a Saturday, but the unthinkable happened and Princess Diana was killed in Paris.

There was a lot of controversy over whether or not the game

should be postponed. Part of the delay was that no one knew when the funeral would be. I was interviewed by a TV crew on the Monday and could only say that, unless we heard anything to the contrary, the match would go ahead as planned. During the day the funeral plans were announced, and that same evening I saw myself on television saying that the game was going ahead.

I was made to look a little callous. Right away I was phoned by Ally McCoist, who said that he had discussed the matter with his wife, Allison, and his mother, and he didn't feel that he could take part in the game if it was to be played on that day. Not long after I had finished talking to Ally, Colin Hendry phoned to say much the same thing. He was doubtful because of injury anyway, but he told me that he could not bring himself to play on that day.

The SFA were in touch with Belarus, but there were communication problems because their president, Yevgeniy Shuntov, could not speak English. He and his general secretary, Vadim Zhuk, were doing their best but, in the end, the conversation had to continue through the president's wife, who could speak English. They proved to be very helpful and the date was changed.

I had no say in the matter, but I was able to represent the players, who were pretty unanimous in their view. I think we were all relieved and happy at the change of arrangements and the game being put back 24 hours. We were all pretty devastated by the reason, though.

As for Rod Stewart, he attended that game, and contacts us regularly to keep in touch with events – a great guy and a great supporter of Scotland.

Sean Connery is another of the world's great superstars who avidly follows the fortunes of Scotland. He is a very busy guy, but he attends matches as often as possible and regularly telephones me for a chat and an update on team affairs. He knows what he is talking about, too.

It is always good to be able to say to the players, 'Oh, by the way, Sean Connery was asking after you!'

On a professional note, I was delighted when the SFA offered me a new four-year contact which I have been happy to accept. I have been to many places all over the world and met many famous people, some of whom have since become good friends. I don't know what road I would have travelled down if I had not entered the football profession, but I did, and I often feel that I have the best job in the world.